REFORM AND REVOLUTION
IN ASIA

REFORM AND REVOLUTION IN ASIA

EDITED BY

G. F. HUDSON

St Antony's College, Oxford

ST. MARTIN'S PRESS   NEW YORK

AFFILIATED PUBLISHERS: Macmillan and Company,
Limited, London – also at Bombay, Calcutta, Madras and
Melbourne – The Macmillan Company of Canada, Limited,
Toronto

CONTENTS

ceased to be sovereign states throughout the age of Western encroachment in Asia—though with very different degrees of success in resisting that encroachment; the other three have emerged from the dissolution of Western empires, and of these three, two—India and Pakistan—took over from the metropolitan power by a peaceful transition, while the third—Indonesia —having asserted its independence with the blessing of a Japanese army of occupation, only obtained recognition of it after protracted warfare against returning Dutch forces.

The armed expansion of Japan over the eight years from 1937 to 1945 was decisive for the historical developments which followed Japan's downfall. It was the final defeat and ensuing occupation that changed Japan's own polity, but it was her previous victories that transformed the countries overrun by her armies, and also India, where the events of 1942 had immediate consequences not to be reversed. The Japanese failed to make a permanent conquest of China, but they did succeed in smashing the central state authority which the Kuomintang had been gradually building up since the government they had established in Nanking had obtained international recognition in 1928; it is very unlikely that the Communists would have come to power in China but for the havoc wrought by the Japanese invasion. To the south of China the Japanese occupations shattered the structures of colonial rule so that they could never be effectively restored. These ascendencies were in any case threatened both by emerging nationalist movements and by the growth of anti-colonial political forces within the metropolitan countries, and the Philippines had already been assigned by legislation in Washington an independence to be effective in the year 1946. But apart from the Philippines the colonial powers were still at the end of the thirties strongly entrenched in South and South-East Asia; there was no prospect of their being dislodged by armed insurrection at an early date and the advance of their subject peoples to independence by consent of their rulers could hardly be expected to be achieved except by a gradual political process. This was vastly accelerated by the Japanese invasions, and the collapse of Japan's brave new empire did not alter the fact that the ascendencies of European powers (other than Russia) in Asia had received a mortal blow.

In the post-war period it seemed at first that the supreme influence of the United States was going to shape the political future of both Japan and China. Apart from Mongolia and Manchuria, where the Yalta agreements had reserved a sphere of influence for the Soviet Union, the war created for the time being an American hegemony which seemed irresistible; in Tokyo a Supreme Commander for the Allied Powers (SCAP), who was an American in command of a mainly American army of occupation, had virtually unlimited power to remake the political fabric of Japan, while in Nanking the Chinese central government, returning to its capital as a result of a victory gained primarily by American arms and dependent on American favour for indispensable aid, was bound to listen with deference to voices which spoke to it from Washington. The outcomes of American political actions in Japan and in China were, however, utterly different. The changes brought about in Japan through the exercise of the authority of SCAP were in the main decisive in setting a new course for the social and political development of the Japanese nation, whereas the American attempts to re-organize China under a Kuomintang-Communist coalition government ended in catastrophic failure. An extraordinary reversal of war-time relations was thus brought about, for militarist and 'fascist' Japan, the war-time foe of the United States, emerged as a demilitarized capitalist democracy bound to America by a security pact, while China, the war-time ally on whom such great hopes had been set, came under the role of a single-party communist regime bitterly hostile to 'American imperialism'. The difference between the success in Japan and the failure in China was indeed partly due to the difference in legal position; the Americans had an authority in Tokyo which they did not have in Nanking. But the contrast was mainly due to the fact that in Japan—under the given conditions of defeat in war—what they were trying to do was in the main acceptable to the Japanese and in line with trends already strongly developed in pre-war Japan, whereas in China American policy pursued the impossible and the only meeting of minds which General Marshall was able to bring about among those between whom he was sent to mediate was in a common resentment of his interference.

In Japan the new Constitution, sponsored and to a large degree framed by the American occupation authority, afforded indeed a great contrast to the Meiji Constitution of 1889, which had been in the main a copy of the political system of Bismarck's Germany and had been likewise intended to provide a measure of elective parliamentary power while retaining a prerogative of the monarch over the armed forces and a governmental executive not responsible to the legislature. The new Constitution reduced the Emperor to the status of a 'symbol of the state', provided that the Prime Minister should be in future elected by the House of Representatives, and got rid of the imperial prerogative of the supreme command of the armed forces by abolishing the armed forces themselves. Japan was thus transformed institutionally into a perfect liberal democracy with the unique distinction—after a war in which its soldiers and sailors had displayed an extraordinary willingness to fight to the death—of renouncing all means of defending itself. This clause, it is true, was not to remain fully in force for very long; the Americans themselves soon repented of having totally disarmed Japan, and ways were found of bypassing the constitutional prohibition so as to allow the creation of a modest 'self-defence force'. The national sentiment of Japan, however, became overwhelmingly pacifist; the utter defeat after years of struggle and sacrifice had produced an extreme revulsion of feeling against military authority, against conscription and against the whole ideology and style of pre-war patriotism. The new 'self-defence force', far from being constitutionally privileged, was barely within the law; it had to lead an almost clandestine existence and lacked any basis of popular esteem and support on which it could aspire to the part previously played by the fighting services in Japanese politics. The supremacy of a democratically elected parliament over the executive power of government was certainly an innovation, but it was not quite such a break with the past as was generally supposed at the time in the West. The Japanese people had been electing parliaments with competition of political parties ever since the promulgation of the Meiji Constitution in 1889—on a restricted franchise before 1925 and thereafter with universal adult male suffrage. It was not a case of a democracy suddenly replacing an absolute monarchy. The Japanese Diet had always been subject to serious restrictions on its power, but it had never been negligible, not even in the period 1940–5, when all the political parties were supposed to have been merged in an 'Imperial Rule Assistance Association', for this was not a new party taking control of the state in the fascist manner, but merely a bureaucratic coordination of politicians who had previously been elected on party tickets. The party politics of post-war Japan continued those of the twenties and thirties, though new labels were adopted by parties which were rather the worse for wear after their involvement in the policies which had proved so disastrous for the nation. The parliamentary politicians carried on as before, with more than half a century of experience behind them, only they were now free from interference by 'our soldier friends' and could themselves make and unmake prime ministers instead of having it done for them by a council of 'elder statesmen'. The Americans by 'democratizing' Japan were thus engaged, not in introducing to the Japanese people a form of politics with which they had previously been unfamiliar, but in freeing its practitioners from curbs which had hitherto been imposed on them, and their intervention was successful in so far as the extra-parliamentary political factors which had formerly been so powerful were now deeply discredited because of the disastrous outcome of the policies they had promoted. Not even the Emperor himself could escape the general disenchantment which followed the surrender; the mystique of a divine monarchy lost its hold on a defeated nation. The retention of the monarchy as an institution entirely without executive power was nevertheless an important element in the new system; it strengthened rather than weakened the democracy. It was not the first time in history that the Japanese imperial dynasty had been deprived of governing power, but its deposition under foreign pressure would have given deep offence to the more conservative sections of the Japanese people, and the restoration of sovereignty after the end of the occupation would certainly have been followed by a strong restoration movement which might have led to civil war. As it was, the perpetuation of the monarchy, with an entirely symbolic and ceremonial function, reconciled to the new regime a large body of sentiment and opinion which would otherwise have been opposed to it. There had not in any case been a revolution in Tokyo in 1945, as there had been in Berlin in 1918; the Emperor had remained in his palace and announced the surrender to the people by a radio broadcast.

The parliamentary democracy set up by the new constitution had two favourable conditions for its operation, both of which were inherited from pre-war Japan: first, a unified and centralized state structure with a highly disciplined and efficient civil service, and secondly, a well-developed industrial capitalist economy with a high level of managerial and technical ability and a plentiful supply of skilled workers. The state structure had been the achievement of the early Meiji reformers in the seventies and eighties of the nineteenth century before the Meiji Constitution had been promulgated; its creation had involved the abolition of the feudal *Kleinstaaterei* of Tokugawa Japan and the gathering of all power into the hands of a central government, which was provided with a well-organized administrative machine for the exercise of direct control over the whole country. This effective centralization of the state was the basic condition of the remarkable progress of Japan in the Meiji era—the development of its modern industry, the liquidation of illiteracy through universal primary education, the building of national military and naval strength and finally the attainment of international status as a Great Power. After 1945 it was the condition of Japan's post-war economic recovery and political renewal. It had not disintegrated under the strain of war and the devastation of nearly all the cities of Japan under air attack, and was still functioning throughout the country when the American occupation forces moved in.

The economic development of Japan before the Pacific War had been unique in Asia apart from the Soviet Union. The decisive transition to modern industry had been made by the end of the nineteenth century when all the models had been economies of private capitalism; nevertheless the state had played an important part in launching new industries, especially those considered important for national defence, and the speed and success of the development had been due less to the spontaneous activities of the Japanese bourgeoisie than to the drive of a governing nationalist élite which sought to promote national independence and power and recognized that a new productive capacity was essential to this end. At all times from the early Meiji era to the outbreak of the Pacific War the armaments industry was a very important sector of the economy, but as against the burden which the requirements of the fighting services imposed on Japan there was the development of a great supply of technical skills in all branches of engineering, and after the war these skills were available for transfer to an almost entirely civilian economy. The immediate post-war period was indeed a time of low ebb in the economy with acute shortages of industrial equipment and goods of all kinds, but once recovery had begun (stimulated before long by injections of American aid) it proceeded rapidly, and soon Japan was enjoying a high rate of economic growth, with virtually full employment and a steady rise in standards of living. The new economy with its vast urban agglomerations created new social problems in addition to many left over from pre-war days, but the size and strength of the middle class involved in the post-war economic revival provided solid support for the political democracy established under the American occupation. It was not a question of creating a modern industry by state action in the absence of sufficient private enterprise; the bourgeoisie was already there, with a fund of previous experience and the ability to push a large export trade in a highly competitive world market in addition to providing great quantities of mass-produced consumer goods for the domestic market. If the Constitution of 1947 represented a 'bourgeois-democratic revolution' which the Japanese bourgeoisie itself did not make, there was at any rate a numerous, active and efficient bourgeoisie there to sustain it after it had come into being.

Two measures enforced by SCAP contributed to the stability of the new regime in post-war Japan. A land-reform law transferred a large part of the agricultural land of Japan from tenancy to peasant ownership and greatly reduced the tensions which had existed in the countryside before the war and might have provided inflammable material for revolutionary agitation in the post-war period had they continued. In the cities the Trade Union Act of 1945 and the Labour Relations Act of 1946 gave Japanese workers the right to organize and strike; the new trade unions took full advantage of their new freedom and Japanese industry was disturbed by disputes which would have been rigorously suppressed under the old system, but the strikes did little to impede the post-war economic growth and the legal scope for industrial action substantially reduced the attractions of revolutionary politics for the Japanese workers.

It was a characteristic of the post-war Japanese political scene, corresponding to the situation in the industrialized democratic countries of the West, that the mass of the industrial workers showed little inclination for revolutionary radicalism, while university students, greatly increased in numbers as a result of a rapid expansion of higher education, came more and more under the influence of the extreme Left, rejecting the new post-war democracy as well as the ideas and institutions of the old *kokutai*. Student demonstrations and riots became a regular feature of Japanese life in the larger cities, and an observer of these frequent eruptions, with their innumerable banners, chanting of slogans and raucous rhetoric, might often get the impression that Japan was on the verge of a great violent upheaval. The degree of alienation of the intelligentsia, and especially of the educated youth, from the social and political order of post-war Japan was indeed a significant phenomenon, yet it amounted to relatively little either in electoral effect or in terms of a potential of violent action. The Japanese people in free elections time after time gave a majority to a party of basically conservative principles and the police had no real difficulty in containing even the most fervent manifestations of student militancy.

In contrast to the conditions existing in Japan at the end of the Pacific War the situation in China was fundamentally adverse to a post-war development on the basis of a democratic polity and a capitalist economy. Instead of the firm, centralized state administration which in Japan had survived the war unbroken there was an anarchy tempered by two single-party dictatorships in different parts of the country. The centralization of government which had been achieved after the Meiji Restoration in Japan had never been brought about in China; on the contrary, in the course of a century of history the forces of fission had prevailed over those of cohesion. China, the empire of the Ch'ing dynasty minus Outer Mongolia, was, of course, many times the size of Japan, and with its vast and largely mountainous interior always had a problem of communications far more difficult than that confronting the Japanese islands. Yet China *was* held together under the old imperial dynasty and this was not simply a matter of military control; the main factor of unity was the civil service, recruited by competitive examination in Chinese classical learning and bearing an almost hieratic authority over the Chinese people. This scholar-bureaucracy co-ordinated a society in which the central government had only slender resources, the proceeds of taxation remained for the most part in the provinces, and the armed forces were extremely decentralized. But the traditional examinations were abolished in 1905 and the monarchy came to an end with the abdication of the last Ch'ing emperor in 1912; the democratic republic set up by a combination of Western-educated intellectuals and ambitious military commanders had no popular roots, and its new-style civil officials lacked the special prestige of the old mandarins. Power fell into the hands of provincial military governors, the so-called 'war-lords', who tore China to pieces with their armed rivalries. The Kuomintang party sought to reunite the country under its 'tutelage'. In 1928 it controlled the principal cities of China and gained international recognition as the *de jure* government, but it still faced a most formidable task of unification with semi-independent forces defying central control in various parts of the country. It was in this disintegrated state that the army of the Chinese Communist Party maintained itself as one of a number of insubordinate military-political entities. Yet the central government increased its authority between 1928 and 1937 and it had a good long-term prospect of overcoming the centrifugal forces opposed to it. The eight years of the Japanese invasion ruined this prospect, destroying whatever central administration existed within reach of the invading armies and creating a huge political vacuum into which the Communists were able to infiltrate with their guerrilla units. Even in those parts of China which the Japanese never occupied, central control was diminished because of the effects of blockade, defective communications, and currency inflation; commanders of provincial forces levied taxes in kind in the areas they held and provided for their troops as best they could. When the war ended, therefore, and the Japanese were repatriated, there was no unified state in China, no functioning national administration and no representative parliamentary body. Nor was there any substantial capitalist class—as distinct from an infinitely numerous petty bourgeoisie; the most important business enterprises had

been in the hands of foreigners—European, American or Japanese
—and Chinese capital formation had been constantly hindered
and thwarted over the years of domestic and external warfare.
The effect of the retreat of the national government to Chungking, with China cut off from the outside world and all the ports
in the hands of the Japanese, had been to diminish the political
influence of the commercial middle class and increase that of the
landlords on whose cooperation the feeding of the armies
depended.

In the circumstances it was impossible for anything like a
parliamentary democratic state to be established in China in the
aftermath of the Japanese invasion. Nor was it possible for the
Kuomintang and the Communists peacefully to merge their
armies and form a coalition government, however hard General
Marshall as the personal representative of the President of the
United States tried to persuade them to do so. China could only
be unified by force and the contest was won by the Communists.
Their first, and so far enduring, achievement was to impose on
the provinces a more thorough and binding central rule than
China had ever known before.

The political and economic system of China after 1949 stood
at the opposite pole from that of post-war Japan. The contrast
corresponded to the cleavage between the Soviet Union and the
United States in world affairs and between the Communist bloc
and the Western democracies in Europe. Japan and China were
thus ranged on opposite sides in the world-wide 'cold war' of
the 1950s, and these alignments were in part the outcome of the
policies pursued by Washington and Moscow after the end of the
Pacific War. The American occupation was decisive for the
shaping of the post-war institutions of Japan; had the United
States agreed to a separate Soviet occupation of the Hokkaido, a
local Communist regime would doubtless have been installed
there, as under the Soviet occupations of East Germany and
North Korea, but General Arthur's refusal to accept any restriction on his authority throughout Japan meant that Japan escaped

the dichotomy of government which afflicted Germany and Korea. In China, as an allied country, there was no general military control by either America or Russia and there was considerable ambiguity in the policies of both powers; nevertheless, the Russians did give substantial aid to the Chinese Communists in Manchuria, and without this the latter might have been hard put to it to prevail in the civil war. But in China, as in Japan, intervention was successful only in so far as it assisted political forces that were strong in themselves and not too greatly dependent on outside support. Nor have either bourgeois-democratic Japan or Communist China remained docile junior partners of their original sponsors. In Japan the political parties of the Left—and not only the Communists—have been vigorously anti-American, and Japanese public opinion has been adverse to any involvement of Japan in American policies in Asia, while the Chinese People's Republic, without relaxing its opposition to American 'imperialism', has become the bitter foe of Soviet 'revisionism' also.

Apart from a claim to have maintained alone the purity of the Marxist-Leninist faith which the Russians and the Russian-supported Communist governments of Europe have abandoned, the Chinese Communists have regarded themselves as uniquely qualified through their experience as a semi-colonial country in the age of imperialism to provide a model of development for all the colonial and semi-colonial countries of Asia, Africa and Latin America. This attitude was bound to bring them sooner or later into conflict with the Russians, who, according to them, could not have the same qualifications, because Russia at the time of the Bolshevik revolution had been herself an imperialist power and had never shared in the colonial or semi-colonial experience. Thus Communist revolutionary movements in all the 'under-developed' countries came to be split between pro-Soviet and pro-Chinese factions, introducing a new complexity into the spectrum of politics, which had been relatively simple in Stalin's time, when all Marxist-Leninists (except for a handful of Trotskyites) looked to Moscow and it was possible to speak of world communism as a single political force. With or without these complications, however, the countries emerging from colonial and semi-colonial conditions had to make a choice between private captalism and state-owned enterprise as the main factor of economic advance; they also had to choose between free-election democracy and some kind of dictatorship as the form of their politics. In territories which had been under Western colonial governments it was natural that the nationalist parties which had been foremost in the agitation for independence should inherit power when it was handed over; these parties, because they sought to mobilize all elements of popular discontent in their societies in their struggles against the colonial regimes, were inevitably inclined towards the Left, but they were not under Communist control except in Vietnam—in India, Burma, Malaya, the Philippines and Indonesia the Marxist label of 'bourgeois nationalist' fitted well enough those who succeeded the old colonial governments in the seats of power.

The new governments had problems in plenty calling for their attention, but one problem they did not have to face was the kind of fragmentation which had reduced the nominal government of China to virtual impotence for most of the first half of the twentieth century. Whatever the Western colonial powers did or did not do, they governed, and they held together the territories under their sovereignty or 'paramountcy' with strong, centralized military and civil services. The inheritance in each case, therefore, consisted on the one hand of a central military and civil bureaucracy and on the other of a population accustomed to obey the central government and to look to a capital city for direction. The events of the Pacific War spoilt the inheritance in French Indo-China and the Dutch East Indies as far as the central administrations were concerned; these were shattered by the Japanese invasions and by the wars of independence which followed, and the new regimes had to improvise administratively when they were at last established. French Indo-China was dissolved into the three kingdoms from which it had been formed and Vietnam was divided into two states ideologically opposed, but the Vietminh government set up in Hanoi derived a great political advantage from taking possession of the former seat of the French Governor-General. In the Dutch Indies, in spite of the deep division between Java and the Outer Islands, the diversity of languages, and the confusion ensuing on the withdrawal of the Japanese, Batavia, renamed Jakarta, remained the seat of authority and the Dutch empire was rebuilt by a state which for want of any suitable native name could only be called Indonesia.

In India, where the British Raj had restored and enlarged the territorial unity of the Mogul domination, where the army and civil service had not been disrupted by a Japanese conquest, and where power was transferred by consent and without a period of insurrection and warfare, conditions would have been favourable for the maintenance of a firm central government over the whole of the British inheritance but for the Hindu-Muslim cleavage which caused it to be divided into India and Pakistan. Each successor state got its share of the army and civil service, but India got not only the bulk of the population but also the capital —Delhi, which had been the seat of Mogul emperors and British viceroys and was now to become the headquarters of a regime secularist at the top and Hindu at the grass roots. Seceding Pakistan was left without any traditional capital—for Karachi had no prestige of history—and was also divided into two widely separated parts, for the process of conversion to Islam in past centuries had left Muslims in a majority only in the western part of the Indus basin and, far to the east, in East Bengal. The odds were against the viability of Pakistan—a state whose very name was an invention of the twentieth century—and yet, at least until the upheaval in Bengal in 1971, it endured beyond expectation and consolidated its national existence in a way that was far from being widely anticipated.

If, however, Pakistan's most remarkable achievement has been to build a state where one did not exist before, India's has been to maintain over nearly a quarter of a century the world's most populous democracy. The record is the more remarkable because, in contrast to the principal parallel Asian democracy in Japan, India had no linguistic unity nor did it have a comparable degree of industrial development or middle-class social formation. So far, in spite of appalling problems of mass poverty and ethnic antagonisms, Indian political democracy has not been superseded either by Communist revolution or by army rule. In Pakistan, on the other hand, the tensions straining the fabric of the new state, and particularly the difficulties of holding together the two geographically separated wings of the nation, led to an acceptance of military rule as necessary to the unity and order of the country. Ayub Khan ruled for ten years, and when he fell from power the disorder was such that a new period of army rule under another general was the only sequel.

In Indonesia a free-election democracy was to be the form of politics after independence, but it was soon replaced under Sukarno's leadership by what he called 'guided democracy'—a coalition of three parties of which one was the Communist. To hold together an archipelago of several large and some thousand small islands he relied on the army, which suppressed armed revolts in the Outer Islands and carried out operations in support of Sukarno's national irredentist policies against the Dutch for western New Guinea and afterwards against Malaysia and the British for North Borneo and Malaya. To prevent the regular army from becoming too powerful Sukarmo devised a scheme for a people's militia which could be used as a check on it, and when the army objected to the arming of this new force he connived at a murderous *coup* against leading generals, which misfired and led to the political fall of Sukarno himself. His semi-dictatorial rule, maintained by clever balancing between Communists and non-Communists, was replaced by army rule under General Suharto, with ruthless proscription of the Communists and a sustained endeavour to restore an economy almost ruined by Sukarno's extraordinary financial extravagance. Under Sukarno, indeed, Indonesia had got the worst of both worlds, for his rule had virtually strangled private capitalist enterprise, native or foreign, without introducing the disciplined collectivism achieved by communist party states.

The five countries whose recent politics are studied in this book thus display examples of three types of state; Japan and India have developed as liberal democracies, China has become a communist party state (with the army since 1966 playing a much more important role than in other communist states), and Pakistan and Indonesia after experiments with democracy have both fallen back on authoritarian forms of government in which the regular armed forces are recognized as essential to the stability as well as to the security of the state. The variety of political developments in these countries, whose inhabitants together number more than fifteen hundred million people, provides a vast field for study and one which, though already history, is also history in the making, so that events still (1972) in the future must soon overtake whatever is written about it. The essays in this book are concerned with special aspects of the Asian political scene in and before the year 1970; though their range of vision has no precise date of commencement, they all belong to the contemporary epoch, and the modernity of their themes can only be fully appreciated if the Asia with which they deal be compared with the Asia which would have confronted a political observer in the year 1870.

CHAPTER II

PREREQUISITES OF MODERNIZATION IN ASIA

W. KLATT

Land provides one of the strongest instruments of power any-where in the world. This is particularly true where land suitable for farming is in short supply, as in large areas of the Indian sub-continent, in Java and in Japan. Where land is available in abundance, man tends to select that portion which best suits his farming methods and is least susceptible to the hazards of an in-clement climate. So, even on the mainland of South-East Asia, where the air traveller may be inclined to register a favourable 'man/land ratio', the man on the ground often has to eke out a meagre existence in fierce competition with his fellows. He may aim at obtaining an optimum return, but often even a minimum may have to be accepted as a kind gesture from the gods.

In this situation man, like land, tends to be part of a balanced system of power relations. Rarely does he live in the state of bucolic happiness that early travellers to Asia were still able to report back to the rapidly changing continent of Europe as it was beginning to build up the tensions of the modern age. To be sure, in some parts of pre-industrial Asia men and women can still afford to be easy-going in an environment which has been kind to them; but on the whole nature, like man, is moody at best and often cruel in the extreme. So life tends to be hard and living conditions often seem squalid to anybody who has been accustomed to a different environment—and this applies to the educated Asian as much as to the foreign visitor or adviser.

It is thus hardly surprising that when, some twenty years ago, new men took over the formerly colonial and semi-colonial countries of Asia, they embarked on modernizing the pre-industrial societies which they had inherited. For the most part, indigenous leaders and their foreign advisers were agreed on rejecting not only the paternalistic political superstructure that was one of the legacies from the past, but also the agrarian basis on which the life of Asia rested. Thus the first decade or so after the gaining of political independence from the European metropolitan powers was marked by efforts at modernizing the new states in such a manner as to make them the equals, in the shortest possible space of time, of those who had been their masters in the past. Where, as in the case of Thailand, the European powers had denied each other control over an Asian territory, the attitudes of its post-war generation differed from those held in former colonial countries in degree rather than in substance. China, which had rarely been penetrated by the white man much beyond the great cities and ports, suffered the humiliation of national defeat and colonial exploitation from the hands of its Asian neighbour Japan. Here the urge to do away with the weaknesses of the past and to emulate, if not to surpass, those who had failed to respect China's sovereignty was particularly strong. To many Asians, whether they had been participants in the Second World War or mere observers of it, there was little to choose between one combatant foreign power and another. Thus the volume of metal and TNT, and ultimately of atomic weapons, hurled against an enemy's strongholds, rather than the record of moral conduct, must have seemed the appropriate measure of the past and therefore of things to come. There were, of course, those who, like Nehru, tried to set standards of international behaviour of the highest order. However, if allowance is made for the lack of national security felt by most of the new nations within their inherited frontiers, it is hardly to be wondered at that steel works and atomic plants ranked high in their order of priorities.

By comparison, agriculture, which, as always, provided work and livelihood for most citizens of the new nations, was at best taken for granted; at times it was even thought to be expendable, together with other features of the past. A highly arbitrary line was often drawn between agricultural and industrial pursuits, as if there were no need in these new nations for the osmotic flow from one sector of society to the other. Of the emerging leaders, mostly educated in Western establishments of higher education, some showed a deep understanding of the history and the workings of European and American institutions, geared to the needs of urban commercial and industrial societies. Few of these new men, however, were equally well briefed on the history of their own nations and on the requirements of the societies which they were about to govern. These societies, more often than not, were frozen in the ways of the Middle Ages when revelation rather than reason regulated the relations between man and deity and traditional human ties had not yet given way to the forms of behaviour that govern modern industrial societies.

Challenge of Ideological Rivals
The issues facing those concerned with modernizing their nations were complex indeed. Moreover, they were agonizingly complicated by the international ideological conflict between rival protagonists in their struggle for the minds of men everywhere. When Mao Tse-tung gained control over China, the controversy could no longer be dismissed merely as an internal squabble between members of the white race. Now the communist system was no longer a reality merely on the continent of Europe. It presented itself also as a viable alternative in the core of Asia, where the traditional values of one of the continent's oldest cultural entities were challenged by the philosophy of historical materialism as interpreted by the new rulers of China. There were those who argued that traditional Asian cultural and religious allegiances would serve as bulwarks against any further encroachment of the communist creed, but they were shown to be

as wrong as their counterparts had formerly been in the European context.

In many respects the doctrine and practice seemed singularly applicable to conditions as they existed in Asia at the time. Being of an all-embracing nature, communism appeared to some well-suited to take the place of any discarded religious belief; but there was more to it than that. Instead of offering to reform outmoded institutions and to progress on a steady, if slow, course from agrarian backwardness to modern industrial society, communists claimed to be able to achieve rapidly the ultimate goal of general prosperity in a classless society, provided all social injustice was swept aside in the course of an uncompromising revolution. So here the nations of Asia, and in particular their politically alert and articulate élites, were faced in the early stages of their new experience with choices that were too far-reaching in their implications to be grasped fully except by the very few. Leaving irrelevant issues aside, the choice was between a long series of reforms and the surgical method of separation from the past by revolution. Who could tell which of the two methods guaranteed success?

The issues were complicated further by the Sino-Soviet dispute. It revealed deep conflicts between the national interests of the two main communist powers, and these were bound to leave their mark on neighbouring Asian nations. The dispute also laid bare differences in the strategies and tactics employed by Russia and China and the communist parties serving their conflicting causes abroad. Of necessity, the schism affected the political life of Asia everywhere, causing multiple splits, as in India's Communist Party, and paralysing the effectiveness of left-wing, non-communist parties, such as the Socialist Party of Japan. There were, of course, also other alternatives of government, ranging from the rule of benevolent autocracies to that of military or party dictatorship, of which the history of the world had provided some tempting examples. Thus there were many systems to choose from. The extent of the agony with which some of the politically less certain leaders must have been faced can only be comprehended fully when it is remembered that absence of such choice is one of the characteristics of traditional pre-industrial society. Considering the dilemma, many of the leaders in Asia acquitted themselves manfully.

The Issue of Law and Order

Taking over from their predecessors, the new men had their hands full with challenging tasks. Invariably the most immediate of them was that of maintaining or restoring a state of law and order, which is the first prerequisite of building a new nation, to say nothing of moving from traditional to modern society. The task which the newly established political authorities were facing would have seemed most formidable to political practitioners of longer and wider experience than any of the new leaders could claim. The assassinations of Aung San of Burma, Gandhi of India, Liaquat Ali Khan of Pakistan, and—last but not least—of Bandaranaike of Ceylon are a measure of the lack of law and order with which the new nations had to contend during their first formative years. But perhaps even more appalling was the loss of life among the ordinary people, not only because of the numbers involved, but even more since death struck so often among the non-committed. They just wished to live their lives as before and had not awoken to the recognition that the process of modernization which they witnessed was bound to be painful at best and often highly costly in men and materials.

There were the losses of hundreds of thousands which occurred in the border states of the Punjab and Bengal between India and the new state of Pakistan. Further losses were caused in parts of Burma and elsewhere by rebels and insurgents who took the departure of the colonial power as a welcome opportunity to switch from fighting the Japanese occupiers to resisting the establishment of a new indigenous authority. Indonesia's 'confrontation' added senseless loss of life and property on her borders in Borneo. But the most serious breakdowns of law and order and the most severe losses of men and materials were caused by those who, instead of cooperating with the new national governments, made the philosophy of guerrilla warfare their own. Parts of the Philippines, Malaya, Vietnam, Laos and Cambodia were chiefly afflicted, but Andhra, Kerala, and West and East Bengal had their share of physical destruction due to the breakdown of the normal processes of government. In these circumstances, it is not to be wondered at that the modernization of the new nations was carried out at times in a somewhat erratic manner and rarely as anticipated.

In fact, with the exception of Japan, which had had its first taste of modernization three quarters of a century earlier than the rest of Asia, no country in the area was able to arrange its affairs in quite the way it had originally planned. All of them were in a hurry, and thus not surprisingly most plans in the economic and social sphere were over-ambitious, placing more trust in the transforming powers of industrialization than was warranted by the endowment of natural resources and the composition of the inherited infra-structure. The first plans were influenced to some extent by the advice given by the non-Asian members of the Colombo Plan, the first international organization to aim simultaneously at both regional cooperation and foreign assistance. It tried to apply to Asia the techniques which, used under the Marshall Plan, had proved highly successful in Europe—no doubt, a misconception in the Asian context. In the course of time, the Asian founding members were joined by almost all other countries in the region, and to the 'old' members of the British Commonwealth were added as donors the United States and Japan. The original plans were marked by their emphasis on the development of agriculture (including irrigation) and of transport, each of which was to take one third of the total funds available, whilst the remainder was shared between the social services and industrialization—which was thus allocated less than 20 per cent of the total estimated cost of development.

Development Priorities

Clearly neither the pace of development nor the order of priorities chosen could satisfy anybody in the region for long. In the eyes of many of the Asian élite, modernization was not going to be achieved in the way the Colombo Plan envisaged it. In the meantime other contenders appeared on the scene: the United Nations with its wide range of multilateral programmes of assistance; the United States, Britain and other industrial nations in Western Europe with unilateral offers of financial and technical aid in both the military and non-military fields; and finally the Soviet Union and other members of the 'socialist camp', specializing in contributions in the public sector and the planning organs of the recipient countries. Original plans were revised or redrawn, and the emphasis was increasingly switched to fixing, before all else, the main pivots of modern industrial society.

It would be erroneous to regard Asia, apart from Japan, at the end of the last war as an area without any kind of modern economy, but what there was had chiefly been chosen under the influence of the colonial powers. As a result, dual economies had developed in which extracting industries, directed by foreigners, such as the tin mines of Malaya and the tea and rubber plantations of India, Ceylon, Indonesia and Malaya, had been superimposed on societies which on the whole continued to live their lives on subsistence farms, untouched by the presence of foreign capital and know-how. Even ten years after the 'emergency' in Malaya, plantation workers, familiar with the techniques used on the estates, could be seen applying subsistence farming methods to their own small plots, i.e. planting closely, tapping prematurely and selling early. The technical and commercial wisdom of the estates was not for them. At the lower end of the dual economy, where land and capital are scarce luxuries rather than the readily available tools of the trade, the workers cannot afford to use the techniques of the estates.

Besides, there were the consumer items, partly produced by Asians for Asians, but partly purchased abroad. Even simple goods, needed for daily use in homes, offices and workshops, had often been imported rather than made domestically. The concept of the international division of labour, cherished in the economic centres of the world for a hundred years or more, had been applied all too often to the disadvantage of Asian communities. It is thus not surprising that industrial self-reliance became the watchword of Asian planners almost everywhere. The excesses resulting from wrong policy decisions bordered at times on the pathetic and the ludicrous. Yet, who could blame those who for the first time applied what they had learned abroad to the conditions they found on returning home? The unnecessary errors committed were, nevertheless, regrettable; they were certainly costly.

Existing Infra-Structure

The existing economic infra-structure varied a great deal from country to country. India had a better system of railways and postal services than most other countries in Asia, apart from Japan. By comparison, China, never entirely under colonial rule, though encroached upon both by European powers and by Japan, was less well served in this respect. The flow of China's great rivers presented natural barriers in the way of a system of communications from north to south, and this was to prove one of the first major challenges with which the new rulers were faced after the Japanese invaders had been driven out. The rule of foreigners over large parts of Asia led to the development of the sea lanes—to the detriment of much else. The large ports of Bombay, Calcutta, Singapore and Shanghai and many small ones besides are monuments to this aspect of the sea-faring nations' activities in that part of the world. Also, the paddy rice economies of Burma, Indochina and Thailand owed their expansion to the opening of the Suez Canal by Western trading interests.

Against this, the resources in the interior of Asia often remained unexplored. It was in the nature of European domination over Asia that bulky and heavy raw materials, such as coal and iron ore, which could be carried to the seaports only at exorbitant cost, were of little interest to foreign explorers and surveyors. Moreover, until landrover, jeep and helicopter became available during the jungle warfare of the early forties, waterlogged territories, such as East Bengal, were closed to all but local travel by river craft for much of the year. The circuit of the colonial district judge was as much circumscribed by the lack of communications as the movements of the culprit whom he had to bring to justice. Only as modern means of transport and communications became readily available to the new governments in Asia, were mineral reserves discovered in remote parts of the continent. China, always believed to be poorly endowed, turned out to have most of the resources on which modern industrialization depends. In some other countries in Asia, however, the shortage of fuel resources has so far acted as a serious brake on indigenous industrial development. Only when atomic energy becomes available at competitive cost will the situation change.

To believe that it required no more than the removal of foreign overlords to release hidden domestic wealth soon proved to be pie in the sky. A great deal of ingenuity and sacrifice was needed to make the break with the past, and to step onto the road towards modern industrial plenty. In this some were more successful than others. By the end of the fiftes most of the ravages of the Second World War had been repaired and the foundations of industrial society had been laid in at least some countries in the area, though others were hamstrung by warfare on their borders or by strife at home. China seemed to have got ahead of its neighbours during its Great Leap Forward, whilst in India the emphasis on heavy industry began to take its toll. The first doubts appeared in official quarters about the choice of planning priorities in the public sector when the farming industry failed to provide the daily diet of the rapidly growing population. In Pakistan, Ayub Khan's regime, relying on the support of a devoted officer corps, a rejuvenated civil service and the initiative

B

of the private entrepeneur rather than the strangely unreal system of 'basic democracies', seemed to be spared the troubles of the Congress Party in neighbouring India and thus to be doing much better than that regime. In Indonesia the political and military leaders, trying to balance antagonistic internal forces by an authoritarian system of 'guided democracy', allowed the armed forces to interfere at all levels with the processes of planning and the tasks of the civil service, thus creating an administrative dualism which proved ineffectual and costly. Economic waste and political uncertainty reigned for many years, during which Indonesia lagged behind all other countries in the area, except for its rate of price inflation and the growth of its external debt. The plantation economies of Malaya and Ceylon and the rice economies of Burma and Thailand could no longer count on the price boom which had followed the Korean War; but if industrialization did not move at a rapid pace, neither was there the same urge to industrialize as in the more densely populated countries of the area. In the meantime, Japan, rapidly recovering from the aftermath of its defeat, surprised all other states in Asia by the speed and diversity with which a renewed modernization took place in all walks of life.

It is still too early to state with certainty to what extent the preconditions of modernization in Asia were established during the sixties, but, judging by the returns available at this stage, the record is unquestionably impressive. Naturally, there have been temporary setbacks. At the same time, certain illusions about economic and social development have been shed. If there is less enthusiasm today for change for its own sake, there is also a growing realization of what is and what is not possible. On the whole, this has not led to widespread cynicism, as it might well have done. At 4 and 6 per cent a year, the overall rates of economic growth (as measured in terms of the volume of gross domestic product), which were achieved in South and South-East Asia during the sixties—and the corresponding industrial growth rates, ranging from 6·5 to 8·5 per cent—can be regarded as impressive, except when set against some of the over-ambitious targets laid down for the end of the first 'development decade'. During this time, Japan did better than the rest of Asia in almost every respect. Expressed in global terms, Japan's annual economic and industrial growth rates reached or surpassed the 10 per cent mark during most of the sixties. This is a formidable achievement by any standard. In most countries of the area the producer goods industries developed faster than those making consumer goods. At the same time, the public sector, which tended to give preference to large industrial units, grew more rapidly than the private sector, though this growth was not necessarily accompanied by a similarly satisfactory record of efficiency. If there was ground for despondency anywhere in Asia, it existed outside rather than inside the industrial sphere of development.

Diversion of Resources

There has, of course, been a certain amount of diversion and waste of human effort and material resources almost everywhere, but it is worth remembering that this was also the case in Europe at the corresponding period of development. In many instances energies were diverted to serve military ends. Pre-industrial countries with meagre public funds at their disposal can ill afford to expend as much as one sixth of government revenue on defence. Yet several countries in the area spent at times up to one third of the public purse in this manner. Indeed, Indonesia at the height of its 'confrontation' with Malaysia allocated more than its total annual revenue to meeting the cost of this adventure. Expressed in a different way, a defence outlay equivalent to not quite US $5 per head as, say, in the case of Pakistan, is a heavy burden for people whose annual income is less than US $100— and these are the orders of magnitude in several countries of Asia. In the case of mainland China, the defence expenditure per head is almost twice as much, or almost 10 per cent of the average annual income of the nation.

Against this, Japan's outstanding success in the post-war

period can, at least in part, be explained by the fact that its so-called self-defence force has so far been kept small—as a matter of constitutional commitment—and the cost involved thus accounts for little more than US $10 per head. This is less than one per cent of the national product against 4 per cent in the case of Pakistan. At Pakistan's rate, Japan would have to divert some US $5,000 million a year, or one third of the country's gross investment, from civilian to military use. This is a measure of the advantage that Japan derives from its relatively small defence budget. In the areas of war or potential war, such as Korea, Vietnam and Taiwan—as indeed in Japan itself—for many years a substantial part of the defence cost has, of course, been met by the United States budget. The same applies to a large portion of the non-military investment programme of countries in Asia outside Japan.

Capital investment cannot usually be financed entirely from domestic savings, although these range from approximately 10–15 per cent of the national income in South and South-East Asia to as much as 30 per cent in Japan, and they are thus not as negligible as is sometimes thought. The foreign contribution to the investment programme varies a good deal from country to country, but it is invariably essential for meeting the plan's foreign exchange component and it is thus vital to the success of any programme of modernization. Of course, the bulk of the funds needed comes from indigenous sources. To give an indication of the orders of magnitude in question, in India the foreign contributions amounted during the period of the third five-year plan to a little less than 5 per cent of the country's total gross domestic expenditure and to about a quarter of its gross investment. In the case of Pakistan, which at the time of the partition of British India was less well provided with the requisites needed for modernization, the foreign contributions were proportionately somewhat larger than for India. By comparison, China has had little foreign assistance, though the loans advanced and the capital equipment supplied by the Soviet Union during China's first five-year plan were critical to the country's early industrial development. In the meantime, China has repaid all foreign debts to the Soviet Union and has financed all economic development for more than ten years from indigenous sources only. This explains to some extent the much reduced rate of growth during the last decade or so. Japan, on the other hand, far from being dependent on foreign financial assistance, has joined the Western donor nations and has become a new exporter of capital. Indonesia has the largest debt *per capita* of any country in Asia. For a long time to come its citizens will have to pay for the extravagance of their late charismatic leader.

Social and Political Implications
The changes which were brought about by industrialization and other forms of development have affected more than the economic structure of Asia. In fact, the social impact, though less amenable to measurement in statistical terms, was often more far-reaching. On occasion, modernization had a traumatic effect on the social fabric of some of the new states. In spite of many years of agitation, when independence eventually came, it came as a shock. The colonial powers had husbanded their own scarce personnel and they had trained far too few 'natives' to take over from them. At the outbreak of the Second World War, the total strength of the Indian civil service amounted to 1,300 men. The Muslim contingent of the administrative élite that was available when Pakistan was founded was less than 150 civil servants and police officers. However, in the years of the struggle for independence, an élite had grown on the Indian sub-continent which had learned as much from Britain as the British had learned from India. By comparison, in Burma, Malaya, French Indochina, and the Netherlands Indies the preparation of the indigenous population for self-rule was conspicuous by its absence. At the beginning of the Second World War, Java had approximately 400 medical doctors of Indonesian and Indian

extraction for a population of almost 50 million people. It still has the lowest rate of physicians in Asia.

In these circumstances, the process of economic modernization was bound to generate major difficulties in the social and political spheres. The strong buffer of a middle class, which had often spared Western society hard knocks from social upstarts, did not exist in most of the new nations. Neither was there an industrial working class of sizeable proportions, except in Japan, where the labour force organized in trade unions today falls little short of the membership of the British Trades Union Congress; in India the number is half as much. Though large in absolute numbers, the organized and unorganized industrial working class is trifling by comparison with the numbers working on the land. At the end of the last war, the need for skilled men in all walks of life was simply enormous. It could not possibly be met from the small reservoir of intellectuals trained in colonial times. In India after independence, some 12,000 seats had to be filled in the capital and the state parliaments alone. In addition skilled men were needed in the new planning administrations, in nationalized industries, in public corporations and in the private sectors. It was hardly surprising that the standards of proficiency declined. The opportunities for political patronage were many and they were not always rejected. In some countries the public services came to be tacitly regarded as employment relief agencies for students who had failed their exams. Almost everywhere over-staffing occurred in the lower grades of the bureaucracy. In 1950, some fifty new entrants at a technical college in South-East Asia, when asked about their plans for the future, expressed satisfaction with the prospect of a clerical, rather than an administrative, post in any of a number of ministries in the capital; all of them were sons of villagers. At that time, the role of the new élite in the changed circumstances after independence had not yet been fully comprehended. Twenty years later in Kashmir, the parents-in-law of a graduate civil engineer assessed the worth of the young man at approximately twelve times the cost of his college educa-

tion. In the intervening two decades social values had changed. A new generation had grown accustomed to regarding itself as an integral part of the new ruling class.

This process of adjustment had not always been easy. It often required a change not only of residence from village to town, but also of loyalties from the religious to the secular authorities. The language of the former colonial power rather than the local vernacular had invariably become the normal form of communication of the administrative and commercial classes. Communal, ethnic and liguistic allegiances came to be questioned, although on the whole existing connections remained well preserved. Most members of the new élite came from established families in town and country. In fact, in most countries in the area social mobility was more restricted than the public pronouncements of the new governments, bent on social justice and equality of opportunities, seemed to imply. All too often birth rather than merit determined public appointment. Broad participation was often limited to such an extent that, contrary to original intentions, social disparities increased instead of shrinking. In the history of development this had always been a feature of modernization, but in the present situation the introduction of universal suffrage at an early stage of development created a novel phenomenon, which could not be ignored for long by indigenous policy-makers and their foreign advisers. Where political dissent was not suppressed, as it was in several countries of the area, the power of the electorate made itself felt increasingly as a factor to be reckoned with. Regional and factional interest began to act as a brake on the operations of the central authorities which, in the absence of developed institutions of mass participation, sometimes wielded an extraordinary amount of power.

In the contest between tradition and change, the armed forces invariably represent an element of considerable cohesion. The traveller to, say, the eastern wing of Pakistan at the time of the assassination of Liaquat Ali Khan would have been struck by the contrast between the muddle in government quarters and the

39

calm competence of the well-trained, well-fed and well-housed officers serving in the armed forces of Pakistan. Their commander was Ayub Khan who some years later ended civilian rule in his country for a decade. In closed societies the temptation to choose coercion as an alternative to persuasion is ever present, and more than one of the new nations in Asia has succumbed to it. At times, the latent antagonism between administrators and politicians— not unknown in Western countries—serves as a direct invitation to the military men to apply their disciplined minds to matters of state. However, as Pakistan and Burma have demonstrated, the military idea of socialism or democracy is no substitute for broadly based civilian government, to which there is no ready return after military rule has been imposed.

Mainland China faced an entirely different problem. Having lost much of the ruling mandarinate when the remnants of the Kuomintang had gone to Taiwan (Formosa), the communist leaders of China had to create most of the new administration from scratch. The system under which the Chinese Communist Party recruited new cadres to its ranks and supervised their lives to the last detail facilitated the formation of an élite to whom the task of modernizing China was entrusted. The methods employed were so different from those applied elsewhere in Asia that they hardly bear any comparison with them. Yet, in China as in the non-communist parts of Asia, the tensions caused by the processes of social engineering led to considerable social and political difficulties. They cannot yet be considered to have been overcome.

Population Pressure

If the new nations of Asia were unprepared for the process of modernization on which they embarked, so were many of their Western well-wishers and advisers. Viewing the situation with hindsight, probably the greatest error of omission originated in the effort of Western medical science to reduce, if not eliminate,

some of the most deadly diseases in Asia. For some considerable time, this laudable action remained unaccompanied by any attempt at reducing the rate of birth and increasing the rate of food production—two operations in the absence of which the control of diseases was bound to cause serious embarrassment to modernizing nations in Asia. Loaded terms, such as 'population explosion', are best avoided in the assessment of any progress made, but there can be little doubt that many problems of the present time would be more manageable had the reduction of human death been accompanied, right from the start, by a full realization of the limited possibilities, in the short term, of controlling human birth and improving farm production. In certain circumstances, a sudden growth of population may well serve as a spur to a society's efforts. In the densely populated parts of Asia this unfortunately was not the case. Instead, there were a number of detrimental effects. The impact on the economic growth rate was the most obvious of them. Whereas during the last twenty years the total domestic product in Asia (outside Japan) more than trebled, it merely doubled in terms of supplies *per capita*. Bearing in mind existing economic disparities, this means that millions of Asians are hardly any better off than they were when their countries became independent.

However, the unexpectedly high population growth rate had other, perhaps less obvious, implications. As the population increased, so the proportion of the young also increased. At the same time, as some of the causes of early death were removed, the lifespan of the old and the incapacitated was prolonged. In consequence, the working population had to labour for a larger number of unproductive members of the community than in the past. In some parts of South and South-East Asia those under 14 and over 65 years of age equal almost half the total population. Against this, in Japan, where the net rate of increase in population is now the lowest in Asia, these unproductive groups account for little more than one third of the total population. The low birth rate has contributed to the Japanese consumers' participation in sharing the fruits of the rate of economic growth, which is higher than anywhere else in Asia.

The effect of the growth of population on the rising rate of urbanization also has to be mentioned. Owing to high urban birth rates and the migration of villagers unable to find work at home, the population of some of the cities in Asia has doubled in little more than ten years. Urban infra-structure could not keep step with this development, and slums and shanty towns have been the result. Since much has been said about the pressure of rapidly growing populations on limited educational facilities in town and country, there is no need to labour this point; but another significant aspect of the phenomenon has escaped public recognition. As more old people stay alive and more young people grow up, the prospects of early inheritance often diminish. Though this is rarely openly mentioned, it has become quite a serious issue in some of the densely populated areas of Asia, where little land lies idle and where therefore more sons have to wait longer than in the past to take over their diminished shares of the family farm. Some of the tension noticeable in villages today would not have arisen, had Western advisers and in-digenous planners thought earlier of the consequences of the unmitigated increase in births without a simultaneous increase in opportunities to work and earn a living. Once again, the social and political implications are as important as those of a purely economic nature.

Western Advice

There are other areas in which Western advice has been disap-pointing and occasionally even misleading. Admittedly, the times when it was assumed that members of the industrial communities of the West knew the answers to the questions of pre-industrial communities have gone. Both sides have become a little more humble in their expectations. Even so, advice is sometimes given all too readily where even the most elementary data on which to base it are lacking and where the assumptions which underlie decisions in industrial society do not apply. Not unnaturally, the enthusiastic newcomer, often unaware of some invaluable historical writings, such as, say, the district commissioners' reports in Burma or the report of the Royal Commission on Indian Agriculture, will feel less restraint in applying his theoretical training to a challenging practical problem than the much maligned former colonial administrator. The latter, though less specialized than the academic graduate of today, tended to regard his assignment as a career for life rather than as a two-year leave of absence from his post at home, and he usually based his advice on an understanding of cultural ties and religious taboos, which nowadays are all too often dismissed as irrelevant to the process of development.

The representatives of the new nations and their Western advisers are confronted with a dilemma in their relations with each other. Having endured foreign tutelage for all too long, Asia's élites wish to attend to the political and social aspects of development without interference from any outsiders. Although modernization is an all-embracing process from which no sphere of human endeavour can be excluded without serious consequences, Western national governments as well as international agencies, in recognition of the limitations imposed on them by the leaders of the new nations, are obliged to limit their advice on the whole to the economic and technical sphere. Not by accident has the United Nations set up regional economic commissions, but these have no mandate, except in very special circumstances, to attend to either the political and social prerequisites of modernization or its political and social consequences. In this situation the economic and technical advisers often gain influence well beyond their professional competence. Economic and technical thinking has frequently influenced the public debate to the exclusion of other aspects of change, and economic and technical arguments have been used at times as excuses for shelving overdue social reforms and for defending outmoded political institutions. Yet some of the traditional institutions present far more difficult hurdles on the ride into the twentieth century than any of the economic and technical details connected with the development of industry, commerce, and the like.

To be sure, economists have been able to bring some valuable tools to the task of helping along the modernization of the new nations. For some time the techniques applied in aggregated and disaggregated models to calculating material balances, input-output relations, inter-sectoral matrices or marginal capital output ratios have been common to planners everywhere. There has been less consensus on the question of the most suitable strategies to be adopted in the interests of economic development. Some economists have stressed the crucial importance of domestic savings and interest rates; others the significance of national specialization within the framework of an international division of labour; yet others the critical role of entrepreneurial initiative and technical innovation. Depending on personal value judgement, some have considered profit maximization or high rates of growth as the chief measures of achievement, whilst others have attributed greater importance to the distribution of wealth and income in the interest of the largest number of participants in the national effort. There is hardly any limit to the alternatives worth consideration. Sometimes growth has been equated with development and development with progress, as if this equation were a part of a sequence, in stages, of a preordained process of evolution. Again, the alternatives of balanced as against unbalanced growth have preoccupied many minds. As most of these various aspects of the strategy of development are bound to become relevant at one time or another, the thoughts of different economic schools have seemed a little academic; as a rule, no two alternatives are mutually exclusive. However, what has often been lacking in the past has been proper timing and consideration of political and social preconditions and implications. In static as well as in well advanced conditions of development no serious harm need come from these omissions; but in the dynamic situations in which many of the new nations find themselves, these aspects of change cannot be treated merely as insignificant extra-economic residuals. Sooner or later they are bound to force themselves to the fore in the national arena. In fact, this situation is already approaching in some parts of Asia where the economic aspects of modernization have been given preeminence whilst growing social tension has been largely ignored.

The Role of Agriculture

In the years in which the national leaders in Asia and their foreign advisers had given pride of place to the development of domestic industries, agriculture of necessity was given a low priority. In many instances no more than one tenth of the investment programme was devoted to the farming industry. On the mainland of China it was less than that. By the end of the fifties, it began to be realized that the order of priorities would have to be altered if disaster were to be averted. In all the countries of the area outside Japan farming represented the largest sector of the community; it was usually also the most neglected. Almost everywhere the rural population accounted for at least two thirds of the total, over half the working population was engaged in agriculture, more than half the average family expenditure was spent on food and well over one third of the gross domestic product was contributed by the farming industry.

In so far as agricultural production had increased up to that time, this was due to an expansion of the acreage under crops rather than to an increase in the productivity of either land or labour. Capital investment allocated to agriculture was largely tied up in slowly maturing irrigation projects, and working capital was used mainly for the purchase of limited supplies of nitrogen fertilizers. These inputs were rarely accompanied by others needed to secure a maximum return, in volume and value, from farm production. As a result, the agricultural output hardly kept pace with the growth of population, thus turning Asia from a surplus producer of grains and other foodstuffs into a substantial importer.

This situation could be faced with equanimity only by countries, such as Malaya, which earned a foreign exchange surplus from the export of plantation products, such as rubber. The situation was more serious in the densely populated parts of South Asia. These became increasingly dependent on the supply of grains from abroad, either under foreign aid programmes or in exchange for scarce foreign currency. By 1959 a report prepared by the Ford Foundation warned that in India grain production would have to be increased substantially within a short period of time, if serious food shortages were to be avoided. These occurred, in fact, in the mid sixties, before the increased supply of farm inputs, such as irrigation water, high-yielding seed varieties, plant nutrients and insecticides, combined with a programme of improved farming practices, had begun to yield results.

In predominantly agrarian societies, such as those of Asia outside Japan, the farming industry fulfils a number of essential functions. Apart from providing a place of work and a source of income for the bulk of the working population, it supplies the foodstuffs needed by both rural and urban consumers and some of the raw materials and manpower used in industry. It also serves as one of the chief sources of government revenue, collected in the form of indirect taxes or export levies, and it thus provides the finance for capital investment in the public sector, whilst some of the rent paid by tenants to landowners finds its way into private investment in industry and commerce. In the course of modernization, the financial and material requirements are bound to increase. It is clearly impossible to meet these needs from a stagnant farming industry; it is thus in everybody's interest to expand agriculture. It is surprising that for a good many years this vital role of agriculture within the context of modernization was not recognized by some of those concerned with the development of the new nations in Asia. They had apparently failed to observe how painful the process of modernization had been in the Soviet Union, where for some forty years the capital required had been extracted from a stagnant rather than an expanding farming community.

The recent shift of emphasis in favour of agriculture is sometimes seen merely as a temporary retreat, similar to Lenin's New Economic Policy of the twenties, and not as a fundamental change of policy comparable to that introduced in Japan after the Meiji Restoration, when it was acknowledged that the intensification of agriculture and the industrialization of other spheres of the economy were interdependent parts of one and the same process. The social and political implications of recent changes in economic policy are not fully comprehended everywhere in Asia either. So far, the 'package programme' of modern farming —which has become possible chiefly as a result of contributions made to development by the Rockefeller and Ford Foundations —has been adopted only by a relatively small number of farmers, well endowed with land, labour and capital, in certain parts of South and South-East Asia where irrigation water is ample throughout the season and the new techniques are not exposed to the effects of drought. This has led to a marked disparity between different farming regions. Even more significant has been the growing polarization within village communities that have participated in the programme. Even its most optimistic supporters do not see the new methods being applied on more than half the farms in the areas where agricultural modernization is under way. This means that differentials in income levels and social status are bound to occur on a significant scale. Tenant farmers and landless labourers in particular will be at a disadvantage in comparison with well-to-do landowners who can afford to spend money on farm inputs and to take the risks involved in applying the new techniques.

Land—A Factor in Modernization

Land is being rediscovered not only as a factor of production, but also as one of the chief sources of social status and political power, which it had always been until industrialization shifted opportunities from the countryside to the urban centres. In the past, administrators, traders and moneylenders returned to 'their' villages once a year to collect their share, as absentee land-owners, of the cultivators' crops. Now many of them have become active farmers employing bailiffs who are expected to apply the new farming techniques and thus to increase their employers' income beyond the previous level of rents paid by the tenants. As a result, land has become scarce; land prices have risen sharply; and tenants have been evicted under escape clauses of the land reform legislation which was introduced with the intention of giving security of tenure and access to land to the under-privileged in the rural areas. Thus in many instances the outcome of the land legislation of the post-war period has not been what it was expected, or indeed intended, to be. Through-out most of Asia the social and political implications of this development are disturbing.

Where agrarian reforms were carried out, they were meant to achieve principally two things: first, to create conditions of security of tenure where previously tenants were at the mercy of their landowning masters; and secondly, to transfer in certain circumstances some land from those who owned it to those who tilled it. These were political steps taken to create some measure of social justice and thus to defuse politically explosive situations. Some economists have argued that these measures are likely to have a detrimental effect on food production, but this need not by any means be so. Their concern is justified only where the state fails to reallocate those of the landlord's functions, such as the maintenance of feeder roads and feeder canals, which some-one has to discharge in place of the dispossessed landowner.

Outside Japan and Taiwan, agrarian reforms were often introduced in a half-hearted manner and were implemented with a maximum of delay and a minimum of effect. They achieved what they set out to do only when the political power of the landowning classes was greatly weakened, as in Japan and Taiwan.

After Japan's defeat, drastic changes became possible which most probably no Japanese administration could have made without the backing of the forces of occupation. In Taiwan the Kuomintang, at the expense of the indigenous landowners and at no cost to themselves, carried out a reform of ownership and tenure which it had been unable to enforce on the mainland of China, where the landowning classes were among its principal political supporters and thus the most effective barrier against any major social reform. Elsewhere in Asia, these social groups were largely identical with the political forces which wrested independence from the metropolitan colonial powers. In victory they had no reason to abdicate the rights of their landed property, as the defeated landowning classes of Japan and Taiwan were obliged to do. In this situation, the failure to carry out agrarian reforms meant the loss of the opportunity of raising food production on tenant farms, of reducing social inequalities in the villages, and of calming the political atmosphere which had become highly charged owing to glaring social and economic disparities. There is now a slowly growing recognition that this state of affairs calls for an appraisal, during the coming decade, of the options open to the countries in the area.

Asian Models

The élites in Asia—whether reformers or rebels—have always scanned the horizon for models suitable to be applied in Asian conditions. Apart from revisionist groups which see the salvation of society in a return to the distant past, most members of the intelligentsia have been attracted by various foreign models. When Britain was defeated at Singapore in 1942, the image of the European colonial powers was shattered beyond repair. As Britain prudently decided after the last war to give up what could no longer be held, the Soviet Union, apparently not only victorious in war but also successful in peace-time planning and development, fascinated many of the new leaders of Asia, many of whom had been affected for some time by State intervention of one form or another. Those who were drawn by the promises of private initiative rather than centralized planning tended to look for leadership to the United States instead of the Soviet Union. However, neither was likely to serve as a model applicable in Asian conditions. Leaving all else aside, both were industrialized well beyond anything that Asian countries—apart from Japan—could hope to achieve in the foreseeable future. Also, both competed for the allegiance of Asia, and in doing so they revealed some of the weaknesses inherent in their status as world powers.

As Japan developed rapidly, outpacing most other industrial nations in the world with its rate of growth, it drew attention to its form of modernization as a pattern possibly suited to other parts of the continent. Being an Asian nation, it began, in spite of its appalling war-time record, to attract interest, though not sympathy, among Asian intellectuals. This interest became intense when agricultural development gained a place of priority in some parts of the area. Japan had been outstandingly successful not only in raising its farm output to an all-time record; it had also carried out one of the few successful agrarian reforms and had thus created some of the prerequisites for viable rural self-government. But, contrary to the views of certain Marxist interpreters, Japan was the only country in Asia with a genuinely feudal historical past, which, though not an unmixed blessing, had enabled the country's leaders to call on the samurai for their contribution to the process of modernization. Elsewhere in Asia neither religious nor industrial and commercial groups were suited to fill this void. The sense of responsibility, on which the leaders of the Restoration were able to count in Japan, had yet to be created when almost a hundred years later the process of modernization gained momentum elsewhere in Asia.

Of the other countries, large in area and population, though not powerful as national entities, those in South and South-East Asia are unlikely to serve as models for others to copy, though the Indian experiment in modernization has at times attracted some other Asians outside the sub-continent. Indeed, at the height of Nehru's premiership, India gave a lead in the area of international relations well beyond the confines of the continent. However, when the five principles of territorial integrity, non-aggression, non-interference, equality, and peaceful coexistence, agreed between India and China in 1954, had to be abandoned eight years later in the war on the Sino-Indian borders, India lost much of its status in the councils of the non-aligned nations. The war with Pakistan did nothing to restore it.

After two wars with its principal neighbours, two failing monsoons and the loss of two prime ministers, India hardly presented a model for others to follow. Yet, in spite of growing disenchantment with the concept of secularism and socialism at home and of non-alignment abroad, India has so far weathered the storms of modernization remarkably well. The institutionalized framework, within which Congress ruled supreme for two decades, has so far held in spite of being challenged by vocal opponents. As the centre lost some of its authority in the wake of the 1967 elections, the regional political élites gained in status, if not always in stature. This process was not reversed by the victories of the Congress Party in March 1971 and in March 1972. Agricultural development brought some badly needed relief on the home front, but it also put rural vested interests in the forefront of political affairs. The landowning classes sometimes now clash openly with small tenants and landless labourers, many of whom belong to the scheduled castes which, in spite of official pronouncements to the contrary, continue to be a fact of life in the rural districts. There is a militant mood abroad in the villages of India—and elsewhere in Asia. This is where China's present position is relevant to the rest of the continent.

The Image of China
The image of China as a model suitable to other parts of Asia has undergone many changes since Mao Tse-tung led the CCP to victory in 1949. Since then, China has become a country

governed by the most gerontocratic bureaucracy in Asia. While the changes that will be introduced after Mao's departure from the political scene cannot be anticipated, the pattern that emerged at the end of the Cultural Revolution will be retained, it may be assumed, for some time to come. China's prerequisites for modernization are unique and thus make its political, social and economic pattern unsuitable elsewhere in Asia. Yet, even under different circumstances the method by which power was seized and retained is regarded as relevant by those who see in guerrilla warfare the chief weapon with which to remove established authority and to replace it with 'peoples' democracy', i.e. with the central control of the Communist Party over all aspects of life.

The CCP seemed to be highly successful in handling the nation's affairs up to 1957, but the course of development was disrupted badly by the Great Leap Forward and the Cultural Revolution which respectively opened and closed the decade following the successful termination of the first five-year plan. In the agricultural sphere in particular, planning has been faulty in the extreme and plan implementation has been disastrous. Though agriculture was declared the 'foundation' of the nation's economy ten years ago, in all probability farm production has merely kept step with the growth in population. The advance which China achieved over India in the first few years after the last war has now largely been lost. This has led to a good deal of disenchantment among former admirers of the Chinese experiment. The established governments in the area fear China's presence sufficiently to treat their powerful neighbour with circumspection, but the times when official missions went to China for guidance and enlightenment on such subjects as agricultural planning and agrarian cooperatives have not yet returned. Pakistan's relations with China are largely dictated by its hostility towards India, which for its part has not yet restored normal relations with China. Russo-Indian relations are influenced by India's fear of the intentions of both China and Pakistan. In any event, as a supplier of aid the Soviet Union is, of course, much to be preferred to China.

Among the overseas Chinese the image of mainland China reached an all-time low at the height of the Cultural Revolution. The new generation of overseas Chinese feel less drawn to their country of origin, the more the country of residence gives way to their desire to assimilate. This does not yet happen, however, in several countries in the area. The outbreak of violence among Malays against the Chinese in their midst is only one recent incident in a long series of anti-Chinese actions in South-East Asia. To consider the overseas Chinese as a potential fifth column of mainland China amounts to a misreading of recent developments in Asia. China's supporters have to be sought elsewhere. They are mainly to be found among those alienated from the ruling groups which they have failed to join, but those who fight them are often also affected by the techniques applied by China at home and aboard. The chief attraction lies in the order of priorities which puts politics 'in command' over everything else. This is often in contrast with the order chosen by governments in the area and by their Western advisers who, of necessity, if not by preference, deprive politics of the commanding position it deserves in the present situation of change.

It would be wrong to exaggerate at this stage the significance of groups that follow the lead from Peking; except in the territories which previously formed Indochina, these groups are mostly small, poorly armed, and at loggerheads with other groups of the Left. However, to underrate their potential impact on the future of Asia could turn out to be a fatal mistake. Brief reference is made here to the activities of the Huks in the provinces of Pampanga and Tarlac in Central Luzon (Philippines); to those of the communist-controlled Peasants' Front (BTI) in Central Java (Indonesia) which ended with the abortive coup of September 1965; and to those of the so-called Naxalites who derive their name from the revolt, in 1967, of cultivators in the district of Naxalbari at the foot of the Himalayas in

West Bengal (India). There are other groups operating elsewhere.

Caution is called for in labelling these groups of discontented cultivators belonging to various tribes and nationalities, as if they were acting under a unified command receiving their orders directly from Peking. This is not the case. However, whereas each group has its specific characteristics which do not fit readily into a general pattern, the conditions under which they operate have certain features in common. As a rule, these groups are based in areas of ethnic or linguistic minorities, where land is scarce, the incidence of rural tenancy is high, the cultivators are poor as a result, and neighbouring areas of plantation farming facilitate political organization of farm labour. In these circumstances left-wing politicians, such as José Sison in Central Luzon, Kanu Sanyal in West Bengal, the late Dipa Nusantara Aidit in Java, and their local agents, have found it of distinct advantage to devote their efforts to these selected areas. Their techniques are usually modelled on those used by Mao during the years when he relied exclusively on the rural areas. They often live frugal lives on a pittance, but holding a wealthy village to ransom or looting a landlord's farmhouse will hardly cause them any qualms. Agitation among dissastisfied villagers, acts of terror directed against individual landowners or officials, and the creation of a highly conspiratorial apparatus furnished with modern means of communication invariably leave their marks in the areas of operation, which are left at short notice for neighbouring jungles or swamps when an attack by the police and the danger of arrest are imminent.

These few details may serve as a measure of the troubles which these small groups of devoted men, trained in the strategy of revolution and the tactics of guerrilla warfare, can cause to the established order, when they seize on a rural population which has genuine grievances. In this situation, to put up a few armed guards, as some landowners in South Asia do, can only be regarded as a rather inept means of facing a highly organized form of political action. Other measures, such as sharing their capital resources and know-how, if not their land, with their tenants and farmhands, are rarely considered by those in danger of eventually losing everything they possess.

The Cultivator's Role

It is true that cultivators rarely turn to organised forms of violence without outside leadership, but where urban intellectuals succeed in infiltrating closely-knit village communities there is usually a pile of grievances waiting to be set ablaze. The view, still encountered at times in government offices, agricultural colleges and manor houses, that in subsistence economies the cultivators' acceptance of hardship knows no bounds can no longer be upheld. The transistor radio, the bicycle and the local bus have facilitated a mobility of the mind and the body which is leading to demands for social mobility and political participation. Even police action cannot suppress these ambitions. The failure of the PKI to gain control over Java in 1965 should not be taken as an unfailing guide to the future. Political chances, like natural hazards, cannot be predicted, and they can only be guarded against by a well-developed system of dams and sluices.

The late D. N. Aidit, probably at the time the ablest of communist leaders within the Asian communist camp, held that the Indonesian revolution was in essence an agrarian affair, although, naturally, it was led by the proletariat, i.e. urban intellectuals devoted to the communist cause. Where effective reforms cannot be introduced and implemented in time, Aidit's concept seems the only alternative left. As the Russian and Chinese revolutions, and other upheavals before them, have demonstrated, revolutions are reforms by other means. Privileged groups have rarely shed any of their vested interests voluntarily and in time, and they may not do so in Asia either. In that case their fate is unlikely to be substantially different from that suffered by those who before them declined the option of re-form—an alternative less costly in human and material values.

The choice is that of the ruling élites and of the privileged groups which back them, and nobody can make it for them. Until their decision is reached and acted upon, modernization will remain one-sided.

Measures designed to raise the economic growth rate, and thus destined, in present circumstances, to enhance the material and social status of the few without the participation of the many, can have a palliative effect for a limited period only. They can buy time, but they cannot avert ultimate disaster. Without measures being taken simultaneously to create the social and political prerequisites of modernization, most of which are still lacking in Asia, tensions are likely to be caused instead of being avoided. If reform is aimed at rather than revolution, in place of the technical 'package programme' of the past decade a much wider one of closely interrelated and well-timed economic, social and political 'inputs' will need to be drawn up and implemented to secure a comprehensive process of modernization instead of the one-sided process of the past. Precedents for such a broad approach can be found at some points in history and in some parts of the world, though there has rarely been a period free from bloodshed. To believe in the process of evolution as if it were a law of nature is a speciality of the Western mind which is not necessarily appreciated elsewhere in the world. Even the limited ground gained in Asia in the last two decades may well be lost again. It need hardly be recalled that much of what was achieved in Europe in the four centuries following the Renaissance was lost for a time, within the lifespan of a generation that is not yet extinct. In Asia, as elsewhere, the road towards modernization will be long. Many hurdles have yet to be taken, and the final goal is not yet in sight.

tion' under Bismarck and Hitler. Now that there is no country which is not involved in the process, there is all the more reason to consider how such a vast and variegated country as China has tackled the problem of modernizing. If, as some experts in development claim, what is important is not economic aid or resources but modern men, *prima facie* the priority China has accorded to changing the public mind would not seem so mad as it has often been thought to be. Handling children, as President Liu Shao-ch'i said, is more important than handling tractor pumps. But the disagreement on *how* to handle them between his ilk and the 'good students of Chairman Mao' was one of the basic issues in the Great Proletarian Cultural Revolution, the story of which contains some instructive lessons for other societies.

The month of December 1964 saw a number of administrative changes and the adoption of measures intended to solve 'contradictions' which had become apparent in the economy and in society. The published reports of the National People's Congress held at this time and other ancillary publicity indicate that the basic outlook of the Party and Government apparatus was then one of strengthening 'rectification' in order to gear the country's resources for defence and prepare for elaboration and implementation of the Third Five-Year Plan, due to begin in 1966. Special attention was given, for example, to the various ministries of machine-building concerned with the production of armaments, and to political consolidation and economic development of the south-western provinces in view of the possibility that they might have an increasing role to play in the widening Indochina war. This approach meant, essentially, using 'politics' to serve as a *means* of attaining the traditional goal of 'wealth and power' (*fu chiang*). Such an approach was alien to the thought of Mao Tse-tung, for whom politics, seen as the struggle for the transformation of man, was the ultimate value. This struggle can be conducted, Mao says, with or without bloodshed; politics plus bloodshed is war, but he agrees with Sun Tzu that the supreme art of war is to win without actually fighting; thus, politics for him ideally is bloodless war by which men are changed—a continuous revolution, by no means the preservation of any *status quo*.

The underlying problem with which both he and the leaders of the apparatus were trying to deal was the creation of a national identity for China, a congeries of groups of diverse ethnic origin hitherto united, as Professor Fitzgerald puts it, by a common culture. This culture must now be chewed over and largely rejected as feudal and responsible for China's past miseries. It was not surprising that the 'struggle between two lines' came to a head during 1965, as the Army, reindoctrinated with Lin Piao's version of Mao's ideology, extended organizational control over an increasing number of civilian administrative structures under cover of the 'Mao-study' campaign. On two key issues the struggle was particularly fierce, and is now well documented: first, on Defence and Foreign Policy (i.e. international relations 'without bloodshed'), and secondly on the handling of young people, especially the education of children and adolescents, the employment of trained manpower, and the 'training of revolutionary successors'. The latter was a problem of securing a sense of *temporal* continuity or 'revolutionary immortality', as described in the work of that name by Robert Lifton,[1] whereas the former was a matter of replacing the old concept of China as a culture-area without definite boundaries, deriving its unity from the moral influence of the Emperor at its centre, by a hard skin, as it were, of precisely demarcated and securely defended State borders. Combination of these processes would have meant transferring the old idea of unlimited *rayonnements* from the spatial to the temporal sphere, with which pre-modern Chinese thought was relatively unconcerned, positing recurrent cycles rather than an infinity. The dilemma was that the methods adopted during the early sixties to meet the requirements of consolidating China as a defensible territory, and so ultimately

[1] Robert J. Lifton, *Revolutionary Immortality*, now available in Penguin Books, London 1970.

59

a modern nation-state, seemed to be incompatible with the other basic requirement. This was to avoid automatic cultural defeat (hence loss of the morale more essential to defence than weapons and logistics) by the very process of modernization which was meant to secure China's future; it was vital, for Mao, to preserve his version of the essence of Chinese culture or personality (*t'i*) while employing (*yung*) the trappings of modern technology. In other words, it was necessary to inspire the emerging nation with the spirit of his guerrilla armies of uprooted peasants and *éléments déclassés*, freed from the traditional culture of 'feudal' China by their life of struggle and his 'rectification' campaigns and endowed with what he considered to be a true proletarian culture, which would prevent China from suffering the fate of other countries that had lost their souls under the impact of the Industrial Revolution.

The two-stream educational and labour systems adopted owing to force of circumstances under Liu Shao-ch'i's 'revisionist' leadership accepted meritocracy, if not aristocracy, in the classroom and privilege in the workshop for established urban and and veteran workers as against young people brought in on contract from the countryside when rural employment was not available. On ideological grounds alone Mao set his face against such division of labour; though European Communists see in this a petty-bourgeois egalitarianism of the small producers, realism too required Mao to make sure that the head of steam generated among the still unremoulded 'petty-bourgeois' masses by the non-fulfilment of their rising expectations should be let off to power a clockwise, rather than counter-clockwise, turn of the wheel of history.

The two problems of Defence and Youth were of course closely linked in the perennial debate on whether soldiers, students and ultimately everyone should be more 'red' (inspired by Mao's proletarian culture) or more 'expert' (adopting an impersonal scientific approach). The logical conclusion of stressing redness was to contend that morale and motivation are paramount, as in guerrilla warfare, the key to morale being a militant enthusiasm (in the technical sense defined by Konrad Lorenz)[1] expressed in terms of hatred for a common enemy, and corresponding selfless devotion to members of one's own group. Stressing expertise is accordingly associated with selfishness and devilishness, isolating one from the group, so that, although it is recognized that experts must be trained in modern technology, it is also necessary to guard against the dehumanizing effects of such an apprenticeship—an idea symbolized in Western folklore by Faust and the mad scientists of popular fiction. In the minds of the Chinese Communist leaders, long accustomed to see everything in military terms, the issue was well symbolized by the question of whether military officers should wear badges of rank, setting them off as an élite of professionals as against the conscript 'masses'.

In the period of sovietization after 1949, the Chinese Army got a Prussian-style officer corps with elaborate uniforms, along with the heavy modern equipment, a regular command system, and technical training purveyed by the Soviet advisers; the same outlook pervaded the civilian establishment as well—Stalinism tended to replace the 'guerrilla style', whether the emphasis was on one-man management (edinonachalie) or the primacy of Party Committees. Both in the Army and in the civilian enterprises whose task, in the last analysis, was to provide the Army with its weaponry and supplies, political work tended to be neglected in favour of the 'purely professional, purely productional viewpoint'. The outlook associated with Liu Shao-ch'i was not unlike that of the manager of a large industrial enterprise—China Holdings—concerned to recruit, train and suitably employ the labour force so as to increase and diversify production, and enhance its competitive strength in the world market, or, if necessary, in the transactions of war. The shareholders in this analogy would be the members of the Chinese Communist Party,

[1] See *Aggression*, by Konrad Lorenz, Bantam Books, New York, 1963, pp. 250, 259–65, on the dangerous nature of militant mass enthusiasm.

collectively owning the means of production and receiving their dividends not so much in cash and prerequisites as in the more satisfying form of status, power and prestige.

Mao Tse-tung's aim was also the self-strengthening of China, but his remedy for the 'national malady'—diagnosed by Sun Yat-sen as disaggregation like a 'sheet of sand'—was a combination of shock treatment to break the old habits and make the patient receptive, and painstaking re-education, drill, and occupational therapy to restore healthy motions to the body politic. The sort of strength which Mao wanted to give to China was to come not primarily from steelworks or atomic weapons made by experts—though these were also seen as necessary—but from the collective energies of the undifferentiated masses, 'liberated' by the stress of the 'mass movement', the highest form of which is people's revolutionary war, and then focused as in a cyclotron by the magical power of Mao Tse-tung thought.

'The great thought of Mao Tse-tung has enabled the revolutionary enthusiasm and creativeness lying in the hundreds of millions of people to burst forth *like atomic energy*[1] (my italics).

The idea behind the emphasis, in Mao's theory and practice, on making everyone participate in mass movements, to learn new patterns of behaviour and culture by doing new things, is not particularly new; one can find the theory of 'remoulding' in Aristotle's *Nicomachean Ethics*,[2] and as early as Sun Tzu military commanders were aware of the need to keep the troops busy and on the move. Modern armies invent pointless exercises and fatigues for this purpose, in order to retain the initiative of command. The new element in Mao's formula is that the movements of mass participation rely so heavily on the more or less artificial stimulation of militant enthusiasm; no doubt this

---

[1] *Peoples Daily* (*PD*), National Day editorial, 1 October 1966.

[2] According to Aristotle the lawgivers of Greek states sought to make the citizens conform to accepted norms by a process of conditioning; *ethizontes tous politas poiousin agathous* (*Nicomachean Ethics*).

feature has much to do with the special quality in Chinese society of repressed aggression against figures representing authority—fathers and elder brothers, educators, bosses and bossy foreigners.[1] The reverse of the coin of submission to, and identification with, oppressive patriarchal authority is suppression of strong feelings of humiliation and indignation (*ch'i*) which must sooner or later burst forth in violent action against the self or some substitute target.

Such phenomena of displacement are, of course, not unique to Chinese culture; a War Office memorandum of 1944 on the morale of the German Army, based on interrogation by psychiatrists of a large number of Nazi officers and troops, explained the process of submission, internal conflict and projection—in this case onto Jews, Slavs, etc.—and demonstrated how the typical personal philosophy of the Nazi believer of that time determined the State philosophy of the Third Reich—encirclement by enemies who are trying to prevent us attain our real greatness, the nobility of war and the qualities it brings out in man, the Wehrmacht as a school, and so on—themes which are found today in the propaganda of Maoism. But the remarkable innovation of Mao's Great Proletarian Cultural Revolution was that it did, at least to begin with, turn the explosion of aggression against figures in authority, or symbolizing authority, such as teachers, heads of universities, party secretaries, and, in the end, the President of the Republic. Whereas the Third Reich solved the problem of conflict between individual impulses and strict social control by seeking freedom, as the wartime analysis put it, not inside but outside, the frontiers, Mao's China, seen as a group personality, rejected this type of solution in favour of the self-punishing attitude reflected in the witch-hunt and approach to civil war characteristic of the Cultural Revolution. From the point of view of the Party, continually exhorted to submit to the criticism of the masses and be a 'willing ox' to serve the people,

[1] See *The Spirit of Chinese Politics*, a psycho-cultural study of the authority crisis in political development, by Lucian W. Pye, M.I.T. Press 1968, Chapter 5 and *passim*.

the psychological mechanism is even more obvious. Instead of blaming the effects of the debilitating internal conflict entirely on outside forces—imperialist encirclement, Trotskyite sabotage or what not—the Party is supposed to expose and get rid of its 'dark side', as Lin Piao put it in a revealing remark. But not everyone in the Party or governmental and educational apparatus had such psychological insight; it may be more than a coincidence that Chief of Staff Lo Jui-ch'ing,[1] who does seem to have advocated exporting China's conflicts 'beyond the passes', was characterized as a jackbooted stormtrooper by his Red Guard critics. Another undesirable feature of Chinese society which the Cultural Revolution did something to redress, at least in its early stages, was the tendency to project onto victims of the successive struggle movements, such as the Socialist Education campaign, so that an outcast group of unpeople or *Gegenreich* (the five kinds of bad elements) was being formed with the same scapegoat function as *finanzjudentum* in the Nazi mythology. This was a logical corollary of the strengthening of the power of Security and Procuratorial organs and the control apparatus of the Party following the anti-Rightist movements of 1957 and 1959.

We know from Lin Piao's statement at the Ninth Congress of the Party that previous efforts to purge the Party and society of its 'dark side' by the tried and tested method of Party work teams stimulating mass criticism and struggle campaigns from behind the scenes had all proved ineffective; according to Liu Shao-ch'i, the 'masses' had become more adept at manipulating these techniques than the cadres themselves.[2] Thus all Communists were agreed that something had to be done; the disagreement was on how it was to be done, and so, in the last analysis, who

---

[1] Lo Jui-ch'ing was removed from his post during 1966.

[2] In a report of 18 August 1964 Liu said 'during the past many movements the class enemies have learned about the several sets of methods used by us. Even in some respects they have studied the Party's policies and principles far better than our Party members have done'. Quoted in 'Selected Edition on Liu Shao-ch'i's Counter-Revolutionary Revisionist Crimes', a Red Rebel publication of April 1967, in *Selections from Mainland Magazines (SCMM)* No. 652, p. 35, 28 April 1969.

was to do the re-educating. What is still mysterious about the events of 1965 is exactly how far and when the views of the so-called Revisionists in the Party really deviated from those of Mao; for up to the last everyone claimed his authority for their policies.

This was particularly noticeable in the great debate on Youth work and education which went on in China between September 1962 and April 1966. Though it centred ostensibly on such questions as the definition of 'all-round development', the proper combination of work and rest and manual and mental labour, the real issue was whether China would ossify into a form of police state, exhibiting many features in common with Nazi Germany and the Soviet Union, or would move back in the direction of Mao's original conception of an emotional rather than organizational solidarity, based on feelings analogous to the *esprit de corps* of a small military unit, adolescent gang, or religious sect.

The dichotomy was already apparent in the published writings of Mao and Liu Shao-ch'i on the nature and role of the Party. While Liu stressed the importance of its structure and organization, in keeping with his managerial view ('you salute the uniform, not the man'), Mao regarded the Party more as a crowd of adepts individually perfecting themselves by 'study' and by labour, without any need for an intermediate hierarchy or structure. To draw an analogy which had also struck some Chinese, the Liuists were like Catholic Royalists, while Mao's forces were like Cromwell's dissenters, especially the Levellers.[1] The Liuists wanted to produce *from among* the proletariat an élite capable of building Communism for everybody, though they might reach it at different times—especially the non-Han national minorities. But the Maoist approach called rather for immediate and universal introduction of the half-labour-half-study system of education, so that everyone should remain on the same level and build communism together. As late as December 1965 the names of

[1] See *Les Nivelours, Cromwell et la Republique*, by O. Lutaud, Julliard, 1967; also article by Melvin Lasky in *Encounter*, January 1969, p. 45.

C

both Mao and Liu were linked with the élitist policy by the Peking newspapers *Kwangming Daily* and *People's Daily*. It was later alleged that 'capitalist roaders' in the Party had taken Mao's name in vain, but the truth of such charges is hard to gauge.

The conflict between the two-stream, élitist policy and what later emerged as the Mao-Lin policy extended from the field of education and youth work to the closely related theoretical problem of blending mental with manual labour—in concrete terms, the training, 'rectification' and employment of professional manpower, both Party and non-Party, cadre policy, management policy, use of intellectuals, technical experts, and other 'upper strata' (including dignitaries of non-Chinese nationalities within the boundaries of the Chinese People's Republic), vocational training of workers, peasants and especially soldiers, and many other matters. Many of these problems came under the heading of United Front Work, and in this and other ways extended even into foreign policy via the links between national minorities policy and foreign relations, the use of foreign experts and expertise, learning of foreign languages, etc., etc. These issues concerned not only the United Front Work Department, but also the Party School and all sorts of other training organs, the Control Commission of the Party and Secretariat and the mass organizations such as the Young Communist League and Pioneers, the All China Federation of Trade Unions and the Federation of Industrial and Commercial Circles. In the Army itself, the struggle between the two lines had been going on for years; in spite of repeated changes of personnel, the Ministers of Defence and Chiefs of Staff seemed by the logic of their positions to adopt the professional viewpoint—all except Lin Piao. Even in the field of secret police work, there was a conflict between advocates of the standard Soviet-style secret police techniques, and the Mao line of mobilizing the masses to hold struggle sessions to unmask and discipline deviationists.

Broadly speaking, the swings in Peking's educational policy since the Liberation in 1949 can be seen in terms of the period of russification, which was followed by attempts to return to something like the style of work of the 'liberated areas' of the civil war times. The mixed motives of these attempts included both practical and ideological elements; on the one hand lack of funds and resources, and on the other a desire to avoid perpetuation of a 'bourgeois' system of education even if the wherewithal had been available.

The educational policy of the Chinese Communists in the war-time liberated areas was, like economic policy, industrial production, and the other ancillary services of the Army, characterized by extreme decentralization and adaptation to the pragmatic local needs and conditions. In accordance with the Army's policy of combining military operations and training (essentially the same thing) with production and political agitation, *study* (*hsüeh-hsi*)—largely spare-time literacy and vocational training for adults—*was added to labour*, in contrast to the USSR where the combination of theory and practice meant rather establishment of workshops in full-time schools.

This aspect of the 'Yenan style of work' was exemplified in the Line and Regulations of Yenan University and reflected Mao's personal attitude to intellectuals in general, as shown in the Yenan talks on literary and artistic work; the intelligentsia must step over to the proletariat by going 'into the thick of practical struggles'.

Yenan's conditions called for, and could only produce, highly motivated generalists. However, after 1949 (as Liu Shao-ch'i said) Mao's military leaders had to take over the entire national economy; there was a swing to specialization and selection with emphasis on quality rather than quantity, in imitation of the Soviet system.[1] Simultaneously, requirements for the self-

---

[1] 'The guiding principle of this system is that institutions of higher learning should aim at training cadres for specific jobs in the highly compex fabric of economic construction. The whole educational procedure reverses the pre-liberation process, which by trying to turn out *jacks-of-all-trades* aimed at lessening the chances of their being unemployed if their own particular "speciality" was already overstaffed.' (Tseng Chao-Lun on Higher Education, quoted in Stuart Fraser (ed.), *Chinese Communist Education*, Vanderbilt University Press, Nashville, USA, 1965, pp. 165–85.)

remoulding of cadres *by manual labour* became less rigorous: it was sometimes implied that study of Marxism-Leninism was enough, or, as Ch'en Po-ta put it, China must now imitate Lenin's Russia.

'Lenin said: "We have now won Russia . . . now we must learn to administer Russia. And to do that we must learn to be modest and to respect the efficient work of the experts in science and technology" . . . According to Lenin a scientist or an engineer will come to accept Communism *through the data of his science and his own way.* This is an important revelation for us.' (my italics).[1]

This policy followed logically from Lu Ting-yi's announcement in 1950 that

'The Central People's Government regards the development of education for workers and peasants and the turning out of *new intelligentsia from among the workers and the peasants* as its foremost cultural and educational task.'

This new intelligentsia, he hoped, would join in the work of industrialization with the 'intelligentsia from other social classes who are likewise determined to serve the country'.

When the imitation of Soviet methods of development was at its height in 1953–4, enrolment in higher and middle schools was decreased. In 1953 the five-year unified elementary school system was abandoned in favour of the old six-year two-part system, in which many pupils dropped out after the first three years. There were not enough teachers or schools. The *People's Daily* pointed to the example of the USSR which in the 1920s 'adopted a policy of educational retrenchment in order to concentrate on industrial growth'. The central authorities were also concerned to maintain and unify standards, in line with the general tendency to centralization, *gleichschaltung* and vertical control.

[1] *Chinese Communist Education*, Vanderbilt University Press, Nashville, USA, 1965, p. 192.

In 1954 the Peking Municipal Party Committee published a decision, drafted under the direction of Mayor P'eng Chen, on raising the quality of secondary and primary education.[1] It allegedly stressed professionalism, examination marks and material incentives, so that the students had no time for political activities.

The defeat in 1954-5 of Kao Kang's anti-Party group left Liu Shao-ch'i and Chou En-lai both in a strong position, the former broadly controlling the Party, the latter the Government apparatus. There ensued a period of transition or indecision. Until 1958 little was openly said about education, though enrolment in the elementary and spare-time schools rose again. In his 1956 report on the training of Chinese intellectuals to replace, eventually, the Soviet experts, Chou En-lai mentioned three ways along which their re-education should proceed.

'One is through observation and taking part in social life; the other is through the work in their professions; and the third is through general theoretical study.'[2]

Typically, Chou here blurs and reconciles three divergent viewpoints.

1. Remoulding is effected by 'going deep into real life'—the life of the masses, i.e. *physical labour* (Lao-tung as against Kung-tso).
2. Intellectuals come to accept Communism 'through the data of', i.e. by working at, one's own art or science, without needing to perform other labour.
3. Intellectuals are cured of bourgeois thoughts by studying *Marxism-Leninism* rather than by any sort of work.

---

[1] See Red Guard material attacking P'eng Chen, translated in *SCMM*, No. 639, 10 June 1967.

[2] Report 'on the question of the intellectuals' delivered 14 January 1956. Foreign Languages Press, Peking, 1956.

The admitted aim of his policy was to create Chinese experts to replace the Soviet experts. However, May 1956 saw the launching of a campaign to counter bureaucratism among mental workers in the Party; in September Chou announced to the Party Congress that redundant personnel would be sent down (*hsia fang*) to lower echelons. Gradually, however, this *hsia fang* seems to have changed from a method of adjusting the *system*, by redistributing its components more rationally, to a method for correcting (or punishing) the 'bureaucratic airs' of *individuals*. With the development of the 'Hundred Flowers' movement into the anti-Rightist Campaign in June 1957, this *hsia fang* reform was widely extended to non-Party mental workers too.

In 1957 Mao allegedly put forward the policy of 'enabling one who receives education to develop morally, intellectually and physically and become a labourer with socialist consciousness and culture', and P'eng Chen's policy was criticized. However, the critics were subjected to struggle meetings and some were sent down for labour reform in 1958.[1]

The 'Great Leap Forward' of 1958 officially combined a *technological* as well as a *cultural* revolution. It saw a certain return to the organizationally decentralized but ideologically unified Yenan style of work, with power centred in Party Committees at each level rather than in ministries in Peking. Instead of a set of 'private kingdoms' based on vertical control from these central bureaucracies, a new set of 'watertight' domains soon emerged based on the 'horizontal' power of Party Committees; one of these was to be the Peking Municipal Party Committee itself.

Following the second session of the Party's Eighth Congress in 1958, in which Liu Shao-ch'i played a prominent part, an important speech by Lu Ting-yi was published in September; it was entitled 'Education must be combined with productive labour' and

[1] See *SCMM* No. 639, 6 January 1969, p. 10: 'Counter-Revolutionary Revisionist P'eng Chen's towering crimes of opposing the Party, Socialism and the thought of Mao Tse-tung'.

reasserted the importance of combining mental and manual labour, of the masses taking part in running educational institutions, and of spreading education widely even at the expense of standardization:

'In the final analysis, the debate on education that has been going on in the recent years boils down to the question of "what is all-round development"?

The bourgeois pedagogues "do not hold with students studying politics and participating in productive labour". When they speak of versatility, they mean extensive book-knowledge. But Communists believe that workers should be peasants and peasants workers, cadres should labour and workers do administration, and so on.

The aim of the Cultural Revolution is to enable all 600 million Chinese people, except for those who are incapable, to do productive work and to study.'

This policy was implemented by such schemes as the rural *min-pan* (people-managed) schools, notably agricultural middle schools, teaching the peasants locally-needed skills. Factories, scientific research enterprises, public offices, civic bodies, armed forces, and cities, and street organizations in cities were told to set up schools: conversely, a Central Committee directive of 19 September 1958 told schools to set up workshops, etc., though in practice this often meant pupils doing work outside the school. However, within a few months Liu Shao-ch'i and Kang Sheng toured the country warning against overshooting the mark in combining study and labour. Kang, later a leader of the Maoist Central Cultural Revolution Group, then quoted Lenin to show that 'a University should not be turned into a simple school of industrial apprentices'; we do not approve of such excesses, he said. In this he agreed with Lu P'ing, head of Peking University, who asked rhetorically, 'am I to be a director of a school or of a factory?'.

In April 1960 the National People's Congress announced educational reforms; the twelve-year primary and secondary course was reduced to ten years, in order to make the graduates available for labour at 16 years of age; part-time labour was to be stressed. However, with the increasing economic difficulties universalization of schooling became even harder and many *min-pan* schools closed or were merged; in Tientsin, for example, they declined from 35 in 1963 to 8 in 1964. During the Great Proletarian Cultural Revolution, it was also alleged that teachers with the purely professional viewpoint had sabotaged these reforms.

Meanwhile press articles had appeared with such titles as 'The work of schools must centre on teaching.[1] Specialization, especially the study of English and other foreign languages, was again stressed. In August 1961 Chen Yi made his well-known speech on the need for expertise as well as 'redness' (political activism). Meanwhile P'eng Chen was surreptitiously carrying out 'surveys' in the Finance and Trade systems and in the Educational system to find and correct the errors of the Great Leap. The media talked of an 'eight-character guideline' (adjustment, consolidation, reinforcement and elevation) on education which stressed quality and gradual development;[2] the goal of universal education receded into the distance:

'Education can only be developed gradually on the basis of the development of production, and the needs of education itself cannot be considered in isolation ... As to the universalization of higher education, this can only be realized after Communism is built.'[3]

The 'Maoist' counter-attack against these tendencies towards

---

[1] Kao Chih-kuo in *Kwangming Daily* (*KMD*) 7 April 1961; cp. interview with Chuh Teh etc. in *China Youth*, 5 July 1961.
[2] See *SCMM* No. 640, p. 21 (on P'eng Chen) and *shih-chieh Chih-shih*, 6 June 1962.
[3] *Shih-chieh Chih-shih*, 6 June 1962.

professionalism and élitism is generally reckoned to have started with his call for class struggle in September 1962, but little overtly happened for a year on the educational front. Then the media began to publicize the 'half-cultivating, half-study schools' and by late 1963 forty million students had been 'sent down' to the villages.[1] It was in May 1963 that Mao had sponsored the 'Ten-point decision' on rural work, setting guidelines for the 'socialist education movement' (this was of course mainly for revolution-ization of the peasantry, categorized as petty bourgeois, not for education in the ordinary sense). According to Lin Piao's story, in order to protect the 'power holders in the Party' this campaign was turned against the mass of lower-level cadres, many of who were 'sent down' for labour reform; actually it spread during 1963–4 to middle- and higher-level cadres and affec-ted non Party mental workers too in the form of a drive for reintegrating their work, including education, with physical labour.

By August 1963 the *Kwangming Daily* was complaining that the year's college graduates lacked practical experience and describing how they were being 'sent down' to farms.[2] But it was argued that the labour must be arranged so as not to interfere with specialized studies. We are now told that Mao's plans for transforming the countryside as well as preparing the revolu-tionization of youth and of culture were all sabotaged by 'Liu Shao-ch'i and his gang'. At any rate, they proved ineffective, as admitted by Mao in February 1967 (quoted in Lin Piao's Report to the Ninth Congress). In July 1964 there began a campaign against allegedly deviationist intellectuals (such as Yang Hsien-chien of the Party School) and in August publicity for half-labour, half-study schools intensified. Chou En-lai reported to the National People's Congress in December 1964 calling for their reintroduction.

[1] Wen Hui Pao (Hong Kong) 10 December 1963, quoted in *Summary of China Mainland Press* (*SCMP*) No. 3120, p. 14.

[2] See e.g. *KMD* 27 August 1963, in *SCMP* No. 3067, 25 September 1963.

Thus there were now at least four converging campaigns, foreshadowing the 'Cultural Revolution' (Chou used the phrase in his report).

1. Mental workers to get rid of their individual bourgeois ideas. (Connected with a drive to rid the collective mind, i.e. the cultural 'superstructure', of such contents in the form of old Peking operas, films and literature and replacing them with 'proletarian' myths approved by Madame Mao, Chiang Ching, and purveyed by the Army's cultural organs.)
2. Cadres and students to be sent down for productive, sometimes corrective, labour.
3. Re-establishment of the half-labour, half-study system in schools.
4. Emulation of the Army and of 'model heroes' in 'studying the thoughts of Mao Tse-tung' as purveyed by Lin Piao.

Key slogans were those of 'politics in command' and 'holding high the Great Red Banner of Mao's thought'. The link in these campaigns was the idea of preparing a climate of opinion for a 'second revolution' to avoid any turning back of the wheel of history.

However, all these campaigns were subject to modification by, if not opposition from, the Party machine. At least one 'model hero', for example, was publicized to celebrate the virtues of the Party Secretariat rather than of the Army cadres as 'good students' of Mao.[1]

Similarly, from spring 1964 until winter 1965–6 there was a press campaign, ostensibly for 'lessening the burden' on students, which was cryptically used to oppose the 'learn from the PLA' campaign. While paying lip-service to Maoism, some authors avoided using Lin Piao's particular slogans and were evidently

[1] Cf. Mary Sheridan in *China Quarterly*, No. 33, January/March 1968, p. 5.

'waving the Red Flag to oppose the Red Flag', as his partisans put it later.

Further, although the Ninth Congress of the Communist Youth League in June 1964 (three years overdue) can be seen in some ways as a preview for a 'Maoist' Ninth Congress of the Party, such as was finally held in April 1969, the actual work of the League in 'preparing revolutionary successors', as Mao wanted, was along lines later condemned as revisionist by the 'Maoist' Cultural Revolution Group. From March 1963 preparations for the congress had been in hand, and various innovations were tried out and publicized, such as 'children activity stations', to strengthen supervision of teenagers in and out of school.[1]

Although the Youth League Congress denounced revisionism and proposed to revise the constitution so as to make Marxism-Leninism *and* the thought of Mao its guiding ideology, most of the reports were delivered by leaders who later emerged as arch-revisionists and during the Cultural Revolution itself the Youth League was bypassed by the Red Guard Movement. It was later alleged that the reference to Mao was omitted from the Party Constitution because of revisionist influence.

During 1964 both Mao Tse-tung and Liu Shao-ch'i reportedly issued 'important intructions' on Education: in his Report at the end of the year, Chou referred to Liu's instructions for a double reform, first of the regular day-schools, which should combine education with labour, and then expansion of the half-study, half-work schools.

Data revealed in the course of the Cultural Revolution, taken with official press articles etc. of the time, suggest that the Peking Municipal Party Committee had much to do with drawing up this so-called 'educational guideline of the Party', which called for gradual long-term application of a double system, with both

[1] Cf. 'Extracurricular activities for teenagers and children actively launched in Ssup'ing City', *China Youth* (*CY*), 14 November 1963, in *SCMP* no. 3120, p. 13.

full-time and part-time schools.[1] However, 'some people' considered the full-time schools to be capitalist, as the Minister of Education said in 1965[2] and this was to be revealed as the line of the Red Guards and their supporters in the Cultural Revolution Group.

On 10 March 1964 the Party Centre published a Mao directive 'concerning the school curriculum and methods of instruction and examination' with Mao's comment that it should be read by P'eng Chen. This document, with another directive by Mao about the 'Kiangsi Communist Labour University', was allegedly pigeonholed by P'eng Chen.

On the other hand, in March–April 1964 the Ministry of Education in Peking and the Peking Municipal Education Department (under P'eng Chen) had promulgated teaching reforms for 'lightening the burden' etc., which were publicized by the *Kwangming Daily* (5,800 extra copies of the relevant issue were distributed to schools) and imitated by education departments in Harbin, Kirin, Changchun, Tientsin, Hofei, Hangchow, Wuhan, Nanking, Chungking, Sian, and Canton. The model for these reforms was the Yü Tsi middle school in Shanghai. An article by its principal in *China Youth*[3] summed up its experience in 'reducing the workload on students'; in September a further article by the Communist Youth League Committee of the School significantly added that 'confusion' caused by too many political meetings and 'duplication of organs' had been overcome, and 'onesided views' refuted.

'Some people believed that the collective should be big, and the bigger the better. In their work, these cadres adopted the "method of filling up", which was what they did with all the spare time of the students in the hope of *controlling their spare-time life*. [my

---

[1] 'Steadfastly promote the part-farming and party-study Education system'. *PD*, 30 May 1965, in *SCMP* No. 3481, 21 June 1965, p. I ff.

[2] *China News Analysis* (Hong Kong) (*CNA*), No. 617, p. 6 (quoting *PD* 13 July 1965).

[3] *CY*, No. 7, 1 April 1964.

italics]. As a matter of fact, they could not control the spare-time life of the students by this means in the first place. In the second place it made the mind of the students inactive. In the third place, it did not help *teaching according to individual capabilities and development of individual aptitudes* . . . [my italics].

The Communist Youth League Committee laid down *inter alia* that:

'1. Meetings should be reduced; with the exception of CYL, Young Pioneer, class union and study groups (plus militia groups for seniors) all small groups were abolished; "study of Chairman Mao's works should be done mainly during the political class".

'2. Unless by consent of the teaching class authorities and except for the labour provided for in the teaching-learning programme and some self-help labour, no class may contract for public service labour outside the school.'

These and other provisions went against the current campaigns for 'emulating the PLA', for setting up special political groups ostensibly for Mao-study, for mass physical and military training, etc. The 'some people' referred to were presumably advocates of this line, for whom 'emulation of the PLA' meant keeping the young people out of mischief with paramilitary exercises and fatigues. Lo Jui-ch'ing, the disgraced chief of staff of the Army, was later accused of stressing physical and professional training at the expense of Mao-study.

'Revisionist' lines were also laid down for rural part-farming and part-study schools and urban part-work and part-study schools (primary and junior middle) and for intermediate agro-technical colleges and technical schools; a similar policy was also implemented at universities. During the period from March to May 1965 a number of specialized conferences were held in Peking by systems of industry, communications, finance and trade, agriculture and forestry and by the trade unions, while work conferences were held by the Army.

These conferences were obviously concerned with furthering the socialist education movement.[1] For example, in May the *People's Daily* reported a national conference on rural part-farming and part-study education, at which Chairman Liu gave 'important instructions' and Lu Ting-yi gave a report. The conference stressed that gradual, experimental operation of the part-time schools, while continuing full-time schools, was a fundamental measure 'for cultivating successors to the cause of the proletarian revolution and preventing capitalist restoration'.

It claimed that since the previous year, in accordance with Chairman Liu's instructions, enrolment in the part-time schools had risen. In future the 'CCP Central Committee's directives concerning two kinds of labour systems and two kinds of education systems' must be further implemented. *Inter alia*, the conference laid down that the part-time schools should primarily try to admit children of poor and lower-middle peasants, but 'as regards children from families of landlords and well-to-do peasants, the conference also favoured admitting them'[2]—allegedly so that they could better be 'educated and reformed'. Similarly intellectuals from families of landlords or other exploiting classes should be accepted as teachers, if they were willing to 'serve the poor and lower-middle peasants'.

'The conference called on all revolutionary education workers to *hold high the Red Banner of the Thought of Mao Tse-tung, promote the spirit of uninterrupted revolution and unite themselves*

---

[1] In his report on the work of the Standing Committee of the Third National Committee of the Chinese People's Political Consultative Conference Ku Mo-jo said on 20 December 1964: 'particularly since the 10th Plenary Session of the Eighth Central Committee of the CCP in September 1962, we have further proposed to launch among the people of all circles a patriotic, internationalist and socialist education movement with class struggle as the central theme. (*PD* 1 January 1965 in *SCMP*, No. 337, p. 13.) This may be taken as the programme of the Cultural Revolution before its Maoist transformation in the spring of 1966. The issue of the *People's Daily* in which it appeared carried pictures of Mao and Liu of the same size.

[2] *PD*, 20 May 1965 in *SCMP*, No. 3481, p. 4.

with the forces in all related quarters'—in particular, the appropriate Departments of Agriculture and Forestry (my italics).

It should be noted that these slogans were not identical with those of the Army's Mao-study campaign, and that the Deputy Premier responsible for agriculture, Tan Chen-lin, was later denounced as one of the chief 'anti-Maoists'.

In July, the *Kwangming Daily*[1] reported on the results of more than ten provincial conferences on rural part-time education held 'in the spirit' of the national conference. It was stressed that 'for a great length of time to come' full-time and part-time schools would coexist. 'The aim is the gradual popularization of primary education with over 90 per cent of school age children being given a chance for education'; the line for agricultural middle schools should call for 'small-sized non-boarding ones' as the important target. Kwangtung province suggested setting up a 'labour university' in every *hsien* and a middle school in every commune, along the lines of experimental models it had set up.

Expanded enrolment, regardless of 'class background', was also now a concern of the Youth League and Pioneers; early in May a plenary session of the League's Central Committee started a movement to organize all possible children, in or out of school. 'Children's Leagues' were organized in some rural areas on the basis of the administrative village and for all children, whether in school or not. An article in *China Youth News*[2] recalled that such Leagues used to exist in the old Kiangsi Soviet area from 1929 to 1934 to organize children between seven and fifteen; between sixteen and twenty-four they joined the Pioneers, and then the Red Guard.[3]

In some areas, including Peking itself, the authorities apparently preferred to expand the Young Pioneers (between ages of nine and fifteen) rather than create these new 'duplicate

[1] *KMD*, 27 July 1965, in *SCMP*, No. 3518, p. 8.
[2] *CY*, 29 April 1965.
[3] See *SCMP*, No. 3745, p. 12 (New China News Agency, 2 June 1965).

organizations'. It was argued that previously too many children had been excluded from the Pioneers, so that the chance of reforming them was missed and 'bad elements in society seized the opportunity to corrupt them'.[1] Naughty children were even sabotaging production and had to be kept usefully busy.

In August 1965 the Ministry of Agriculture held another conference at which Liu Shao-ch'i gave 'an important directive concerning the revolution in education', which was not published.

Meanwhile, the part-time policy was also being extended in organizations under the Finance and Trade Departments. For example, in July the *Ta Kung Pao* published articles on the running of part-time schools by supply and marketing coopera- tives. It said that 'supply and marketing cooperatives all over the country have seriously implemented the CCP central committee's instructions concerning the enforcement of two labour systems and two education systems and have experimentally run a number of part-work part-study schools'.[2]

From the experience gained, it said, Finance and Trade Departments had learnt that the system would be suitable for training recruits for the ever-expanding staff of Finance and Trade Departments and for further universalization of education under present conditions, because the students could wholly or partly pay for their living and tuition expenses out of the remuneration from the factories etc. where they did their part-time work. These articles used language closer to the 'Mao-Lin' vocabulary than those concerned with rural schools, and referred to 'the working style of the Yenan anti-Japanese university' (which was headed by Lin Piao). We may recall that since the holding in June 1964 of a national conference on political work in finance and trade departments (i.e. banks, shops, etc.) the transfer of demobilized servicemen to clean up and supervise such commercial organizations had been stepped up[3] and 'political departments'

[1] *Fu Tao Yuan* (Instructor), 20 August 1965 and see *SCMM* No. 471, p. 1.
[2] *Ta Kung Pao* (*TKP*), 4 July 1965, in *SCMP* No. 3508, p. 6.
[3] See *CNA* No. 581.

established in the relevant offices at the level of provinces and major cities as well as in ministries. In Peking, however, the Municipal Party Committee apparently sought to do things in its own way[1] although 1,400 servicemen joined financial and commercial offices there in the spring.[2]

In February 1965 a second national meeting was convened at Tientsin by Finance Minister Li Hsien-nien, an old soldier and member of the politbureau. It appeared that a central 'Finance and Commerce Political Department' had been set up. This was in order to implement Lin Piao's slogan to 'give prominence to politics', to judge from the report by its deputy head Yang Shu-ken, a former military commander of the Canton area.[3] It was decided to set up political departments down to county level. In at least one province (Heilungkiang) it was ordered that the former Finance and Commerce departments of Party Committees in each town and county should be turned into Political Departments. This meeting was followed by the usual provincial meetings, but work proceeded slowly. In May, the *Ta Kung Pao* published an article cryptically suggesting that the transferred soldiers knew Mao's thought but knew nothing about their new jobs and were meeting with opposition.[4]

The main thrust of the decisions taken at a simultaneous Tientsin conference of the State Economic Commission was to intensify a so-called 'revolution in management', which called for getting rid of the Soviet-type, large-scale, all-round and self-contained *Kombinat* and favouring specialization and cooperation of small and medium-sized enterprises. This campaign was mainly concerned with the machine-building industry[5] and was

[1] By 'sending down' superfluous personnel of its own offices to make investigations on the spot, ferret out concealed stocks, correct abuses, etc., in factories and enterprises. See for example the article on 'New Atmosphere in public Organs' in *Ta Kung Pao*, 14 August 1965. See also *Ta Kung Pao*, 11 April 1965.

[2] *TKP*, 14 August 1965, in *SCMP* No. 3528, 31 August 1965, p. 9.

[3] *TKP*, 27 March 1965.

[4] *TKP*, editorial, 10 May 1965.

[5] See *PD*, 12 May 1965, in *SCMP* No. 3473, p. 5.

theoretically based on 'the principle of economic rationality *and the strategic* needs of national defence'[1] (my italics). However, it was combined with a campaign to reduce and 'send down' administrative personnel to 'uproot revisionism' and to give 'prominence to politics' (Lin Piao's slogan), on the ground that enterprise management was part of the socialist education movement.[2] Thus there were signs of a clash between 'professionals' and 'politicians' on these issues—in concrete terms, a struggle for control of defence plants.

In October 1965 another article on the Yü Tsai model school appeared in the *Kwangming Daily*.[3] It referred again to the 'confusion and chaos' caused by the drive 'to turn students into revolutionaries' in the second half of 1964, which had involved 'heavy schedules of militia training', and it recommended the policy of 'less but finer' in school work. As for 'tasks assigned by sources outside the school', it laid down that they must be 'transmitted by the administrative authority of the appropriate education department'. The general effect was to negate the Army's campaign for Mao-study with military and physical training[4] by limiting them to an hour or two once a week. In particular, it openly stipulated that 'no special group is to be formed for the study of Mao's works'.[5]

At the end of 1965 a conference on part-time education in cities was convened by the Ministry of Education 'under the direct guidance of the Party Central and Chairman Liu Shao-ch'i'. The *Kwangming Daily* said that the matter was being followed with the closest interest by Chairman Mao and Liu; in the cities factories should establish schools and schools factories, but standards should not be lowered; experimentation should go on for five years and implementation of the system should take ten years.[6]

---

[1] *Shih-shih Shou-tse*, No. 8, 21 April 1965, in *SCMM* No. 473, p. 10.

[2] See series of 5 *PD* editorials on management, especially 24 September 1965, in *SCMP* No. 3555.   [3] *KMD*, 5 October 1965, in *SCMP* No. 3560, p. 8.

[4] *KMD*, loc. cit., p. 13.   [5] *KMD*, 7 December 1965.

[6] *China Youth Daily*, 13 July 1965, in *SCMP* No. 3519, p. 8.

The 'Liuist' educational guideline was also applied in universities; a typical article by the Communist Youth League Committee of Tsinghua University in Peking advocated cutting down militia training, physical labour and extra-curricular political activities.[1] It stressed the role of the Party and Youth League Committees and forbade anyone to 'onesidedly increase the frequency of meetings and activities' (i.e. 'Mao-study'). Teaching and student cadres had learnt that it was necessary not only to *give prominence to politics*, but also to pay close attention to the student's *professional studies* and *physical training*.[2]

In December 1965 the President and First Party Secretary of Nanking University, Kuang Ya-ming, published an article ostensibly on 'lightening the burden' on students which not only advocated reduction of meetings, labour, etc., but also relief of overcrowding—by sending second-stream students to a half-work, half-study group under the 'double system'. A camp for this was established at Li Yang, some distance from the University. Significantly, it was at this branch school that all the trouble started on 2 June 1966, the day after Peking Radio publicized the big-character posters put up by Maoist 'rebels' at Peking University (Peita) on 25 May, the event which officially set of Great Proletarian Cultural Revolution.

As late as December 1965, the *Kwangming Daily* was still saying that the educational reform must be carried out gradually, without lowering standards. However, those who regarded the full-time schools as 'capitalist' were getting stronger. What seems to have been happening behind the propaganda smoke-

---

[1] Cf. 'We should fight against the tendency of discriminating against the children of workers and peasants'—*KMD* in *SCMP* No. 3999, 5 February 1965; 'Bourgeois educational system condemned for persecution of children of poor and lower middle peasants'—*Yung Wan Pao* in *SCMP* No. 3743, 12 July 1966, p. 12: contrast article by Sun Pao-lung of Nanking University in *CY* No. 24, 1964, *SCMM* No. 456, 9 November 1964, p. 8.

[2] Here we see combined the lines stressed by Lin Piao 'politicals' and the 'professionals' such as P'eng Teh-huai and Lo Jui-ching. The writers attacked by 'Maoist' propaganda at the opening of the Cultural Revolution and defended by P'eng Chen were accused of trying to rehabilitate Marshal P'eng Te-huai. Lo was accused by the Red Guards of stressing training and tournaments at the expense of Mao-study.

screen was, briefly, this. The selection of pupils for 'sending down' to labour on graduation, or relegation to the second-line half-and-half schools, often discriminated[1] against children of the less-educated workers and peasants who come to boarding schools in town and could not cope with their tasks there, whereas children of former 'bourgeois' or Party cadres were at ease in the school milieu and favoured by the examination system. The half-and-half system was largely intended to keep them from dropping out altogether, and much evidence suggests that simply keeping them busy was an important consideration. But the two-level educational system, like the similar distinction between veteran skilled and young contract labour in industry, generated fierce resentment, which was mobilized by elements of the Party in the Army's General Political Department under cover of the 'Mao-study groups' and emerged as the 'Red Guard Troops' movement (*Hung Wei Ping*). It may be noted that the Army itself represented a younger group than the Party cadre.

At this stage, however, the Cultural Revolution was still meant to be run along the lines of an ordinary Party-inspired mass movement, like the rural socialist education movement: that is to say, by officially-despatched work-teams. Mayor P'eng Chen of Peking headed a five-man planning team in charge of it until his overthrow in the spring of 1966. After P'eng's arrest by Red Guards in December, Chou En-lai publicly noted the difference between the Great Proletarian Cultural Revolution and all previous mass movements; they had been both from the top to the bottom and vice versa, but the GPCR was essentially a movement from bottom to top. But, he went on to say, 'we cannot detach ourselves from the supreme leadership', i.e. of Mao and the Party Centre. This speech of Chou's marked the beginning of efforts to bring under control the spontaneous revolutionary forces loosed by the ultra-Maoists.

The first shot in the 'Maoist' takeover of the ongoing Cultural

[1] *Cultural Revolution in China*, by L. Delyusin, Moscow, Novosti publication, No. 1967, p. 7.

Revolution was fired in November 1965, in the form of an article by Yao Wen-yuan of the PLA's Political Department cryptically attacking the Peking Municipal Party Committee by way of denunciation of literary works published by Vice-Mayor Wu Han. In the new year, the Army's paper began to 'feature articles of a clearly directive nature', as a Soviet account[1] puts it, over-shadowing the Party's own organ, the *People's Daily*. An article in the *Southern Daily* (Canton) on the reform of full-time schools said that 'after learning in a big way from the political-ideological work experiences of Tach'ing[2] and of the PLA' *some schools had established political offices* and many had stepped up labour education and Mao-study. The teachers had overcome the idea of trying to prepare many of their students for higher education, and more and more primary school drop-outs were going down to the farms of their own accord. However, the last two paragraphs repeated all the themes of the earlier articles on 'lightening the burden' and ensuring proper rest for the students (as at Yü-Tsai 'model' school).

A report about progress of the Yü-Tsai-type reforms in Tsinghua University was presented at a meeting of Peking's city offices for schools of higher education and published on 9 April 1966 in the *Kwangming Daily*. It said that the reforms followed instructions received from Mao in July 1965; they stressed not only 'combining labour and rest' but 'overcoming subjectivism and formalism'.

The municipal elections in Peking had taken place on 3 April 1966. Mayor P'eng Chen reportedly kissed a baby 'like a bourgeois politician' and told it 'in 20 years' time I shall vote for you as a Mayor'. He was already fighting for survival. From 9 April to 12 April 'the secretariat of the Central Committee' was in session under Premier Chou to hear P'eng severely criticized by K'ang Sheng and Ch'en Po-ta; it was decided to

---

[1] *PD*, 11 April 1966, p. 2.
[2] Tach'ing oilfield was a 'model' for integration of city and countryside, worker, peasant, soldier, and intellectual, in accordance with Mao's thought.

repudiate the 'February outline report' (of his five-man group originally in charge of the Cultural Revolution) and set up a new Cultural Revolution drafting group for approval by Mao and the standing committee of the politburo.

From this moment dates the transition from the 'Socialist' to the 'Great Proletarian' Cultural Revolution. Significantly, it was on 11 April that the New China News Agency released a report about another conference on education, which acknowledged that 'the five principles of Comrade Lin Piao giving prominence to politics apply also to schools of higher learning and must be implemented'.[1]

A few days later in April 1966 the *People's Daily* began to publish letters from Party Branch secretaries of provincial secondary schools which criticized the 1964 teaching reform as individualistic and capitalist; though the system had been changed, it had not got out of the circle of 'education for education's sake'. It was necessary to learn the methods of the PLA—and so on.[2]

According to the Red Guard account, P'eng Chen and his group in the Peking Municipal Party Committee now published in their Press organs the 'April 16 editorial note' and held the 'April sinister meeting' to fight back against their Maoist opponents. P'eng Chen remained in touch by telephone, although attending a Central Committee meeting between 16 April and 20 April. On 18 April the Army newspaper openly demanded a 'Cultural Revolution', i.e. something more than a debate about poisonous weeds in literature. On the 27th P'eng returned to Peking, but according to East European sources the guard on his office was changed and he had to work from his residence; the process of 'overturning' him had begun, and a Maoist 'notice of the Central Committee' repudiating him had already been drafted; such a document was circulated on 16 May.

On 1 June 1966, the *People's Daily* published a call to 'organize

---

[1] *PD*, 14 April 1966, p. 2.
[2] *PD*, 1 June 1966.

and encourage children to participate actively in the present great socialist cultural revolution'. It said that the class struggle between socialism and capitalism was raging 'not only in the school education of children but also in the upbringing of children of pre-school age'.[1] Next day, apparently on Mao's orders, the *People's Daily* published the big-character poster put up by 'rebel' members of Peking University to denounce its authorities for suppressing the Cultural Revolution. According to Lin Piao's Report to the Ninth Congress, the poster itself was inspired by the 'Party Central', though at the time it was torn down by other students.

The *People's Daily* now changed its masthead, symbolizing a shift of power in Peking. On the 6th it carried a story on a new model day-school (not Yü-Tsai) which had got rid of the idea that a school was for study. On the same day, a girls' school in Peking addressed a letter to the Central Committee proposing complete abolition of the educational system; others demanded the abolition of examinations. Accordingly, on 13 June a decree was issued in the name of the Central Committee and the State Council for reforming the educational sytem and postponing enrolment of new students. The reform was explained in an editorial of the *People's Daily* on 18 June; it was to 'establish Chairman Mao's line in the educational system and completely eliminate the bourgeois line'.

In practice, school activities were now paralysed and the young people left free for 'Red Guard' activities. After the Eleventh Plenum of the Central Committee, Mao attended on 18 August the first great review of Red Guards, in military uniform. To Lin Piao, now officially his 'closest comrade in arms', he said:

'This is a very great movement. It has really mobilized the

---

[1] Thus the article took up the theme of up-bringing of children by parents (especially by those who were of 'good class origin' and officials) which had been stressed in a number of articles during 1965. It was argued that mere birth could not guarantee proletarian virtue. See *SCMP*, no. 3494, pp. 5–6.

masses. It is of the greatest importance for the revolutionizing of the consciousness of the people all over the country.'

It seems likely that Mao then believed Lin to have found the 'magic weapon' which would bring about all that the socialist education campaign had failed to achieve. However, it is hard to determine how far the 'movement' was spontaneous, and how far it was remote-controlled by the Army's political and cultural departments; it is significant that many of the leaders involved in this first phase of the Cultural Revolution were later purged as 'ultra-Leftists' who had only used Mao's words to oppose him.

We must remember that, parallel to the developments in the educational field outlined above, the years 1965–6 also saw a similar debate over trade union work and the use of skilled manpower: the real issue was the establishment of a sort of parallel power structure of 'political', actually military, commissars[1] which usurped the powers of the constitutional Party Committees. As in the *Kwangming Daily*, articles appeared in the *Ta Kung Pao* and *Kung Jen Jih Pao* (*Daily Worker*) which superficially followed the campaign to 'learn from the Army', but cryptically opposed aspects of it by stressing, for example, that trade unions should look after the health and cultural and material interests of the workers 'under the unified direction of the Party Committee' in each enterprise. In June an article on management opposed political movements, excessive overtime and 'championism' and emphasized that the principal task of a factory was production.[2]

But, after a five-week rectification session for leaders in industry, communications and TV work, this view was heard no more, and on 11 March Lin Piao wrote a symbolic letter to a certain defence plant on 'living study and living use of Mao's

---

[1] 'The political work cadres transferred from the PLA are the hardcore of a political organ. Their role should be properly developed'. (*Ta Kung Pao*, editorial, 1 August 1965.)

[2] Cf. 'Chinese factories urged to build up a revolutionary industrial Army', Peking *Daily Worker* editorial of 3 February 1966.

works' in these fields, the concrete meaning of which was that his line had gained control of them: henceforth, the main purpose of factories was to produce revolutionized men, not material products.[1] This letter was, of course, not published until June.

During April the Central Committee of the Youth League held a 2-day meeting 'under the solicitude and leadership of the Party' and 'in the spirit of rectification'. While repeating Lin Piao's slogans ('giving prominence to politics', etc.) and admitting that the League's work in this respect 'shows a big gap as compared with that of the PLA', the report on this meeting still stressed the leadership of the Party Central Committee and the Party Committees at all levels; it noted that the socialist education movement was 'the best classroom for promoting revolutionization of youth', and tried to make out that the *socialist* Cultural Revolution currently unfolding was a "class struggle *in the ideological realm* (my italics) i.e. a matter of organizing young people to analyse and criticize books, films and other literary and art works containing "poison"'.[1]

This was essentially the line attacked by the 'Leftist' backers of the Red Guards. Indeed, it can be argued that the socialist education movement, in the form of the *four-clean* drive against spontaneous capitalist tendencies of the peasants and erroneous working style of the grassroots cadres, was not a forerunner of, but a rival to, the policy of the Cultural Revolution as it developed after 16 May. The *four-clean* drive was operated by Party work teams sent from above, as was the first phase of the Cultural Revolution allegedly run by P'eng Chen and masterminded by Liu Shao-ch'i. In his confession the latter admitted his mistake in using work teams during the first 'fifty days', but nothing proves that Mao's attitude really was as it was later said to have been. It will be remembered that the 'first set of ten directives' on socialist education in the countryside (apparently submitted by Mao as a draft to members of the Central Committee on 20

[1] See *SCMP* No. 3697, 13 May 1966, p. 2 ff.

May 1963) were not officially ratified by the Central Committee until the Eleventh Plenary in August 1966; in between times, two further versions appeared, in September 1963 and in 1964. They in effect concentrated on the reform of cadres first and masses afterwards, instead of promoting what Mao meant by 'class struggle'. Finally Mao superseded these attempts to get it right with his 'twenty-three articles', which reintroduced stress on contradictions and class struggle within the Party and referred to persons in authority taking the capitalist road.

16 May was later declared to be the terminal date of the socialist education movement; the 'overturning' by Red Guards of the academic authorities and the Party Secretaries who supported them rapidly led to a situation in which rural cadres and other victims of the movement labelled as bad elements by the work teams were able to 'rebel' and demand a reversal of the verdicts, on the ground that they had been passed by capitalist-roaders sent by Liu Shao-ch'i. The Leftists in the Central Cultural Revolution Group encouraged the rebellion of these repressed elements in the countryside in the same way as they exploited the rancour of the under-privileged school children and contract workers; the revolt of elements condemned to labour under supervision or sent to the countryside in previous rectification campaigns played a large part in the 'Revolution' of the spring of 1967. According to Chiang Ch'ing herself, rationalizing a development that was probably not so well thought out in reality, the 'Ultra-Left' began to be active in May 1967, and managed to 'blind some of the masses'. At that moment, she said, 'we took measures to separate Wang Li from Kuan Feng and dealt with Chi Pen-yü in another way, so that measures concerning him were spaced out in time'. All three men, it will be remembered, were members of the Central Cultural Revolution Group and held controlling positions in its Press organs (Kuan Feng on the *Liberation Army Daily* and the other two on *Red Flag*). Although Chi Pen-yü distinguished himself by encouraging the Red Guards to denounce Liu Shao-ch'i and drag him out of Chungnakhai for a

struggle meeting, the real policy of the group appears to have been to spread *small* struggle meetings at unit level in which the public could actually 'overthrow' the officials that they had normally come in contact with, and who represented the Party and regime in their everyday understanding: the policy of the rest of the Centre turned out to be to concentrate on very large-scale rallies to denounce top leaders like Liu, Lo and P'eng who were too far removed from the life of the ordinary people for the rally to be more than a somewhat unreal psychodrama of the type portrayed in George Orwell's *Nineteen Eighty-four* (the hate sessions in cinemas against an all-purpose mythical heretic). The small-unit sessions were bound to produce anarchy and chaos where the mass rallies only produced catharsis and militant enthusiasm. After the Wuhan incident of July 1967 the Ultra-Leftists were purged, and *Red Flag* ceased publication until July 1968. In the autumn it became apparent that the media had been giving a falsely Leftist and activist impression of the Central leaders' policies, or else that these policies had moved to the Right.

On 1 September 1967, Kang Sheng complained that the small groups (i.e. of Ultra-Leftists) were no longer getting clearance for their activities from the Premier, Chou En-lai; on 1 October the watchword went out against 'polycentrism', after measures had been promulgated to strengthen the attitude of the Army units against Leftists and an article had been published by Yao Wen-yuan, ostensibly against two books by Tao Chu, which warned in Aesopian fashion that those who had risen to commanding position in the Press and propaganda apparatus were due for criticism. The crisis had probably come during August, when the Army paper published a report that 'under the direction of the Party Committee of the General Staff grouped around Yang Cheng-wu' proletarian rebels of the General Staff had armed themselves with the 'spirit of beating the dog in the water': the meaning of this was that struggle must be continued to the end against officers who had committed mistakes, thus extending to the Army the Leftist principle of having the rank and file attack and purge their immediate superiors. This article followed the publication by the Centre of documents aainst P'eng Te-huai, the contemporary meaning of which could be taken in various ways. It was not until six months later that it became clear that it was Chief of Staff Yang Cheng-wu himself who was to be disgraced, and not the many less senior officers who had done something wrong but had carried out self-criticism. But to break the Left Lin Piao had first to move against the Right; the Army's Cultural Revolution group was retooled and joined by Lin's wife Yeh Chün: it was then possible to proceed against the ambitious 'young Colonel' types who were trying to clear the Old Guard out of the way under the slogan of 'dragging out the handful' (of capitalist-roaders) from the Army.

The Army thus being put back on the right road, normalization of the other sectors gradually followed. This development can be traced back to the decisions taken in the second half of January 1967, theoretically limiting the spontaneous nature of the rebellion, bringing in the Army to control it and laying down that the achievements of the four-clean drive must not be tampered with.[1]

The factionalism of the Red Guards and Rebels had proved the impossibility of inspiring united and coherent action by general, ideologically expressed directives without an intermediary hierarchy to give them specific application on the spot. On 25 July 1968, Mao rebuked Red Guard leaders and threatened them with direct military control. Thereafter, instead of the young intellectuals, led by a group of propagandists, teaching revolutionary purity to their elders, hundreds of thousands of former Red Guards were sent to work in remote villages, often under Army supervision. Industrial workers' teams were to run schools in the towns, while in the rural areas they were to be run by the production brigades, that is, by the poor and lower middle

---

[1] Quoted by Melvin J. Lasky in 'The Metaphysics of Doomsday', *Encounter*, 1969, p. 45.

peasants. But ultimate control rested with Army men who supervised the worker and peasant teams. To a certain extent, this meant in practice that influence passed from the lowest Party officials, many of whom had been demobilized after the Korean war, to younger veterans working through the militia structure rather than the Party.

What the new system will mean in practice is still uncertain. It does not fully conform to 'Draft Recommendations on Educational Reform' which were disseminated by posters at the height of the Leftist wave in January 1967. According to these, schools were to set up 'political organs' and send the original political cadres for manual labour; they should introduce the 'military formation system'; schools should be like Lin Piao's Anti-Japanese University at Yenan, with political commissars. Control by specialists and professionals, and the titles of professor, teacher, etc., should be abolished. The thinking behind this was evidently the same as that which led to the abolition of ranks in the PLA.

Analysis of the personalities most attacked in the Cultural Revolution shows that apart from their alleged policy and the posts they held at the time, there was often something in their past history which might explain the real reason for their being denounced. Many of the high-ranking cadres of the cultural and propaganda establishment, and among scientific and technical personnel, were members of long-standing cliques such as the 'prison cadres' who were once authorized by Liu Shao-chi'i to make confessions to their captors in order to survive and those involved in the 9 December movement of 1935 led by Liu Shao-ch'i and P'eng Chen. This group included the Minister of Higher Education, Chiang Nan-hsiang, and Lu P'ing, head of Peking University. Other cliques of purgees can be identified as 'white area' cadres—those who were working underground in enemy-controlled cities before the liberation—and people personally linked with Kao Kang in Manchuria, with Marshal P'eng Te-huai or with Marshal Ho Lung. (Kao fell in 1954,

P'eng in 1959 and Ho during the Cultural Revolution.) The Cultural Revolution contained an element of factional struggle against these groups of old-timers by groups of different background and loyalties, among whom can be identified, for example, the younger propagandists Yao and Chang from the Shanghai party organization, who attached themselves to Madame Mao, also from that city. These factional struggles clouded the real doctrinal issues; but the main issue was clearly the choice between 'less but finer' (the twin-stream system) or 'more but worse'. The economic situation would not allow of universalizing education, even if it had been desirable to do so, without completely changing the content of the education given, to suit it to the needs of a mass, not a traditionally narrow élite.

The policy which one may caricature as 'more but worse' was probably not so much a thought-out programme as a series of *ad hoc* measures to keep the lid on an increasingly troublesome boiling of problems; broadly speaking, it went through the stages of first trying to keep the swarming adolescents busy with paramilitary exercises, indoctrination sessions and manual labour or fatigues, and then removing the lid to let their seething discontent scald the Establishment. Now, however, the lid is on again; though the 'Workers' and Peasants' Mao Tse-tung Thought propaganda teams' and other authorities have continued to search for a magic formula and have come up with some interesting experiments, the inevitable restoration of power to regular teaching staff and to managerial bureaucracy has led at the time of writing to continuing obstruction against practical application of the new ideas. Reporting a forum on Mao's July 1968 instruction (we must still run universities . . .) the New China News Agency on 22 July 1970 quoted a conversation between the Shanghai leaders of the Cultural Revolution, Yao Wen-yuan and Chang Chun-chiao, and representatives of technical colleges, in which the latter complained that the relevant industrial departments took no notice of their efforts to combine production with learning (e.g. of producing chemicals while teaching chemistry) and would not allocate the necessary raw materials.

In this, of course, China is not unique. Spokesmen of British manufacturers have said that university graduates are unemployable without expensive retraining, because their courses are really taught by academics to produce more academics, not practical engineers, chemists and other technicians. Lord Butler, like Mao, has advocated a fundamental reappraisal of the role of universities so as to produce more technicians. It is also notorious that our system keeps going only because six out of seven young people never present themselves for higher education at all. In less developed countries, such as those of Francophone Africa, the authories have been equally concerned at the unsuitability of a traditional academic education for their needs, and like China they face the problem of their modernization programme taking the wrong turn and producing deplorable social effects. In China, as in some other countries suffering the pangs of modernization, things are further complicated by the conflict of 'second revolution versus restoration'. In our own case, Cromwell had to repress his fanatiques and Levellers, who wanted to carry the Revolution through to the end: even their slogans were Maoist—'Overturn, Overturn!' (Ezekiel 21 : 25) and 'the kingdom is not to be maintained by Lawes, but by Perfect Men'. They were strong among the élite troops (then the cavalry; nowadays it is the air and mechanized forces that give trouble, as in China). According to a recent French study, their ideas influenced the French Revolution of 1789. In the end, General Monk brought about the Restoration. In Nazi Germany, too, the National Socialist German Workers Party took the path of the Kuomintang (as a Chinese might see it) when Hitler put down the SA and linked up with the military-industrial complex. In China the old fighters, united by their common 'front-experience', are still in charge; in a sense, their management of what promised to be a second revolution has prevented one. No Chinese SS has emerged, in spite of Moscow's exaggerated charges; the real effect of the

95

CHAPTER IV

MAO'S CONTINUING
REVOLUTION

ARMY AND PARTY IN COMMUNIST CHINA

RALF BONWIT

(Written in July, 1970)

I

Commenting on the outcome of the Chinese Communist Party's Ninth Congress, the Shanghai paper *Chiehfang Jih Pao* (*Liberation Daily*) said on 22 May 1969:[1]

'After three years of the rectification (*cheng feng*) movement, and following the Seventh Party Congress (in 1945),[2] the whole Party achieved unprecedented unity, ensuring the victory of the war of resistance against Japan (1937–45) and the war of liberation (1946–49) and building the dictatorship of the proletariat. The recent Ninth Party Congress was convened after three years of the great proletarian cultural revolution, which has liquidated the renegades, enemy agents and diehard capitalist-roaders headed by Liu Shao-chi who have sneaked into the Party. Now we have gained a clear understanding of our political and

---

[1] BBC, Summary of World Broadcasts, second series, FE/3062/B/5. If not otherwise indicated, quotations below are from the B/II sections of this document; all references are to the FE (Far Eastern) issues.

[2] Every CCP Congress elects a new Central Committee which is numbered after the Congress; sessions of a Central Committee are numbered separately—thus the 'enlarged' session, meaning one attended by non-members of the Central Committee, which expelled Liu Shao-ch'i in October 1968 and prepared the way for the Ninth Party Congress in April 1969, is known as the Twelfth Session of the Eighth Central Committee.

D

organizational lines and of our ideology. Thus our Party has again achieved unprecedented unity.'

This passage is interesting for various reasons. For one thing, the 'unprecedented unity' of the Party is more stipulated than real, as is shown by the frequent appeals to establish such a unity around the new Party Central Committee.[1] But the appeal to precedent links together the *cheng feng* of 1942–4 and the cultural revolution of 1966–9—both in character and duration. The *cheng feng* campaign has been acclaimed as a movement 'as mild as spring rain'—and leniency towards deviant Party members has become a characteristic of directives on the current campaign for Party consolidation, which, as stated in a *Hung Chi (Red Flag)* article on Party-building at Peking University published in July 1970,[2] has become the main purpose of the cultural revolution. If we accept three years as the significant period of the cultural revolution before the Ninth Party Congress, we would have to set the beginning in April or May 1966. The Ninth Party Congress endorsed the expulsion of Liu Shao-ch'i and elected a Central Committee of Mao-Lin nominees, thus enabling Mao and Lin Piao to drop the mystique of the 'proletarian headquarters'[3] and assume the mantle of a Communist Party Central Committee headed by Mao, with Lin Piao as his deputy. Liu Shao-ch'i was no longer disguised as 'China's Khrushchev', but became a 'remnant traitor' exorcized by name.

The beginning of the decisive phase of the cultural revolution can be set in May 1966, when two important documents were drafted: the Party Central Committee Circular of 16 May, which established a Cultural Revolution Group under the Party Central Committee, and Mao's letter to Lin Piao of 7 May, now known as Mao's '7th May Directive', which laid down the overall

[1] Written in July 1970.
[2] Summary 3425/B/2.
[3] See below.

direction for what was to follow.[1] The '7th May Directive' is exceptional in that it is really a directive from Mao to the head of the military establishment—unlike most of 'Chairman Mao's latest instructions' which are passages from not-always-published speeches or from an article in *Hung Chi* or most frequently from a 'joint editorial'.[2]

We can find a Mao directive denoting the end of the high-level political phase of the cultural revolution in his appeal for 'unity' to the Ninth Party Congress—one of the few passages from his speeches to the Congress revealed by the Chinese press. Lin Piao in his Political Report—the key document of the Congress—said that Mao 'recently' pointed out that the proletariat was 'the greatest class in the history of mankind . . . It can and must unite the overwhelming majority of the people around itself so as to isolate the handful of enemies to the maximum extent and attack them'. A 'Mao instruction' in these terms appeared in the Peking press on 2 May 1969.[3]

[1] Published by the Chinese news agency NCNA (Hsinhua) again in February 1969, Summary 2992/B/11; it said:

'While the main activity of the workers is in industry, they should also study military affairs, politics and culture . . . While the main activity of the peasants in the communes is in agriculture . . . they, too, should study military affairs, politics and culture . . . They should run some small factories. They should also criticize the bourgeoisie. This holds good for the students too. While their main task is to study, they should . . . learn other things, that is, industrial work, farming and military affairs . . . The period of schooling should be shortened; education should be revolutionized and the domination of our schools by bourgeois intellectuals should by no means be allowed to continue. While conditions permit, those working in commerce . . . and in Party and government organizations should also follow the same course.'

[2] This usually means an article simultaneously published in Peking in the Party paper *Jenmin Jih Pao* (*People's Daily*), the Party journal *Hung Chi* and the organ of the People's Liberation Army (PLA), *Chiehfang Chün Pao'* (*Liberation Army Daily*). Such joint editorials appear regularly at the New Year, on 1 October, National Day, and on the Party anniversary on 1 July. In most years (but not in 1970) they have also appeared on 1 August, anniversary of the Nanchang uprising celebrated as Army Day, and on the anniversary of the 4th May youth movement of 1919; any major event, such as a Party congress, the establishment of an important provincial revolutionary committee, the republication of a Mao article, etc., may give rise to a joint editorial containing fresh 'instructions'.

[3] The relevant passage occurs in Part IV of Lin Piao's Report, for which see Summary 3060/C.

99

In a wider sense the cultural revolution has neither beginning nor end. Its far-off origins lay, theoretically, with the anti-Japanese demonstrations which in 1919 initiated what became known as the 4th May youth movement. Mao's statement of 20 May 1970 (see below) made it clear that the Chinese revolution will only be completed when the world revolution against imperialism has been successful. This is also the meaning of a joint editorial of 25 June on the twentieth anniversary of the outbreak of the Korean War.[1] The connection between the Chinese and world revolutions was also stated in Lin Piao's Political Report. He had previously discussed it in his treatise on 'people's war', published on the anniversary in September 1965 of the end of the war against Japan.[2]

In the opening section of the Political Report, the cultural revolution is seen in wider perspective. Lin Piao states:

'In 1957, shortly after the conclusion of the Party's Eighth Congress, Chairman Mao published his great work "On the correct handling of contradictions among the people"[3] . . . in which he comprehensively set forth the existence of contradictions, classes and class struggle in socialist society . . . and set forth the great theory of continuing the revolution under the dictatorship of the proletariat . . . This great work . . . has laid the theoretical foundation for the current great proletarian cultural revolution.'

The same section of the Political Report mentions another work by Mao which has been mentioned frequently in the Ninth Party Congress documents: Mao's report to the Second Session of the Seventh Central Committee held at Shihchiachuang, south

[1] Summary 3413/A3/3.
[2] This treatise also foreshadowed the general direction of the cultural revolution; see R. Bonwit, *The Chinese PLA and the great proletarian cultural revolution*, in St Antony's Papers, No. 20, Oxford, 1967, pp. 64–5.
[3] There are, in fact, two essays by Mao on the problem of contradictions, one written in 1937 and the 1957 essay on, specifically, contradictions among the people. Both have been mentioned in cultural revolution literature, but it is usually the 1957 essay which is meant—and which is discussed here.

of Peking, in March 1949. Lin Piao quotes the following passage from the 1949 report.

'After the country-wide seizure of power by the proletariat, the principal internal contradiction is that between the working class and the bourgeoisie. The heart of the struggle is still the question of State power.'

Lin Piao's elucidation of Mao's thesis of contradictions provided the theme for a fresh analysis of this work in *Hung Chi* of October 1969.[1] After quoting Mao's essay on the relative importance of economic base and superstructure, the paper says:

'Marxist-Leninist philosophy has always held the view that the superstructure is determined by the economic base; meanwhile, the superstructure itself also provides a driving force for the economic base; it is understood that the political power of the State is the core of the superstructure.'

This implies that Party leadership is the core of the superstructure. The expression 'core group' has been used lately with increasing frequency to describe leading groups—not otherwise defined—in certain contingencies.

A previous *Hung Chi* article, of September 1969,[2] contrasted Mao's theory of the relationship between the power structure and the State with that held by Soviet revisionists and by Liu Shao-ch'i. It accused Khrushchev of having told the Twenty-Second Congress of the CPSU that proletarian dictatorship was no longer essential for the Soviet State. Brezhnev, too, had failed to

'recognize the existence of classes and class contradictions in

[1] Summary 3208/B/1.
[2] Summary 3187/A2/1—the references to Liu Shao-ch'i in this article are to his book *How to be a good communist*—renamed *On Self-Cultivation* in the cultural revolution literature.

socialist society; nor does he mention the necessity of the use of violence by a socialist State for the suppression of the overthrown classes. This does not mean that the handful of renegades want to negate the role of violence . . . They are constantly stepping up the use of counter-revolutionary violence for the suppression of the proletariat . . . Yet, because of a guilty conscience, they insist on hoisting the signboard of the 'State of the whole people'.

The same article accused Liu Shao-ch'i, 'China's Khrushchev', of having argued that it was the function of the State to 'organize social life'. This had been part of his attempt to transform the proletarian into a bourgeois dictatorship.

The underlying controversy turns on Lenin's concept of the 'withering away of the State', as put forward in his *State and Revolution.* The presumption that the State will ultimately disappear, because the disappearance of classes and class struggle will make it redundant, cannot be reconciled with the assumption in Mao's 'Contradiction' essay that class struggle will continue for the forseeable future. This may be a marginal difference, but it operates on a margin of 'hundreds of years'. Since Mao has also ruled out the possibility of 'socialism in one country', in that the Chinese revolution can only succeed as part of a successful world revolution, the revolution must either be a 'continuing' process or will end in 'counter-revolution' through an imperialist reconquest of China or through revisionist corruption—or possibly through a combination of these two 'colluding' forces.

The theoretical background of this issue was explored by two provincial papers. One of these, the Canton *Nanfang Jih Pao* (*Southern Daily*) of 9 May 1969,[1] said:

'Chairman Mao's theory on continuing the revolution under proletarian dictatorship greatly enriches and develops Marxism-Leninism and forms the third milestone in . . . its development.

[1] Summary 3072/3.

Marx and Engels established the theory of scientific socialism, but they could not then solve the series of important problems of making revolution under proletarian dictatorship. Lenin saw that class struggle still existed after the proletarian seizure of political power . . . and that it was necessary to strengthen proletarian dictatorship for a long time. However, Lenin died too soon to solve these problems . . . Stalin dealt with a large number of counter-revolutionary bourgeois representatives sneaking into the Party, but did not admit theoretically that classes and class struggle existed in society during the whole historical period of proletarian dictatorship . . . Chairman Mao . . . put forward the theory of continuing the revolution under proletarian dictatorship and personally initiated and led the great proletarian cultural revolution . . . He correctly solved the . . . problem of strengthening proletarian dictatorship and preventing capitalist restoration and has developed Marxism-Leninism to a brand-new stage.'

The implication is that Marx and Engels were unpractical theorists and that Lenin might have changed his views, had he lived longer. Stalin's terror regime is seen to be lacking in political orientation, since it failed to detect and destroy those who, after his death, abandoned proletarian dictatorship in favour of rule by a revisionist bureaucracy. But Mao saved the purity of Marx's concept by adding the principle of the continuing revolution.

The *Heilungkiang Daily* of 5 July 1969 said in an article[1] about Lin Piao's Political Report:

'A great contribution was made by Marx and Engels to the theory of the dictatorship of the proletariat . . . Marx said "What I did that was new was to prove (1) that the existence of classes in only bound up with particular historical phases in the develop-

---

[1] Summary 3120/B/5.

ment of production; (2) that the class struggle necessarily leads to the dictatorship of the proletariat; and that (3) the dictatorship itself only constitutes the transition to the abolition of all classes and to a classless society." . . . [This] was the first milestone of Marxism. Marx and Engels lived in an era in which capitalism was developing. However, capitalist contradictions had already become visible . . . They also led the great struggle of the proletariat in the exercise of dictatorship . . . [They] summed up the fundamental experience in and lessons drawn . . . from the Commune and developed further the theory of the dictatorship of the proletariat . . . [They] felt that the only revision that should be made in the Communist Manifesto should be [that] . . . the proletariat must destroy the old State machinery and exercise the dictatorship of the proletariat.

A great contribution was also made by Lenin . . . With genius, Lenin resolved the question of whether socialism can triumph in one country and raised Marxism . . . to the stage of Leninism . . . [He] transformed the theories of the dictatorship of the proletariat put forward by Marx and Engels into reality by building the first socialist State of the dictatorship of the proletariat . . . He perceived the danger of the restoration of capitalism and the protracted nature of the class struggle after the seizure of power by the proletariat. He said explicitly: 'The transition from capitalism to communism represents an entire historical epoch . . ."

Chairman Mao has also made a great contribution to the theory of the dictatorship of the proletariat. [He] . . . has comprehensively summed up the historical experience of the dictatorship of the proletariat with genius, both in the positive and negative aspects, put forward the great theory of continuing the revolution under the dictatorship of the proletariat, and initiated, led and is still leading the great proletarian cultural revolution, the first of its kind in the history of mankind. He has resolved . . . the most important contemporary question: how the proletariat, after seizing political power, consolidates the dictatorship of the proletariat and prevents capitalist restoration—thus developing Marxism-Leninism . . . to a higher and completely new stage . . . He has analysed contradictions, classes and class struggle in society scientifically . . . the first such analysis in the history of the development of Marxism . . . Chairman Mao . . . puts forward the basic line of our Party for the whole historical period of socialism.

Lenin once stated that "the new bourgeoisie was arising from among our Soviet Government employees" . . . Chairman Mao explicitly pointed out that the main target of the revolution under the dictatorship of the proletariat are the representatives of the bourgeoisie who have sneaked into the Party, the handful of Party persons in authority taking the capitalist road.'

The *Heilungkiang Daily* stresses the interest shown by Marx in the Paris Commune—an interest which Mao shares with Marx and which may help to explain the choice of the term 'people's commune' for this Chinese attempt at a short-cut to communist society—and it credits Lenin with having demonstrated the practicability of a proletarian dictatorship—even though at the price of seeing socialism triumph in one country only. Lenin is said to have stipulated 'an entire historical epoch' as the duration of the transition from capitalism to socialism—which is not the same as Mao's proposition that this transition will, in practice, never end. In this respect, Mao's 'continuing' revolution goes beyond his previous concept of the 'uninterrupted' revolution. Both terms may occasionally be found in one and the same pronouncement, e.g. in a *Hung Chi* commentary of November 1969[1] on the duties of cadres to 'persist in struggle'. This takes issue with the revisionist ideal of 'peaceful evolution' and gives warning that 'lack of political consciousness of making uninterrupted revolution' may make cadres 'go after fame, position and salaries' and thus give class enemies opportunities to 'undermine the new-born revolutionary committees'. The

[1] Summary 3233/B/6.

article ends with an appeal to members of revolutionary committees at all levels to 'adhere to Chairman Mao's great theory of continuing to make revolution under the dictatorship of the proletariat, for ever maintain our Party's revolutionary tradition of hard struggle and plain living, and overcome bureaucratism, so that our revolutionary committees will become even better and our dictatorship of the proletariat will become still further consolidated'.

The difference between uninterrupted (*pu tuan*) and continuing (*chi hsu*) revolution has not been defined by Maoist writers. It appears to be a difference of emphasis; both refer to a revolution proceeding by stages, but the continuing concept is the wider one in that it assumes underlying factors valid for all stages. This makes it easier to go forward or backwards in history and to attach contemporary significance to past pronouncements made in a different context.

II

Mao's continuing revolution, as Lin Liao's Political Report says, has to be seen in the context of Mao's theory of contradictions as outlined in his 1957 essay, and of the principle that 'One divides into two'. This principle has political as well as philosophical meaning. Its opposite—that 'two combines into one'—has been condemned as a symbol of revisionist liberalism, since it presupposes the ultimate harmony of opposites. In political terms this represents Liu Shao-ch'i's theory of the 'dying out of the class struggle' and revisionist 'capitulationism', i.e. readiness to strike bargains with capitalists at home and with foreign aggressors.

One practical aspect of Mao's principle of innate dualism, of 'One divides into two', is that it makes people look at different aspects of the same phenomenon; thus they will tend to consider nothing perfect—since anything good has its bad qualities, just as nothing is irredeemably bad, since it has its good side. Dualism makes it possible to reclaim 'bad' people by bringing out the good in them through 'remoulding' and 're-education', and it preserves good elements from the folly of righteous assertion of absolute merit gained in the revolution. Mao-study on these lines is recommended as a corrective for shortcomings in cadre work and Party-building, friction within revolutionary committees, and difficulties over production and distribution in industry and agriculture. A *Jenmin Jih Pao* editorial note of 4 July 1970 says:[1]

'One-sidedness means thinking in terms of absolutes, that is, taking the viewpoint of regarding everything either as positive or negative . . . If we see only the good and regard everything as positive, we shall become conceited and complacent, adhere rigidly to traditional forms and customs and we shall not be able to continue the revolution and our advance. If we see only the bad and regard everything as negative, we shall lose confidence and the courage to march forward . . . Our great leader Chairman Mao teaches us: We must learn to look at problems from all sides. This is the dialectical method of Marxism-Leninism.'

We see here evidence of a Maoist tendency to bring in the principle of continuing revolution and the dualist approach to reinforce elementary practical advice. It would, however, be a mistake to dismiss this dualism as a mere peg on which to hang banalities. Lin Piao and others have paid tribute to Mao's 'genius' and to his achievement in having 'enriched' Marxism-Leninism by this concept—meaning that Mao made an original contribution to Marxist dialectics. Mao's special merit is that he established a new relationship between economic base and cultural-political superstructure and modified Marx's *Unterbau-Überbau* relationship to make it less deterministic. Marx argued that the alternative to successful proletarian revolution would be chaos—but he

---

[1] Summary 3431/11.

apparently did not expect chaos to ensue. Lenin toyed with the idea of eventual harmony in a classless society. Mao regards chaos—in the form of a reversion to capitalism or perversion through a revisionist pseudo-class bureaucracy—as a real threat to the revolution which can be avoided only by eternal 'vigilance' and 'struggle'.

Much of this can and has been stated by Maoists in Marxist dialectical terms. There would therefore be no need to dwell on 'contradictions'—a term which is not a mere Chinese colloquial translation of 'dialectics'. The Chinese term (*mao-tun*) is a very concrete expression, meaning 'spear and shield' and referring to a classical story of someone who claimed to be able to supply customers with shields which nothing could pierce and spears which nothing could withstand.

On the other hand, it would be tempting to equate Mao's dualism with the Hegelian formula of thesis-antithesis-synthesis, and some concepts of the cultural revolution come very close to this, notably that of 'struggle-criticism-transformation', in the superstructure. But Hegel envisaged an eventual goal and end to this process, whereas Mao does not. His 'Contradiction' essay of 1957 insists that contradictions will always exist, although some of them are 'friendly' and can be resolved, while others are between 'hostile' class elements and must be dealt with by force—war or dictatorship. To deny the existence of contradictions, for Mao, is a symptom of 'counter-revolutionary' attitudes, be it in literature, the arts, economics, politics or military affairs. The crimes of Liu Shao-ch'i, P'eng Chen, Lu Ting-yi, Chou Yang, Peng Teh-huai and the economist Sung Yeh-chaung can be brought under the common denominator of anti-dualism and the 'denial of class struggle'. Mao is convinced that the revolutionary principle of 'One into two' will prevail—and that its momentum will create an eternal dichotomy.

It may be useful to look at Mao's dualism in a Chinese setting. There are striking parallels between Mao's theory of contradictions and some precepts of the Yin-yang school of philosophy and of Taoism. The second chapter of the *Tao Teh Ching* says that action to further beauty will result in creating ugliness, and that action to foster an absolute good will create evil. High and low, big and small, long and short, indeed existence and non-existence are relative, 'mutually created' phenomena. Chapter 25 of the *Tao Teh Ching*, which discusses the nature of Tao, makes it follow a circular route in which its power is known as that which 'departs'; this becomes 'distant' and then 'returns'. The beginning of Chapter 42 says that the birth of Tao gives rise to one, this to the birth of two, this to three, and this to the 'ten thousand things'. A passage which brings the image of Tao very close to that of flowing water—and which also presents an interrelation between momentary enlightenment and historical necessity, occurs in Chapter 4 of the *Tao Teh Ching*:[1]

'The Tao (or Current) must drain away and spend itself in order to replenish itself. What a turbulent abyss! It contains the multitude of things. It is sharp but blunts its own sharpness. It is confused but creates order out of its disorder. It shines with brilliance but brings the harmony of shade to its blinding light. Thus it can identify itself with its own materialization—which is this world. How calm it is, as if it never moved! I do not know whose father's son it is. Certain is that it existed before heaven and stars existed.'

There are passages in the *Tao Teh Ching* for which parallels in Mao's teachings on politics, administration and war can be found. There is, for instance, a parallel between Mao's guerrilla strategy and the passage in Chapter 36 which says that the supple and weak can overcome the strong and unbending.[2] The

[1] My translation. Readers may prefer to consult a published translation of the *Tao Teh Ching*, notably Arthur Waley's *The Way and its Power*. I would, however, suggest that the water image of Tao—certainly in the passages quoted here—gives easier access to the practical implications of this work, which is in many ways a treatise about government and about the relations between rulers and ruled.

[2] The word *jou*, meaning 'weak and supple as a child', is used in the Japanese terms denoting the art of unarmed combat (*jujitsu, judo*); this does *not* mean the 'gentle' art.

following passage in Chapter 66 might be of relevance to cadres and students 'sent down' to the countryside to be 're-educated' by the peasantry.

'The reason why rivers and the sea can be masters of the hundred streams is that they know how to put themselves lower than these streams . . . That is why the sage who wants to be above the people, must put himself in what he says below the people; if he wants to precede the people, he must, in his person, put himself behind them.'

In similar vein, it is said in Chapter 17:

'If the great ones rule, their inferiors do not realize that the great ones exist . . . How careful they (the rulers) must be in what they say! The work they accomplish is in accordance with the state of things. Then the nameless ones say: It's we who have done this; it's we who wanted it done!'

This passage is reminiscent of Mao's preoccupation with the 'mass line' and the fear that leaders may become 'divorced from the masses and from reality'.

There have been, it is true, Maoist condemnations of popular Taoist superstitions, but there have been no denunciations of Taoist philosophy. On the other hand, Confucianism has been condemned as a 'feudal' philosophy used by the ruling class to oppress the people—and Liu Shao-ch'i has been condemned for being a Confucianist of sorts. Like the *Tao Teh Ching*, Maoism shows a special interest in the control of currents, as in the 'helmsman' song about Mao and the saga of Mao's Yangtse swim, when he miraculously covered a distance beyond the reach of ordinary swimmers, certainly of men of his age. It may well be that the logic of Mao's contradictions has a special appeal to a people on whom the Yin-yang philosophy has had such a strong impact. It is not unlikely that Mao's upbringing in a peasant family may have endowed him with a knowledge of Yin-yang imagery and other ideas enshrined in the work attributed to the mythical sage Lao Tse. We know that Mao writes poetry in the classical style, which is deeply imbued with Yin-yang symbolism. When Mao 'enriched' Marxism-Leninism, he may well have done so by combining it with Taoist statecraft. Mao is in a way the epitome of the Taoist sage-ruler (*sheng jen*), diametrically opposed to the Confucian scholar-statesman (*chün tse*). In cultural revolution terms, this is the difference between leaders 'serving the people' and 'authorities' divorced from the masses.

Another Taoist aspect of Maoist practice is rejection of teaching by the spoken word only. The Taoist saying that those who know do not speak and those who speak do not know (*chih che pu yen*) finds its echo in Maoist exhortations to 'combine theory with practice' and study with work. Inherent in Maoism and Taoism is a conviction that there is a 'natural' way in the essence of things which, if followed, will produce results; it is for the 'helmsman' to steer the right course which will make the ship drift in the right direction, just as it is for the Taoist sage to arrange things in such a way that there remains nothing further to be done (*wu wei*) to them. Both employ the principle of applying the greatest possible leverage.

III

The nature of the continuing revolution makes it possible to attribute to an event of a past period a significance relevant for the future. This method has been used more widely since Lin Piao's assertion in his Political Report that the continuing revolution is the guiding principle of the cultural revolution. Even before then there had been a pronounced ideological reversion to the Long March and Yenan periods.[1] The events of

---

[1] See R. Bonwit, *loc. cit.*, p. 62—the main periods of the Chinese revolution are: first civil war 1924–7, second civil war 1927–36, war against Japan 1937–45, war of liberation 1946–9; the end of this war meant the beginning of the period of socialism.

those days continue to inspire—and sometimes to warn—Army Party and people in the present tasks of 'revolution and construction'.

Some major documents of the Yenan period have been republished, together with commentaries or joint editorials on their significance in the present context; such was the purpose of the *Hung Chi* article of October 1969 on Mao's 1957 'Contradiction' essay.

An important publication of such a historic document took place in November 1969—after the Twelfth Session of the Eighth Party Central Committee. The document chosen was Mao's report to the Second Session of the Seventh Central Committee in March 1949. A joint editorial of 25 November 1969[1] discussed the need to study this document in the light of Mao's 'latest instruction' about learning from historical experience. An NCNA note on the publication of the 1949 report said that the following points made therein were of special importance: the shift of the main tasks of Party work from rural to urban areas, China's transformation into an industrial country, and the transition from a new-democratic to a socialist society.

The 1949 report contains some recommendations similar to policies now attributed to Liu Shao-ch'i's revisionist school of thought, such as reliance on 'positive factors' in capitalism, a 'prudent' and 'step-by-step' transformation of agriculture, and combination of private, State and mixed ownership in the industrial sector. But there are already indications in the document of the ideological war to be waged against imperialist economic and cultural influences. These are held responsible for the evils of Kuomintang misrule. Mao calls on the Party to 'conscientiously unite the entire working class, the entire peasantry and the broad masses of revolutionary intellectuals' as the 'leading and basic forces' of the proletarian dictatorship. He gives this advice:

[1] Summary 2935/B/2.

'Proceeding from the desire to unite with them, we should carry
out serious and appropriate criticism or struggle against their
errors and shortcomings in order to attain the objective of unity.
It would be wrong to adopt an accommodating attitude towards
their errors or shortcomings. It would also be wrong to adopt a
closed-door or perfunctory attitude towards them. In each big
or medium city, each strategic region and each province, we
should develop a group of non-Party democrats who have
prestige and cooperate with us.'

Since the Ninth Party Congress, much has been heard of the
importance of 'open-door' methods of Party-building. The
attitude recommended in 1949 for correcting shortcomings of
non-Party democrats is in line with the often-quoted motto of
'curing the sickness to save the patient'. The following section
of the 1949 report contains a warning against 'sugar-coated
bullets' which has become a mainstay of cultural revolution
propaganda:

'With victory, the people will be grateful to us and the bourgeoisie will come forward to flatter us. It has been proved that
the enemy cannot conquer us by force of arms. However, the
flattery of the bourgeoisie may conquer the weak-willed in our
ranks. There may be some Communists who were not conquered
by enemies with guns . . . but who cannot withstand sugar-
coated bullets; they will be defeated by sugar-coated bullets.
We must guard against this situation.'

There follows a reflection about the long-term character of the
Chinese revolution:

'After several decades, the victory of the Chinese people's
democratic revolution, viewed in retrospect, will seem like a
brief prologue to a long drama. A drama begins with a prologue,
but the prologue is not the climax. The Chinese revolution is

great, but the road after the revolution will be longer, the work greater and more arduous. This must be made clear now in the Party.'

Mao's 1949 report figures prominently in Lin Piao's Political Report. Lin Piao observes:

'As early as March 1949, on the eve of the transition of the Chinese revolution from the new-democratic to the socialist revolution, Chairman Mao explicitly pointed out that after the country-wide seizure of power by the proletariat, the principal internal contradiction is 'the contradiction between the working class and the bourgeoisie'. The heart of the struggle is still the question of State power.'

Lin Piao then traces the development between 1949 and the 'Contradiction' essay of 1957.

'Our Party waged intense battles in accordance with the resolution of the Second Plenary Session of the Seventh Central Committee and the Party's general line for the transition period formulated by Chairman Mao. In 1956, the socialist transformation of the ownership in agriculture, handicrafts and capitalist industry was in the main completed . . .'

—a reference to the success of land reform, agricultural co-operatives, and the anti-bourgeois campaign in the cities. Lin Piao continues:

'That was the crucial moment [deciding] whether socialist revolution could continue to advance. In view of the rampancy of revisionism in the international communist movement and the new trends of class struggle in our country, Chairman Mao, in his great work, "On the correct handling of contradictions among the people", called the attention of the whole Party to the following: "In China, although in the main socialist transformation has been completed with respect to the system of ownership . . . there are still remnants of the overthrown landlord and compradore classes. There is still a bourgeoisie as well as the overthrown landlord and compradore classes. The remoulding of the petty bourgeoisie has only just started."'

Mao in his 1957 essay, continues Lin Piao, took issue with the

'fallacy put forward by Liu Shao-chi in 1956 that "in China, the question of which wins out, socialism or capitalism, is already resolved". Chairman Mao specifically pointed out: The question of which will win out, socialism or capitalism, is still not really settled . . . The class struggle . . . will continue to be long and tortuous and at times will even become very acute.'

Lin Piao adds:

'Thus, for the first time in the theory and practice of the international communist movement, it was pointed out explicitly that classes and class struggle still exist after the socialist transformation of the ownership of the means of production has been in the main completed and that the proletariat must continue the revolution.'

The struggle was led, continues Lin Piao, by

'the proletarian headquarters headed by Chairman Mao in the direction he indicated. From the struggle against the bourgeois Rightists in 1957 to the struggle to uncover Peng Teh-huai's anti-Party clique at the Lushan meeting in 1959, from the great debate on the general line of the Party in building socialism to the struggle between two lines in the socialist education movement—the focus of the struggle was the question of whether to uphold the dictatorship of the proletariat or to restore the dictatorship of the bourgeoisie.'

The reference to the period 1956–9 is also important from another aspect. This was the period when Soviet policy, in the Maoist view, diverged from the revolutionary path. In this, the Maoists alleged the Soviet Leaders had the open or disguised support of Liu Shao-ch'i and of Army leaders centred around Peng Teh-huai. This aspect of the controversy about revisionism was stressed in a *Hung Chi* article of 24 September 1969.[1] It said:

'The programme adopted by the Soviet revisionist renegade clique at the 22nd Congress (of the CPSU) undisguisedly declared that the dictatorship of the proletariat "has ceased to be indispensable to the USSR". Khrushchev alleged: "Some comrades . . . are of the opinion that the dictatorship of the proletariat should be retained until the final victory of communism has been achieved . . . This approach . . . is scholastic."'

As for Brezhnev and his group, says *Hung Chi*, they

'donned Khrushchev's mantle and are murdering and repressing the proletariat . . . at home and energetically pushing social-imperialist policies abroad. Moreover, these renegades have taken over the mantle of the old Tsars and are engaged in colonialist aggression by plundering and oppressing their "fraternal countries".'

There follows an attack on

'China's Khrushchev—the renegade, hidden traitor and scab Liu Shao-ch'i . . . After the victory of the war of resistance against Japan, he trumpeted "the new stage of peace and democracy", alleging that "at present the main force of the struggle of the

---

[1] 3187/A2/1.

Chinese revolution has changed from armed struggle to non-armed and mass parliamentary struggle", and advocated the parliamentary road. In his sinister book *Self-cultivation*, which he carefully put out in 1939 and revised and republished in 1962, Liu Shao-ch'i viciously omitted Lenin's important conclusion that "the dictatorship of the proletariat is essential" . . . Chairman Mao . . . has set forth the great theory of continuing the revolution under the dictatorship of the proletariat. This is Chairman Mao's epoch-making contribution to Marxism-Leninism.'

One can see here implied in the theory of the continuing revolution a theory of the continuing counter-revolution, which stretches from the Tsars to Brezhnev and from the controversies over tactics and strategy of the 1920s and 1930s—notably on the question of cooperation with the Kuomintang—to the controversies ventilated at the Lushan conference.

Much of the 1959–65 controversies revolved around the Mao-Lin 'proletarian headquarters' and Liu Shao-ch'i's 'bourgeois headquarters'. The location of either 'headquarters' is somewhat nebulous. The 'bourgeois headquarters' seem to have been in control of the Eighth Party Congress. The 'proletarian headquarters' have now given place to the Mao-Lin Central Committee elected at the Ninth Party Congress. As for the 'proletarian headquarters' themselves, no special location was ever indicated for them. For a time, the stronghold of Mao and Lin Piao appears to have been the Central Committee's Military Affairs Commission, especially after Lin gained effective control of the armed forces in 1960—but this has never been proved. Now that Liu Shao-ch'i has been expelled from the Party, his 'headquarters' should have completely disintegrated, but it remains a bugbear of the cultural revolution.

The continuity of the Maoist revolution is reflected in the required study material for indoctrination and Party-building. This has always included Mao's three 'much-read' articles from the Yenan period, including a tribute to the Canadian doctor,

Norman Bethune, entitled 'Serving the people'. Mao's 'Talks at the Yenan Forum on Literature and Art' of 1942 have, acquired a new meaning in the light of the 'sending down' of young intellectuals to be 're-educated' in the countryside. To these writings have been added the documents of the Ninth Party Congress, including Lin Piao's Political Report and the new Party Constitution—and also Mao's speeches at the Congress; these have been discussed at provincial gatherings but have not been published. More recently, two documents, usually referred to as 'the two resolutions', have been added to the basic study material for Army-building, Party-building and, especially, Party-building in the Army. They are the resolution of the 1929 Kutien Conference (although that date is not often mentioned), also known as Mao's article 'On correcting mistakes within the Party', and the resolution of the 'enlarged' session in 1960 of the Military Affairs Commission, said to have been drafted by Lin Piao and approved by Mao. Although this is not often stated, the Kutien Conference was not a Party conference, but a meeting of Party cadres of the then Red Army. The Kutien resolution was the subject of an article in *Fukien Daily*—the paper of the province in which Kutien is situated—of December 1969.[1] This notes that Mao 'personally presided' over the Conference. The Kutien resolution, says the paper,

'was born in the fierce struggle of the second civil war, when Chairman Mao's revolutionary line smashed the opportunist line. It is the great programme for our Party and our Army.'

The paper adds that Lin Piao said in 1962:

'"The resolution of the Kutien conference points out the direction of our Army building." We must follow this instruction [of Lin Piao] . . . We must give prominence to proletarian

[1] Summary 3266/B/2.

politics and launch the "four good" and "five good" movements
. . . Rather than study the Kutien resolution only once, we must
study it repeatedly every year, every month and every day . . .
We must persevere in building our leading groups with Mao
Tse-tung thought. Our great leader Chairman Mao has taught
us: "Cadres are a decisive factor, once the political line has been
determined".'

This exhortation to study the Kutien resolution uses the standard
formula for the study of key documents, such as the new Party
Constitution. The paper stresses the importance of the 'four
good' company and 'five good' fighter campaigns in the PLA
(see below). It stresses the importance of 'leading groups'—a
term which can, but need not, refer to Party organizations proper.
It explains:

'Those at basic levels can work in leading organizations, while
cadres of leading organizations can also work at basic levels.'

The paper quotes from the Kutien resolution Mao's warning:

'There are various non-proletarian ideas in the Communist Party
organization in the Fourth Red Army which greatly hinder the
application of the Party's correct line.'

It goes on to quote Lenin:

'The spontaneous forces of the petty bourgeoisie come from all
quarters to surround, stain and corrupt the proletariat.'

It then denounces

'all harmful characteristics of the petty bourgeoisie, such as
disunity, individualism and disappointment deriving from
fanaticism . . .'

and asks those responsible to be

'good at helping our comrades to overcome all erroneous ideas. Eclecticism, conciliationism, being wordly-wise and playing safe, and being irresponsible [with regard] to the revolution— all these are wrong . . . We must make a complete break with all old traditions. . . We must put "destruction above everything", destroying and constructing in a big way . . . The splendour of the Kutien Conference will shine forever.'

Here the emphasis is on Mao's dictum that 'destruction comes before construction'—a maxim increasingly applied to Party consolidation.

The history of the Kutien resolution has been chequered. So far as the text of Mao's article, 'On correcting mistaken ideas in the Party', included in the first volume of Mao's Selected Works,[1] gives an indication of the purpose of the Kutien Conference, this was an attempt to purge the Red Army of doubtful elements, to instil some degree of discipline and to restrict interference in inner-Party affairs by outsiders. It asked for the elimination of all traces of the 'ideology of roving bands' and of 'absolute egalitarianism', and for closer integration of worker and poor peasant elements into the Red Army. It was as much an Army as a Party occasion and it enshrined the principles of Army conduct which were laid down in the 'three-eight' formula[2] still used as the model of behaviour in Mao's China. In this way it prepared the way for the close relationship between army and people, the 'fish in water' symbiosis, which has remained a guiding principle of China's revolutionary establishment.

[1] Page 105 of the English edition published in Peking in 1965—for problems involving this text, see Stuart Schram, *Mao Tse-tung*, Pelican, 1966, p. 141.

[2] These consist of three rules of discipline: (1) obey orders, (2) do not take a single needle or piece of thread from the masses, and (3) turn in everything captured; and four 'points for attention': Speak politely, pay fairly for what you buy, return everything you borrow, and pay for everything you damage (these are expressed by eight Chinese characters).

But the Kutien resolution also contains certain organizational proposals of relevance to the cultural revolution. It calls for the widest possible use of special propaganda teams—forerunners of the PLA 'Left-support' teams of the cultural revolution, especially after the Shanghai events of January 1967. It calls for the creation of committees of soldiers and workers, forerunners of the 'three-way alliances' which formed the basis of the revolutionary committees, and it includes specific warnings against the 'small group' mentality, at present the main obstacle to the rapid formation and smooth functioning of revolutionary committees. The Kutien Conference was an emergency conference of the cadres of a Red Army without a secure base and in danger of disarray. Here was indeed a situation where 'destruction' had to precede 'construction' to create a viable revolutionary force. The Kutien Conference has lately been acquiring a significance hitherto reserved for the Tsunyi Conference of 1935, which in Communist hagiography represents the point where Mao assumed control of the Party.

IV

The resuscitation of the Fukien Conference and Military Affairs Commission session resolutions coincided with the revival of the more strictly 'cultural' controversies of the cultural revolution. In May 1970, Peking papers published revised texts of several 'model' theatrical works, and there were special broadcasts of these. Tribute was paid to the initiative in these matters shown by Mao's wife, the former actress Chiang Ching. Mao's personal interest in the modernization of theatrical works as early as 1964 was mentioned, e.g. in a *Hung Chi* editorial of June 1970 on the opera *Shachiapang* and on Mao's 1942 'Talks at the Yenan Forum on Literature and Art'.[1] Revisionist theatrical producers were castigated for their reluctance to use the music of 'East is Red' as a leitmotiv to illustrate the meaning of references on

[1] Summary 3400/1.

stage to the morning sun, the Party and its leadership—the music identifying them with the 'Reddest sun in our hearts', Chairman Mao. There were fierce attacks on Chou Yang and other 'rogues' in literature and art. The connection between the disputes over theatrical works in 1964—when rival versions were performed on May Day in Shanghai and Peking—and the estrangement between Mao and the Peking Party Committee headed by P'eng Chen was stressed.

In this way, the cultural revolution has come full circle. It started as a literary controversy with political overtones; it returns to the fray now that many of the actors on the 'cultural' stage have disappeared, writers and politicians into limbo and many Red Guards into the countryside. But the manner of the revival of literary and artistic feuds is important.

The Yenan Forum resumes in retrospect a significance going far beyond the sphere of literature and art. This emerges clearly from the joint editorial published on 22 May 1970[1]—only two days after Mao's statement on the ultimate aims of world revolution—to celebrate the twenty-eighth anniversary of the Yenan Forum Talks.

The joint editorial asks for a 'deepening of the cultural revolution' to accomplish 'the fighting tasks of the Ninth Party Congress . . . now that we are engaged in the great cause of continuing the revolution under the dictatorship of the proletariat . . . an unprecedently great struggle for transforming the objective world'. The editorial quotes Mao's observation at the Yenan Forum that 'literary and art workers should go . . . for a long period of time unreservedly and wholeheartedly among the masses of workers and soldiers'. This is now used as justification for letting

'the masses of revolutionary cadres and revolutionary intellectuals . . . take the road of integrating themselves with the workers, peasants and soldiers by settling down in the countryside as

[1] Summary 3387/C.

commune members, entering '7th May'[1] cadre schools, going down regularly to factories and villages to take part in physical labour, or working in selected basic units to get experience to guide overall work, and by other ways.'

This statement may foreshadow a mitigation of the 'sending down' policy for most cadres, and possibly also for some students, in that they would stay at basic levels in rotation.

There is one aspect of the current controversy over the re-writing of Peking opera and other stage works which has a bearing on the character of the continuing revolution. Much of the discussion turns on the role of 'armed struggle' and 'people's war'.

This comes out clearly in a *Hung Chi* article of September 1969 on a film about the fall of Changchun, called *Beleaguered City*.[2] The article complains that the film

'completely ignores the part played by the revolutionary army and the revolutionary masses . . . We see no scene showing the invincible march forward and the strong political offensive of our PLA, or showing the wall of iron which the broad masses of the revolutionary people have built to support revolutionary war. PLA appearances on the screen are in fleeting scenes in which the PLA plays an unimportant supporting role. As for the broad masses of the revolutionary people, they are not allowed to participate in the people's war.'

The article asks:

'How was Changchun liberated? It was liberated because the PLA troops, directly commanded by Comrade Lin Piao, resolutely and thoroughly carried out our great leader Chairman Mao's

[1] Named after Mao's 7 May 1966 Direction and used for retraining cadres up to provincial level in farm camps.
[2] Summary 3172/B/1.

important instruction on 'building and consolidating the bases in the North-East' and his other important instructions. Moreover, they waged a tit-for-tat struggle against Liu Shao-ch'i's capitulationist line promoted by P'eng Chen and Kao Kang.'

The juxtaposition of P'eng Chen and Kao Kang, the North-Eastern leader who died in mysterious circumstances in the 1950s, is interesting.

Chiang Kai-shek, *Hung Chi* observes, went to Shenyang (Mukden) but could not save the garrison besieged in Changchun. They were compelled to surrender 'as the result of armed struggle. The decisive factor here was still the gun and the people's war'.

The *Hung Chi* article of June 1970 about the opera *Shachiapang* quotes Mao's 'On problems of war and strategy' for this observation:

'In China, war is the main force of struggle and the army is the main form of organization.'

The last scenes of the revised version were written, says *Hung Chi*, after Mao had given instructions 'that armed struggle should be the play's main theme'. Referring to the two main characters, a man representing the Red Army and a woman representing the civilians helping it by espionage among enemy troops, *Hung Chi* observes:

'The original scenes have all been retained and the principal vocal parts have not been curtailed. But the relationship between armed struggle and secret work, which is one between the principal and the secondary, has been straightened out and clarified.'

These observations follow a passage in which Mao is quoted as saying in 'Problems of War and Strategy':

'In most of China, Party organizational work and mass work are directly linked with armed struggle. There is not, and cannot be, any Party work or mass work that is isolated from armed struggle.'

The new version of the opera, observes the article, also shows 'the role played by militiamen and the tremendous power of people's war'.

The attempts to refashion the opera were nearly marred, says *Hung Chi*, by the intrigues of Li Chi, who 'then usurped the position' of Director of the Propaganda Department of the Peking Municipal Party Committee, headed by P'eng Chen. Li had tried to keep in the script scenes which 'confuse the relationship between armed struggle and underground work, put underground work above armed struggle and place armed struggle under the leadership of underground work'.

This argument about the Army and secret work may have some bearing on the dismissal of Lo Jui-ch'ing from the position as PLA Chief of Staff, probably in the middle of 1966. Lo had once been in command of the security forces, and there is reason to believe that he wanted to create a security empire—possibly on the model of the NKVD. The ambiguous role of security forces in incidents in Kunming, which led to the suicide of the leader of the Yunnan provincial Party establishment, and in the Wuhan riots, indicated a possible rift between them and PLA units loyal to Mao and Lin Piao.

The argument about the security forces was elucidated in a *Jenmin Jih Pao* editorial of 12 July 1968.[1] This accused Liu Shao-ch'i of having

'attempted to place the government and law enforcement organs under the control of the 'bourgeois headquarters' and to turn these organs into counter-revolutionary tools for . . . suppressing the masses . . . Chairman Mao pointed out time and again . . .

[1] Summary 2754/B/14. For Lo Jui-ch'ing's position, see also R. Bonwit, *loc. cit.*, p. 59.

since 1957 that in the work of suppressing counter-revolutionaries and in security work it is necessary to rely on the masses.'

The PLA organ *Chiehfang Chün Pao* in November 1969 carried an article denouncing Peng Teh-hai and Lo Jui-ch'ing for their 'towering crimes in sabotaging militia-building'.[1] It described the Chinese militia as

'an armed organization of the masses which our great leader Chairman Mao founded. The militia is an important component of our revolutionary armed forces which are led by our Party. It is Chairman Mao's consistent strategic thinking and the core of the theory on people's war to carry out the "three-in-one" combination of regular forces, local forces and militia . . . Chairman Mao comprehensively and systematically put forward the theory, line, principles and politics on people's war of mobilising the people and arming them, so that everybody is a soldier.'

Peng Teh-huai is accused of having

'clamoured: "The existence of the militia system is no longer appropriate to the current new situation". At this vital moment, Chairman Mao issued an important instruction that, so long as imperialism exists, militia work must be strengthened . . . In September 1958 Chairman Mao issued a great call to the people of the country: "The imperialists are bullying us in such a way that we will have to deal with them seriously. Not only must we have a powerful regular Army, we must also organize contingents of the people's militia on a big scale. This will make it difficult for the imperialists to move a single inch in our country in the event of invasion."'

Today imperialists are not the only potential enemies whose

[1] Summary 3241/B/2.

threatened invasion would be drowned in the 'ocean of a people's war'. The article goes on to say that

'since 1962 Chairman Mao has given many more important instructions on militia-building . . . Lo Jui-ch'ing feigned compliance but actually opposed Chairman Mao's instructions. Lo Jui-ch'ing tried . . . to block or sabotage the implementation of these instructions. He alleged that in doing militia work the first thing was to do it politically, and that this should serve as a basis for doing it organizationally and militarily.'

In other words, Lo proposed to do for the militia what Lin Piao with his 'four good' company campaign has been doing for the PLA: putting political-ideological work above technical training. However, says the article, this was a case of

'waving "Red flags" to oppose the Red flag. The militiamen are armed masses who are not divorced from production; so it is impossible to carry out militia work politically before carrying it out organizationally. In fact, Lo Jui-ch'ing was consistently opposed to giving prominence to proletarian politics.'

The real charge against Lo appears to be that he was unwilling to allow the existence of a powerful paramilitary force, a non-professional army. It was the existence of the militia, says the article, which during the civil war and the war against Japan kept secure military bases which

'provided no sanctuary for traitors and enemy agents . . . Moreover the militia consolidated the revolutionary political power, safeguarded production by the masses and provided our Army with a stabilized rear.'

The question is asked:

'Is the militia system now outdated? Absolutely not! . . . The larger the scale of war and the more complicated the war situation, the more necessary it is to bring into full play the role of the masses in war and to turn the whole nation into soldiers. So long as imperialism exists and there is class struggle within the country, the militia system will never become outdated.'

This implies that the continuing revolution is inseparable from a military-political establishment in which 'everybody is a soldier'. The article clinches the argument by stating:

'Chairman Mao has always taught us: "Politics is the commander, the soul in everything". In building the militia the question of whether to put proletarian politics to the fore and whether to arm the minds of hundreds of millions of militiamen with Mao Tse-tung thought determines whose hands control the barrel of the gun.'

Power, it appears, not only 'grows out of the barrel of a gun'; care must be taken that the gun does not fall into the wrong hands. It is the militia—which is organized by county-level armed forces' departments under the PLA—and not an armed political police which protects the proletarian dictatorship. In the the later stages of the cultural revolution, a movement began for organizing a 'workers' provost corps' in the cities and for new 'organs of the proletarian dictatorship' to replace the security organs, people's procurates and special courts, discredited by events such as the Wuhan incident. The above article blames Lo Jui-ch'ing for having discouraged the study of Mao's works by the militia and says:

'We should educate the militiamen with Chairman Mao's great theory of continuing the revolution under the dictatorship of the proletariat, so that they never forget the class struggle and the dictatorship of the proletariat, recognize the aggressive nature of US imperialism and [Soviet] social-imperialism, heighten their vigilance and are fully prepared against wars of aggression.'

This picture of China as a permanent military camp is also inherent in one of the Mao teachings constantly quoted nowadays: 'Be prepared for war, be prepared for natural calamities and do everything for the people'.

V

The need to 'fight for the further consolidation of the dictatorship of the proletariat' was the theme of the joint editorial of 1 October National Day 1969.[1] Mao, it said, had defined the task thus:

'To sum up our experience and concentrate it into one point, it is this: The people's democratic dictatorship under the leadership of the working class (through the Communist Party) and based upon the alliance of workers and peasants.'

The twenty years since the foundation of the Chinese People's Republic had been years of struggle for the consolidation of this dictatorship. Mao's 'thinking on continuing the revolution under the dictatorship of the proletariat' had become deeply ingrained in the people. The further consolidation of the proletarian dictatorship required 'serious attention to be paid to further strengthening and perfecting the three-in-one revolutionary committees at all levels'.

The article affirmed that the proletarian dictatorship was

'effected through the leadership of the Communist Party. The whole Party, the whole Army and the people of the whole country should rally closely around the Central Committee of the Party with Chairman Mao as its leader and Vice-Chairman Lin

[1] Summary 3191/C/8.

E   129

as its deputy leader . . . We must conscientiously carry out the work of consolidating and building the Party.'

Mao had stated:

'The second function of this dictatorship is to protect our country from subversion and possible aggression by external enemies.'

The Mao quotation puts the militia-type function of the armed forces and their internal security role on an equal footing with their external function of warding off foreign aggression. The article stresses the leading role of the Communist Party over other organizations and the masses, affirmed in the new Party Constitution.[1] But it also implies a dual leadership of Party branches and revolutionary committees at all levels below the Party Central Committee.

The leading function of the Party was restated in the joint editorial on the forty-ninth anniversary of the CCP on 1 July 1970.[2] Paraphrasing the Constitution it says:

'The . . . glorious and correct CCP is the vanguard and the highest form of organization of the working class. The working class exercises its leadership through the Communist Party . . . The whole Party must observe unified discipline and be subordinate to the Central Committee. The organs of State power of the dictatorship of the proletariat, the PLA and the Communist Youth League and other revolutionary mass organizations, such as those of workers, the poor and lower-middle peasants and the Red Guards, must all accept the leadership of the Party . . . and carry out to the letter the line, principles and policies of the Party's Central Committee . . . All individuals and organizations

[1] Summary 3061/C.   [2] Summary 3113/C.

must pay attention to the point that they should on no account put themselves in a wrong position in relation to the Party.'

There follows a reminder that Mao warned the Ninth Party Congress that

'in the . . . cultural revolution, some tasks have not yet been fulfilled and they should now be carried out, for instance, the task of struggle-criticism-transformation. We must . . . consolidate and develop the revolutionary great alliance . . . further consolidate and develop the revolutionary three-in-one combination [also known as the three-way alliance] . . . and continue to do well in the work of purifying the class ranks. In units where purification of the class ranks is by and large completed, it is necessary to take firm hold of the work of consolidating and building the Party and other tasks of struggle-criticism-transformation.'

The last sentence confirms that Party-building is the outstanding task of 'transforming the superstructure' but that this has in many cases not even started. There follows a reminder that the first task in Party-building is 'to consolidate the Party ideologically'—rather than organizationally. Later on the article says that in Party consolidation

'it is most important to make a good job of consolidating and building the leading bodies. In the revolutionary committees at all levels, according to their own conditions, a strong core of Party leadership must gradually be formed.'

This article admits, in fact, that a Chinese Communist Party as a viable nation-wide organization at all levels does not yet exist— and that it will take a long, 'gradual' struggle to bring it into existence. Meanwhile it leaves the revolutionary committees as caretakers—where they exist.

To appreciate the inter-relationship between Party groups and revolutionary committees we must revert to the time when the last Chinese provinces had formed their revolutionary committees and thus prepared the way for the convocation of an 'enlarged' final session of the Eighth Party Committee. It was this session which ended what one might term the 'Cultural Revolution Group' phase of the cultural revolution, expelled Liu Shao-ch'i and prepared the way for the Ninth Party Congress and the election of the Mao-Lin Politbureau. One of the last key committees to be set up was the Szechwan Revolutionary Committee. At its inauguration in Chengtu on 31 May 1968, its Chairman, Chang Kuo-hua[1] was quoted by Chengtu radio[2] as referring to Mao for a definition of the cultural revolution as 'a continuation of the struggle between the CCP and the Kuomintang reactionaries'. A joint editorial of 2 June 1968[3] on the Szechwan event said that the basic distinction between the CCP and Kuomintang turned on 'whether to protect or oppress the broad masses of the people'. This comparison has two implications. It is a warning to the Party not to fall into the error of 'becoming divorced from the masses'. It is also a warning to the PLA not to try to replace the broken-down Party machine by a purely military dictatorship.

A situation in which the Party had been discredited and the mass organizations of youth, workers and intellectuals—including the Chinese Communist Youth League and the All-China Federation of Trade Unions—had been disbanded or suspended required a new type of organization under strong, but not exclusive, PLA control, if a purely military dictatorship was to be avoided. The solution was the revolutionary committee. It is not certain that it was Mao's first choice. There are indications that the original aim of the Shanghai workers' 'January rebellion'

---

[1] Former commander of the PLA forces in Tibet, whose transfer to Szechwan presaged the collapse of the 'independent kingdom' of Li Chi-chuang, one-time Secretary of the South-West China Regional Bureau of the Party Central Committee.
[2] Summary 2786/B/4   [3] Summary 2786/B/7

of 1967 was to set up a 'Shanghai Commune' in the image of the Paris Commune so beloved of Marx, Engels and Mao. Instead, the Heilungkiang 'rebel' committees became the model of the new power structure. In essence the revolutionary committee was to be a council of workers, poor and lower-middle peasants and soldiers, although often Red Guards played a part in its formation. The initiative came in many cases from the armed forces, whose intervention was sanctioned by Mao's appeal to the PLA during the Shanghai events to 'support the Left'. Even before October 1968, a connection between revolutionary committees and Party consolidation had been stated in some provincial pronouncements. A Kweichow directive[1] is still one of the most explicit instructions on Party consolidation available; broadcast on 8 September 1968, it quotes Mao's instruction that revolutionary committees at all levels should tackle Party rectification by setting up 'Party leadership core groups' and revive the 'organizational life of the Party'. However, it observes,

'organizational life at present . . . consists mainly of studying and applying Mao Tse-tung thought creatively, repudiating China's Khrushchev's [Liu Shao-ch'i] counter-revolutionary revisionist line on Party-building and combating self-interest [which includes "factionalism"] and repudiating revisionism. Party members who have committed serious mistakes must conduct self-criticism; suspected traitors and spies must not be allowed to take part in the organizational life of the Party for the time being . . . In the admission of new members, priority should be given to outstanding workers, poor and lower-middle peasants, PLA fighters and revolutionary little generals [Red Guards] filled with the proletarian spirit of the revolution . . . Work concerning new admissions to the Party must be strictly organized.'

The directive provides that acceptance of

new Party members in all units subordinate to the Kweichow

---

[1] Summary 2879/B/20.

Provincial Revolutionary Committee must be approved by the various leadership groups [not further defined]. Acceptance of Party members at district, factory, etc. level must be approved by the Party leadership core group of revolutionary committees at county level and above and their equivalent.'

Where a unit does not yet possess a Party leadership core group, admissions may be

'discussed and examined by Party members of the Standing Committee of the Provincial Revolutionary Committee and referred for approval to the Party core leadership groups of higher-level revolutionary committees.'

Nearly all provincial revolutionary committees are chaired by leading members of the local PLA command. The PLA, by definition, is represented in the 'three-way alliances' which form the basis of revolutionary committees. There is another leverage which gives the PLA further authority—the abrogation of the regional bureaux of the Party Central Committee. This has left the PLA Regional Commands[1] one step above the top level of committees.

A 'three-way alliance' is, nominally, one of representatives of the PLA, revolutionary cadres and revolutionary mass organizations. In practice, the PLA has the veto power concerning the

---

[1] With some exceptions—Sinkiang being one—a PLA Regional Command embraces several provinces, and troops are deployed between these. There is also a PLA Railway Corps which helps with the construction and maintenance of railway lines and whose Mao-thought teams have played an important part in settling disputes between 'contending factions' among railway workers—or between railway administrations, e.g. between Chengchow and Wuhan over alleged hoarding of wagons. How sensitive the Chinese authorities are to threats of 'factionalism' on the railways—with memories of sections of track operated by independent war-lords in the 1920s—was shown when Premier Chou En-lai made leaders of two 'contending factions' from Chengchow come to Peking and helped them to compose their differences. The PLA in Sinkiang and Heilungkiang—and more recently in some other areas—also operates a Construction and Production Corps for water conservancy and other tasks.

formation of an alliance or committee and the vetting power over the admission of new Party members and the disciplining of existing or 'former'—the distinction is not always clear—Party Committee members through the revolutionary committees controlled by it. Ultimately, Party-building is thus controlled by the highest political organ of the PLA, the Military Affairs Commission of the Party Central Committees. The use of its 1960 decision as one of the 'two resolutions' to be studied for Party-building has enhanced its authority. In fact, the PLA's control over revolutionary committees goes one stage further back in their formation. In order to have 'representatives of mass organizations' participate in a 'three-way alliance', such mass organizations must first be created. Especially in the case of trade unions, this may prove difficult, when they are split into pro- and anti-Mao factions. Chinese reports in such cases speak of 'the two contending' organizations or groups. The instrument chosen to bring harmony into this discord is usually the PLA. A PLA Mao-thought propaganda team, usually unarmed, arrives at the factory, district offices, railway station, government department or other unit concerned and makes the contending factions participate in 'Mao-study', where suitable Mao instructions are expounded and a reconciliation is effected. Bloody clashes—'struggle by force' in Chinese Communist parlance—are usually ascribed to elements among the masses 'hoodwinked' by revisionist class enemies or blinded by 'factionalist' self-interest. It is often the intervening PLA group which decides which faction should be recognized as Maoist and which 'persuaded' to give in. In this manner the PLA is instrumental in creating a new trade union or other functional group called a 'great alliance'. In theory the sequence is: struggle, leading to 'great alliances', which combine into 'three-way alliances', which form revolutionary committees. The only constant element in this process is the PLA team backed by the PLA command.

Lin Piao restated the all-pervading role of the PLA in a passage in his Political Report:

'The People's Liberation Army is the mighty pillar of the dictatorship of the proletariat. Chairman Mao has pointed out many times: from the Marxist point of view, the main component of the State is the Army.'

VI

The military aspect of the continuing revolution was further stressed by Mao's statement of 20 May 1970.[1] It told the Chinese people that their revolution would not be complete until all suppressed peoples of the world had been liberated. It called for world-wide unity against the US imperialists 'and their running dogs', protested against the extension of the Japanese-US Security Treaty—which it denounced as an attempt to revive the Greater East Asia Co-prosperity under American supervision—and expressed the Chinese people's solidarity with the three Indochinese peoples and 'all other' oppressed peoples—a formula implying that Chinese help is not meant to include active military intervention. An attitude of friendly support short of war is also implied in the assertion that 'a small and weak country can defeat a big and strong country'. This, says Mao, 'is the law of history'. There are echoes in this Mao statement of the Chinese Communist victory over the US-supported Kuomintang forces and of China's victory over Japan—as the course of the Pacific War has been interpreted, for instance, in Lin Piao's treatise on the 'people's war'.[2] It so happened that the 'people's war' operas were published in revised form in the same month of May which saw the issue of Mao's statement. It proclaims the existence of a *de facto* 'state of people's war' between the Chinese and the imperialists for a long time to come. Since, according to Maoist logic, external aggression and internal class sabotage go together, such a state of permanent war tension is also a state of permanent class struggle.

[1] Summary 3384/C.   [2] See R. Bonwit, *loc. cit.*, p. 68.

This justifies a siege economy, a siege ideology and an establishment in which the Army is 'the main component of the State'. It does not necessarily involve military action—although this is not ruled out and would probably follow an American invasion of North Vietnam or North Korea or Soviet encroachments beyond the frontier rivers or the Sinkiang border. In talk about Chinese 'war-preparedness', actual war threats are scarcely distinguished from latent hostility between China and the two Big Powers. To be 'prepared against war' is as necessary as to be 'prepared against natural calamities'. Indeed, adequate 'preparedness' may make the dreaded events unlikely to occur: well-maintained dykes prevent floods, and a nation fully prepared to 'drown any invading aggressors in the ocean of a people's war' may deter him from attacking at all.

The theme of the 20 May statement was repeated with only slight variations about one month later on the twentieth anniversary of the outbreak of the Korean war. This occasion was celebrated extensively by both the Chinese and the North Koreans, tributes were paid by both sides to their solidarity and to the gallantry of the Chinese People's Volunteers. There were again denunciations of the Japanese-US Security Treaty, and there were further references to Chinese solidarity with the peoples of Indochina. The Chinese commemorated on this occasion not only the anniversary of 'American aggression against Korea' but also that of the 'American occupation of Taiwan', and the Koreans supported China's claim to this 'sacred part of the Chinese motherland'. The Korean war, said the Chinese joint editorial on the occasion,[1] proved that US imperialism was a 'paper tiger'—a power to be watched with vigilance but not to be feared. The editorial quoted this passage from the 20 May statement:

'Ever since World War II, US imperialism and its followers have been continuously launching wars of aggression and the people

[1] Summary 3413/A3/4.

137

in various countries have been continuously waging revolutionary wars to defeat the aggressors.'

The editorial accuses certain quarters of trying to 'offset the growing unity of the Asian peoples by fraternising with the Japanese reactionaries and even maintaining dirty relationships with Lon Nol and the like'—a reference to the continued presence of a Soviet diplomatic representation in Phnom Penh after the fall of Sihanouk. The US imperialists are described as 'teachers by negative example'.[1] The editorial ends with an assurance that the Chinese people are 'determined to fight shoulder to shoulder with the people of Asia and the whole world to defeat the US aggressors'—again a formula which expresses sympathy without committing China to going to war.

We have here projected again a situation in which the Chinese people are permanently threatened by a hostile world but are confident of their ability to contain these threats at the price of eternal vigilance. The danger of foreign aggression and of internal counter-revolution and the need to contain both are the *raison d'être* of the continuing revolution. As long as imperialism—and also 'social-imperialism'—exist, there is need for a Chinese establishment geared to the need to be prepared for a defensive 'people's war' and for a proletarian dictatorship ready to prevent a revisionist reversal. The instrument of this dictatorship is the Army and its protagonist a Party fashioned in the image of the

---

[1] The Maoist concept of learning from past events by doing the opposite and thus treating people or institutions as 'teachers by negative example' has been applied notably to Chiang Kai-shek and the Kuomintang, US imperialism and—once by Lo Jui-ch'ing, speaking as Chief of Staff—to the Munich agreement (see R. Bonwit, *loc. cit.*, p. 60). Since the cultural revolution, the Soviet revisionist leaders have become the most frequently cited 'negative examples'. As Liu Shao-ch'i was—and occasionally still is—called 'China's Khrushchev', the function of treating revisionist leaders as 'negative examples' is to polarize disputes between contending sections of Maoists and anti-Maoists in Party and other organizations. There has been less of this talk since the Ninth Party Congress and Mao's appeal for greater unity. One has heard very little about 'negative examples' in the PLA, bitter as the dispute between Lin Piao and the Peng-Lo 'clique' has admittedly been.

PLA and controlled by it as to the character of its membership. Party-building and continuing the revolution go together.

This connection was outlined about the time of the twelfth Session of the Eighth Party Central Committee in a *Hung Chi* editorial of 15 October 1968.[1] It included two passages which were proclaimed to be Mao's 'latest insructions'; they contained the biological image of Party renewal—'letting in fresh blood and getting rid of waste' and the definition of the working class as the source of all political power. The editorial welcomed the establishment of the twenty-nine provincial revolutionary committees and said that this event 'proclaimed the recapture by the proletariat of all the power which was usurped by China's Khrushchev and his local agents and proclaimed their loss of all posts in Party, Government, finance and culture; this is self-evident and has long been an objective fact'.

In these words, the editorial anticipated the expulsion of Liu Shao-ch'i from the Party. It will be noted that there was no reference to any action contemplated against the PLA. The editorial interpreted the establishment of the revolutionary committees as seizure of power by the proletariat; since in theory the Party is the vanguard of the proletariat, the revolutionary committees are seen to be standing in for the Party. And since these committees are controlled by the PLA, the Army stands in for the Party, too.

The PLA controls the civilian sector through its Mao-thought propaganda and 'three-support and two military task' teams.[2] In a situation of permanent 'war-preparedness' and readiness to wage a 'people's war', the Army can also control civilians as

[1] Summary 2901/B/1.

[2] There are 'three support' and 'two military' tasks for which such teams are deployed. They concern 'supporting the Left', i.e. arbitrating in disputes between 'factions', usually at factories or universities, helping agriculture and helping industry; and providing military and political training, usually at schools and colleges. Since 27 July 1967, when a worker-PLA Mao-thought propaganda team entered Tsinghua University, Peking, long-term work by such combined teams has become frequent. One PLA unit famous for the work done by its 'support teams' at various Peking factories and colleges is Unit 8341, possibly a unit of the Peking Garrison Command. The first two digits may refer to the PLA's 'three-eight working style'.

members of the militia. For the militia, which includes men and women, the county-level people's armed forces departments are responsible, and these are in turn responsible to the provincial PLA command. The first blueprint of a revolutionary committee organization at provincial level, the Heilungkiang revolutionary 'rebel' committee plan[1] provides that 'militia work shall be handled by the Provincial Military District'.

In order that the PLA should continue to hold these extraordinary powers, an extraordinary state of semi-war has to exist; Mao's 20 May 1970 statement asserts that such a state will exist as long as imperialism exists. In theory the oppressed peoples should be strong enough to overthrow the imperialists—that is the message of Lin Piao's September 1965 treatise on the 'people's war' with his image of the non-capitalist 'countryside' surrounding the capitalist 'city' on a world-wide scale—but in practice this will involve a long struggle. For the immediate future the real task is to prevent a further extension of the imperialist—and 'social-imperialist'—sphere of domination and to be prepared to defeat any attack on China and any revolt or ideological betrayal inside the country. Chiang Kai-shek and the American forces are 'negative examples' of military aggression and of how to defeat it; the Soviet Union and the CPSU since Stalin's death are 'negative examples' of the corruption of a Communist power élite from within. The latter danger constitutes the more real threat to the future of the Maoist regime in China. There must be 'vigilance' against the erosion of the Communist power structure through revisionism and a 'reversal of verdicts'. The cultural revolution abounds in examples of alleged attempts by Liu Shao-ch'i's followers and other class enemies to 'reverse the verdicts' pronounced on them.

VII

The concept of the continuing revolution has become since the Ninth Party Congress the *vade mecum* of leadership groups of all

[1] Summary 2388/B/33 and 2389/B/44.

descriptions in Mao's China; it is the guiding principle of Party-building, of economic planning, with hints at new 'leaps forward', especially in industry; it is the main subject of Mao-study of the 'tasks set by the Ninth Party Congress' and of the Party Constitution adopted by it. According to the 20 May statement, it is also the underlying principle of world revolution and thereby of the road to the ultimate fulfilment of the Chinese revolution. It is all-embracing.

It is also so vague as to be almost meaningless. There is no true continuity of this 'continuing' process in recent Chinese history. According to Lin Piao, the continuing revolution concept was put forward by Mao in his 1957 essay on 'Contradictions' and became the theoretical basis of the cultural revolution. But it is only since the Ninth Party Congress that it has been projected in this light; it was not the main theorem of the 16 May Circular or the 16-point Central Committee decision on the cultural revolution of August 1966. It was not stressed in the 15 October 1968 *Hung Chi* editorial which foreshadowed so many of the decisions by the Eighth Central Committee and the Ninth Party Congress. Like 'boundless loyalty to Chairman Mao', 'continuing the revolution under the proletarian dictatorship' may mean different things to different people in different contexts. It is a shell of a concept.

In this it reflects a situation where the shell of a Chinese Communist Party is assumed to provide leadership for all organized forms of political, cultural, and economic life—*vide* the new Party Constitution. We know that there is a new Party Central Committee, members being listed 'by order of strokes of their Chinese characters', i.e. by the Chinese equivalent of alphabetical order, so as to make it difficult, if not impossible, to guess who controls whom—except for Mao and Lin Piao whose positions as head and deputy head are enshrined in the Party Constitution. There are various kinds of 'core groups', leadership groups and Party committees. And there is the Party apparatus in the PLA which appears to be relatively intact. One does not come across references to 'former' Party committees in the PLA, as one does with provincial and lower-level Party committees.

One may well say that where the Communist Party has survived the cultural revolution relatively intact, it has done so within the armed forces, notwithstanding individual changes at top and medium levels. As far as one can deduce from current Chinese reports, Party consolidation is making fairly rapid headway within the PLA.

Outside the PLA, there appears to be no properly constituted Party authority below Central Committee level, although a beginning is being made with forming new Party committees at village, commune and county levels. Some 'former' provincial Party committees are leading a shadowy existence, with members sent off to '7 May' cadre farm-schools to improve their minds and 'change their world outlook'. Others have advanced to the stage where there are provincial Party 'core groups' or leadership groups, not always clearly distinguishable from the leadership provided by relevant revolutionary committees and the PLA representatives on them. Indeed, the relationship between revolutionary committees and Party groups or branches at various levels is still far from clear, either side being urged to respect and 'support' the other, and the PLA being exhorted to help both.

There is now much talk about rebuilding the Communist Youth League. Less is heard about rebuilding the trade unions, but the movement to set up a 'workers' provost corps' has started in Canton and several other cities, together with organizing Red Sentinels, in the image of the Red Guards, in some factories. A high proportion of the middle school pupils and university students who, as Red Guards, provided the impetus for the 1966–7 'Bombard the headquarters' phase of the cultural revolution, have been sent to the countryside to settle down to become 're-educated' by the poor peasants while providing a leavening of elementary technical knowledge—e.g. book-keeping for production brigades—badly needed to prepare Chinese agriculture for its eventual modernization and to narrow the social and income gap between town and countryside. Meanwhile Red Guard congresses continue to function in some fashion in the cities and to send delegates to provincial 'four good' congresses and other gatherings, where the virtues of Maoist conduct and style of work and study are expounded, with special reference to PLA experiences in this field. The PLA 'four good' company movement—in which the 'first good' of being loyal to Mao's thought outweighs the technical 'three goods' of military training and discipline[1] without, however, being allowed to supplant them—is becoming a model for colleges, rural communities and factory workers. A civilian 'four good' movement has recently got under way.

A complicating aspect of Party-building is the attempt to strengthen industrial working-class representation within the Party. This trend was given prominence when Mao personally invited 10,000 workers from the twenty-nine provinces to a special reception at the Great Hall of the People for the National Day celebrations in October 1968. From the reports which these delegates made upon their return home, it would appear that National Day was followed by some sort of workers' forum together with leading members of provincial revolutionary committees, many of them PLA commanders or political commissars, who stayed on in Peking to attend the 'enlarged' session of the Eighth Party Central Committee. A stronger workers' contingent in Party branches will help to give the Party a more 'proletarian' character—hitherto 'proletarian' in the Chinese context tended to mean 'poor and lower middle peasants'. All

[1] A useful summary of the precepts of the 'four good' company, 'five good' fighter and similar movements can be obtained from the 'four firsts', which Chinese reports define as follows: (1) as between man and weapons, give first place to man; (2) as between political and other work, give first place to political work; (3) as between ideological and routine tasks in political work, give first place to ideological work; (4) in ideological work, as between ideas in books and living ideas currently in people's minds, give first place to living ideas currently in people's minds.

this reflects the growing importance of the industrial sector in a developing economy. In this regard the resuscitation of Mao's 1949 report with its stress on urban problems merits attention.

In a confused situation, cohesion is provided by the PLA, its 'support' teams, its Mao-thought study teams co-operating with workers' teams at universities and schools, its control over the peasant militia and, more indirectly, over the workers' provost corps and other urban militia-type organizations and, through them, over the new 'organs of the proletarian dictatorship'. There are Party branches and political departments at various levels of the PLA. The PLA Railway Corps in particular, and the PLA Logistic Command in general, seem to exercise some kind of supervision over the economic sector.[1] There is not only a nationwide campaign for the people to 'cherish' the Army and the Army to 'support' the people; there is also a corresponding campaign to foster solidarity between Army and 'Government'. How the 'Government' continues to function is far from clear, but function it apparently does, if claims of bumper harvests and fair performance in industry and transport are to be believed.

What then is the ideological justification for this degree of military control? It is twofold. For one thing, the Chinese PLA is in theory—and largely in fact—a thoroughly indoctrinated Communist force of largely peasant origin with a more recent intake of a larger worker contingent through conscription. It is a national army, as distinct from the war-lord armies of the 1920s and from the Kuomintang forces in which the war-lord element was still prevalent. It is loyal to the *idea* of the Party, as represented by the Central Committee and its Military Affairs Commission. It has been brought up on the principle of 'serving the people' and of relying on the people's active support in 'people's war'. It has a strong sense of discipline and of comradeship between officers and men—or commanders and fighter as they have been called since the abolition of rank badges in May 1965. It is, in fact, what the Party is expected to become after

---

[1] And so, presumably, do military departments connected with nuclear research.

its consolidation under the principles of the new Party Constitution: a revolutionary proletarian vanguard force.

The other factor justifying the predominant position of the PLA is the warlike atmosphere of a China of continuing struggle against saboteurs at home and potential aggressors from abroad. The 20 May statement, by proclaiming China's obligation to help the cause of the world revolution of the oppressed peoples and by proclaiming this to be the final aim and justification of China's own revolution, appointed the PLA caretaker of the Chinese revolution. To the Party ,not to the Army, is applied Mao's dictum that 'destruction precedes construction' which must make the process of Party-building a time-consuming one. While the country stands in danger of imperialist aggression and revisionist subversion, a non-existent Party apparatus cannot ensure its safety. This task devolves on the PLA. At the same time, the Party apparatus within the PLA represents the Party-in-being and helps to keep the PLA a communist force.

In political terms, the concept of the continuing revolution represents a compromise between Army and Party leadership. It was the participation of military leaders representing provincial revolutionary committees at the 'enlarged' Central Committee session of October 1968 which set the seal on the victory of Mao over Liu Shao-ch'i. But it appears likely that a price had to be paid for this. Chou En-lai was able to assert Government authority over the Red Guards and other 'rebel' groups;[1] Chiang Ching's role became restricted to the reform of Peking opera and related art forms, and the Cultural Revolution Group of the Central Committee received honourable mention in the Political Report but ceased to have any clearly-defined function. The prestige of the Military Affairs Commission was enhanced by the elevation of its 1960 session's resolution to the level of guidance

---

[1] Chou did this very explicitly at a rally held in September 1968 to celebrate the 'China all-Red situation' after the establishment of twenty-nine provincial revolutionary committees. Chiang Ching on this occasion pleaded for kind treatment of the Red Guards in view of the valuable work they had done for the cultural revolution—see Summary 2870/B/17.

document for Party-building, together with the 1929 Kutien resolution which was primarily a statement by Mao on Army-building. The Army maintains indirect control over lower-level Party branches via the revolutionary committees controlled by it. And the Army remained as exempt from Party interference—other than through the Military Affairs Commission and the Party apparatus within the Army—as it had been under the provisions of the 16-point directive on the cultural revolution.[1] Dreams of creating a network of cultural revolution groups at various levels with a supreme group at central level had to be abandoned. Compromise took the form of the coexistence of revolutionary committees and Party branches, with no effective control by either over the PLA. This has left open the way to eventual rebuilding of the Party at all levels—under indirect PLA supervision—and the eventual assumption of Party control over those activities which are to be controlled by the Party according to its new Constitution.

But this can only take effect when there is again a Party in existence at all levels. This will take a long time under the careful procedure outlined in the Kweichow regulations quoted above. Meanwhile, the PLA remains the guardian of the pro-letarian revolution. There is no time limit for this. What Mao hopes to ensure by entrusting the caretakership to the PLA, 'created by him and commanded by him', is that a regenerated Party will be 'forever loyal' to Mao Tse-tung thought. The need for a time-limit is avoided by resort to the concept of the continuing revolution, on the assumption that final transition to communism may take several generations. Since the same time-scale is applied to confrontation with the Big Powers, the inevitability of 'armed struggle' and the means of waging it for a long time to come follows—and from it the continuation of PLA caretakership. This is the institutional significance of Lin

[1] Section 15 of this document says: 'In the armed forces, the cultural revolution and the socialist education movement should be carried out in accordance with the instructions of the Military Affairs Commission of the Central Committee of the Party and the General Political Department of the PLA.' Summary 2507/B/26.

Piao's appointment as Mao's successor under the Party Constitution. It is an implied condition that the PLA should remain
'boundlessly loyal to Mao Tse-tung thought' even after Mao's
death and that it should never forget its formative Yenan period
where its survival depended on the ultimate identity of Army,
Party and People—an idea now propagated vigorously by
professional and amateur theatrical troupes performing Peking
operas and ballets on the 'people's war'. To forego the principle
of revolution through 'armed struggle', to believe in the possibility of 'peaceful evolution', represents in Mao's China the
utter heresy of revisionism; so does any attempt to create a
Party bureaucracy 'divorced from the masses'. To a Soviet
citizen the Maoist picture of the Soviet State and Party since 1956
may appear as a caricature. To a thoughtful Chinese, it may be
a fair description of many of the anti-progressive features of
Kuomintang rule and of the Mandarinate of the days of what
Marxists term China's 'feudal' past. The remedy against a
reversion to anything like this is an ideological 'people's war',
and the safeguard of 'democratic dictatorship' is a PLA created
and maintained in it. As Mao has said: 'Without a people's army,
the people have nothing.'

CHAPTER V

THE MISHIMA AFFAIR:
A POLITICAL FORECAST

G. R. STORRY

In Japanese culture one of the oldest and most deeply cherished ideals has been that of *chowa*, 'harmony' (as in the Expo 70 slogan, *ningen no shimpo to chowa*, 'the progress and harmony of mankind'). *Chowa* is synonymous with 'stability' and also with 'peace'. Yet during the present century—to go back no further—*chowa* has been shaken from time to time by eruptions of astonishing violence; of which by far the most startling in recent years has been the Mishima Affair of 25 November 1970.

The details of this melodrama are familiar to all who follow Japanese affairs. It is sufficient to remind ourselves that the writer, Mishima Yukio, and four young stalwarts of his ultra-nationalist Tate-no-kai ('Shield Society') were received by the commanding officer of the Ground Self-Defence Force Eastern Corps Headquarters at Ichigaya in Tokyo; that they tied the general in his chair when he refused to allow Mishima to make a public appeal to the officers and men of the Headquarters; that under duress the general gave way, whereupon Mishima addressed about 1,000 members of the Force for some ten minutes, after which he committed ceremonial suicide (*seppuku* or *hara-kiri*) in the general's office. Mishima's *kaishakunin* (assistant or second at *hara-kiri*), having beheaded his principal, stabbed himself and was in turn decapitated by another member of the Tate-no-kai.

But it is not so much the incident itself as its likely significance that demands attention. Will this prove to be, like the assassination of Asanuma Inejiro in 1960, an isolated act, a lightning flash seemingly portentous, yet bringing no downpour in its train? Or will it turn out to be, like the attack on Hamaguchi Yuko in 1930, the signal for a change of mood, the first terrorist outrage in a series that will jerk the country off course and along a new route at present unforeseen, and indeed undesired?

It could be argued that the parallel with the Hamaguchi Affair is so faint as to be invalid. In November 1930 Japan was torn by the political convulsion that arose from the London Naval Treaty and by the economic and social consequences of the world depression. The situation today is very different. There is no political debate comparable with the fierce controversy that surrounded the London Treaty. The Liberal-Democrats are firmly in the saddle. Their hegemony was strengthened by the electoral victory of 1969, itself an indication of general popular satisfaction at the conclusion of the Okinawa Agreement, which guarantees the attainment of a long-sought fundamental aim of national policy. There may be all kinds of reservations, even anxieties, about the details of the Okinawa settlement. But the prospective recovery of the Ryukyus is a solid achievement—as is apparent once the eye turns to the intractable problem of the 'northern territories'. The contrast with 1930 is of course still more remarkable in terms of the country's economy and social life as a whole. Four centuries, not four decades, seem to separate the thriving nation of colour TV and the family car from the Japan of the stricken, half-starved, Tohoku farmers and Osaka unemployed. Where discontent simmers it has manifold outlets for expression. In 1930 mass protest could debouch only into the perilous channel of nationalist hysteria. Moreover, it could be claimed that the huge improvement of material conditions and the inescapable impact of the uncensored mass media have produced a degree of psychological change, and thereby a new outlook, that does not respond sympathetically to attitudes and behaviour now thought to be almost ludicrously out of date.

Thus the jeers of the Self-Defence men, listening to Mishima's speech from the balcony at Ichigaya, struck a note of cruel but healthy scepticism. ('We can't understand you, Dad!' 'Quit the heroics!') It was as if D'Annunzio had been pelted with rotten onions at Fiume.

What does the defence of Japan mean? It means the defence of a culture and history centred on the Emperor. Could such words from Mishima's last appeal stir the heart of anyone under forty in Japan in 1970? Mishima had once declared: 'What must be protected is not democracy but the Three Sacred Treasures'. Could this really mean anything at all to the younger generation? These questions appear rhetorical at first sight. But they demand an answer which only the passage of time will provide.

Among Japanese sociologists there is a school of thought that dwells on continuities.

'In the course of modernization Japan imported many western cultural elements, but these were and always are partial and segmentary and are never in the form of an operating system. It is like a language with its basic indigenous structure or grammar which has accumulated a heavy overlay of borrowed vocabulary; while the outlook of Japanese society has suffered drastic changes over the past hundred years, the basic social grammar has hardly been affected.'[1]

That comment is concerned with the framework of social relationships. But the inference must be that if 'the basic social grammar' has hardly been affected, the political grammar of Japan may have been less affected by 'the borrowed vocabulary' of the past hundred years than has been widely believed. Another sociologist, writing about the farming community, appears to take much the same view.

---

[1] Chie Nakane, *Japanese Society* (London, Weidenfeld & Nicolson, 1970), p. 149. The book is her own translation of her *Tate-shakai no ningen kankei*, 'Personal Relations in a Vertical Society' (Tokyo, Kodansha, 1967).

'Rational individualism expressed in principled independent behaviour, the democratic spirit which permits rational cooperation with mutual respect for individual independence—these are things which the farmer has yet to learn.'[1]

On the other hand, Mishima himself, it should be observed, was profoundly depressed and disheartened by the changes, by the sharp break in continuity, after 1945. In an interview with *Asahi* eight weeks before his suicide he expressed with characteristic frankness his pessimism so far as Japan's future was concerned. 'Everything will get worse. There will be absolutely no improvement at all.' A country that 'cannot shake itself free' from defeat in war 'cannot create a national culture'.[2] And in the manifesto containing his last thoughts Mishima declared that post-war Japan had forgotten the very source of its being, and that the national spirit (*kokumin seishin*) had been lost.

Mishima's despair, then, is evidence that, in his view at all events, the 'basic grammar' of Japanese society has indeed been deeply, perhaps fatally, affected by the reforms and innovations of the past twenty-five years. All that was best in Japan, including the Emperor, had been devitalized by the aftermath of the lost war. Such was clearly Mishima's conviction. For although his valediction at Ichigaya was *Tenno Heika Banzai!* ('Long Live the Emperor!') Mishima seems to have had very little respect for the present *Tenno*. In conversation just a week before his death he remarked that he was not interested in the Emperor, who had doubtless an agreeable personality but had become, since his official abrogation of divinity, no more than 'a popular parlour figure'.[3] The root of all the trouble was to be found in the post-war Constitution. Indeed, in a well-publicized statement Mishima declared that the present Constitution had destroyed Japan's morale.[4]

[1] Tadashi Fukutake, *Japanese Rural Society*, trans. R. P. Dore (Tokyo, Oxford University Press, 1967), p. 216.
[2] *Asahi Shimbun*, 22 September 1970.
[3] *Shukan Gendai*, 12 December 1970, p. 122.   [4] *Asahi Shimbun*, 22 September 1970.

But if the situation seemed beyond repair, did Mishima hope nevertheless to fan into flame, through the example of his *seppuku*, the embers of the burnt-out spirit of the traditional Japan which he loved and claimed to understand? The motive of the *seppuku* at Ichigaya has provided many yards of printed argument in Japan and elsewhere. The action has been described as an attempted *coup d'état*, a gesture of self-dramatization, a homosexual love suicide, and so on. Certainly it was the culmination of a long-standing obsession with death; and there is in Mishima's death-wish something reminiscent of Saigo's attitude in the 1870s. Yamamoto Yuzo, in a play about Saigo Takamori and Okubo Toshimichi, makes the latter say of Saigo: 'He is continually seeking a place to die'.[1] But, granted that Mishima thought primarily in terms of the method, place, and timing of his death, he cannot have been indifferent to the possible effect his *seppuku* would have on Japan in the 1970s, and indeed on posterity. Some measure of keen calculation could not have been absent. Japan had lost her national spirit. But was all of it, every bit of it, lost? And for ever? If even a little remained, then surely his kind of suicide could create a legend that would help to rescue the national spirit from complete extinction.

A British journalist who knew Mishima well recorded his impression 'that Mishima has in fact sown a seed'.[2] Against this we have the comment by the Director-General of the Defence Agency, Nakasone Yasuhiro: 'I think few people in this well developed society will sympathize with this fanatical action'.[3]

It so happened that the Mishima Affair took place on the day that the Prime Minister addressed both Houses at the opening of a new session of the Diet, an occasion of some historical significance because of the presence in the Diet of members (seven in

---

[1] Yamamoto Yuzo, *Saigo to Okubo* (Saigo and Okubo) (Tokyo, Kadowaka Bunko, 1954 ed.), p. 84, cited by Hilary Conroy, *The Japanese Seizure of Korea* (Philadelphia, University of Pennsylvania Press, 1960), p. 31.

[2] Henry Scott Stokes, 'How I Trained with the Tatenokai', *The Financial Times* (London), 3 December 1970.

[3] *The Japan Times*, 26 November 1970

all) representing, for the first time since the Pacific War, the Ryukyu Archipelago. Sato Eisaku's speech was remarkable for the attention it paid to a single theme, summed up in his phrase, 'no growth without welfare'. The government party has keen antennae; but in any case it could scarcely have ignored the groundswell of opinion reflecting an entirely new popular attitude to the *keizai seicho*—economic growth—of the past ten to fifteen years.

By the latter part of 1969, if not earlier, a descriptive term for *homo nipponicus*—coined, it is alleged, by Zulfikar Ali Bhutto, Foreign Minister of Pakistan—had gained currency throughout Japan. The term in question was 'Economic Animal'. Whether or not, when first employed, this description was meant to be pejorative, it was regarded by the Japanese people as decidedly uncomplimentary, not to say unkind. In the first place there was the gratuitous choice of the word 'animal', which seemed insulting in itself. Secondly, the use of the adjective 'economic' implied a concentration on materialist aims that took no account of anything else. Seen in this light, the appellation 'Economic Animal' was of course a caricature, and one of a peculiarly ungenerous type. For the Japanese could feel that, having devoted their energies wholeheartedly to the praiseworthy tasks of economic recovery and expansion, they were now being despised for their success in the arts of peace, just as in the past they had been resented for their success in aggressive diplomacy and war.

Nevertheless, if the caricature had borne absolutely no relation to the truth, it would not have been so generally taken amiss. Building on the basis of 'no welfare before growth' and 'economics before politics', the Ikeda and Sato governments of the 1960s had raised the Gross National Product to a height that was the envy of the world. But a by-product of this development has been the phenomenon known as 'the Showa Genroku age', glittering with conspicuous consumption, including a proliferation of largely expense-account entertainment that makes Babylon or pre-war

Shanghai seem, by comparison, a monastery garth.[1] The foreigner on a brief visit to Tokyo, or a resident of South or South-East Asia observing the dedication of Japanese businessmen eager for new markets and sources of supply, could be excused the error of believing that in Japan purely materialist values were supreme.

Be that as it may, discussion in the Japanese press and other organs of publicity about the controversial label 'Economic Animal' provoked serious self-examination, and this was sharpened by the realization that pollution—what was known as the problem of *kogai*, 'public hazards'—had reached an alarming level. For the smog in Tokyo during the hot-weather months of 1969 could not be ignored by anyone, since even suburban residents who stayed at home were conscious of the acrid smell that pervaded the air, making throat and nostrils smart in an uncomfortable, if not actually painful, way. Disenchantment with economic growth *per se* was beginning to infect the public mind.[2]

The winter of 1969–70 gave Tokyo and other cities some relief. (It is the heat and strong sunlight of the five months from May through September that produce the worst conditions.) But the *kogai* season of 1970 turned out to be even more trying than that of the previous year. A report, in the early autumn of 1970, did not exaggerate when it declared: 'Japanese society appears to be absorbed *en masse* in the problem of environmental pollution.'[3] For the problem, needless to say, is not confined to air pollution but includes the contamination, by industrial waste, of

[1] It is alleged that the money spent in 1969 on entertainment in city night-clubs amounted to some 2 per cent of the GNP, roughly equivalent to what was spent on expenditure for defence. (*This is Japan*, No. 17, Asahi Shimbunsha, 1969, p. 248: Richard Hughes, 'The Free Ride is Ending.')

[2] Car exhaust fumes were chiefly responsible for the summer smog. From 1960 to 1968 car ownership quadrupled and oil consumption increased by 450 per cent. (Kobayashi Setsuo, 'Environmental Pollution', *Japan Quarterly*, Vol. XVII, No. 4, p. 402).

[3] *Institute for Economic Trends (Japan)*, Economic Monthly Letter No. 060, 1 October 1970.

rivers, coastlines, and inshore fishing grounds. Noise, too, constitutes *kogai*.[1]

Accordingly, the Premier in his speech at the opening of the Diet was correct when he told his audience that the *kogai* problem was 'the matter of greatest present concern to the general public'; and it is not surprising that most of what he said was devoted to this subject. Good intentions were proclaimed, with promises of remedial legislation. Then, leading into his peroration, the Prime Minister (no doubt with the spectre of the Economic Animal in his mind) declared:

'Twenty-five years after the end of the war I feel that we Japanese are on the threshold of a period of great change, in all senses of the term. It means that the true happiness of human beings cannot be attained by mere material progress: that we have to find our purpose in life by building up true culture and refinement and rich sensibilities.'[2]

So on the same day in Tokyo two outstanding public figures—the successful writer, the brilliant pessimist, and the successful politician, the down-to-earth, experienced, optimist—appealed through a 'captive audience' (Self-Defence personnel and Diet members) to a larger constituency, namely the people of Japan. For Mishima it was a savage hope, for Sato a sober conviction, that the people were ready for a change. For at least some of the way the instincts and aspirations of Mishima and Sato ran along parallel lines. Neither was satisfied with mere material affluence,

---

[1] The 'development' of Yokkaichi on Ise Bay provides a good example of all that can be implied by the term *kogai*. In his Dyason Memorial Lecture in Australia in 1964 Professor Tsuru referred to the petro-chemical industrial plant that had been built on reclaimed land at Yokkaichi. 'Residents suffer, day and night, from what they call "vibratory noise". Again, almost all residents of the older part of the city suffer from air pollution; and many have succumbed to respiratory diseases. Then, there is a fishing village nearby where the oil-soaked dirty water is drained and the stench damage on fish caught has now become so serious that the fishing industry there is on the way out.' Shigeto Tsuru, *Essays on Economic Development* (Tokyo, Kinokuniya, 1968), p. 245.

[2] *The Japan Times*, 26 November 1970.

personally or in terms of national wellbeing. Mishima was able to indulge a love of the bizarre to both luxurious and austere extremes. Perhaps more than most Japanese writers he was at ease with foreigners and had expensive, cosmopolitan tastes. These meant little, we may be sure, beside his concern for what he believed to be the intangible, dying, traditions of his race. Sato, the nurse and tutor of economic growth, has been wise enough, shrewd politician that he is, to wait for the moment when the generation that never knew the war, and the older generation that has half forgotten it, would begin to hunger for a national purpose which will link Japan's destiny more closely with her past. And if there was a single aspiration, relating to a specific public issue, which could be said to have been shared by Mishima and Sato it was the desire to see the existing Constitution revised.

It is sometimes forgotten how soon after its adoption the post-war Constitution came under government scrutiny, with a view to eventual revision. As early as the autumn of 1953 the Prime Minister, Yoshida Shigeru, instructed the Legislative Bureau of the Cabinet Office to study the Constitution and suggest amendments. A year later, shortly before Yoshida was succeeded by Hatoyama Ichiro, the Legislative Bureau reported that seven articles of the Constitution should be amended. These were Articles 1 (the Emperor's position), 7 (the Emperor's functions), 9 (renunciation of war), 69 (dissolution of the House of Representatives), 79 (popular review of Supreme Court judges), 93 and 95 (popular election of prefectural governors).[1]

Yoshida—as Premier—was always very cautious in any remarks he made about the Constitution. But Hatoyama made no secret of his personal wish to see it revised. Indeed, he is reported to have said that Occupation policy had been based on a policy designed to reduce Japan to the status of a third-rate power. He stated, furthermore, that Japan's national rehabilita-

[1] Iwao Hoshii, 'Japan's Controversial Constitution', *Orient/West* (Tokyo), Vol. 7, No. 5, May 1962, pp. 11–12.

tion had been retarded by the Constitution,[1] a point of view very close to Mishima's.

The failure to secure a two-thirds majority in the Diet has, of course, prevented every conservative leader, from Yoshida to Sato, from bringing in legislation to revise the Constitution. And until the General Election of 1969 it was generally believed that time was on the side of the Opposition political parties. The Liberal Democrats won successive elections, but each victory reduced, albeit slightly, their overall majority in the Diet—until December 1969, when they were returned to office with their parliamentary strength enhanced. Moreover, the main socialist party, the Shakaito, suffered particularly heavy losses. This came as a notable shock to most political pundits in Tokyo—the largely Left-wing intelligentsia of journalists, editors, and social scientists in the universities. They were taken aback in December 1969 in much the same way (although to a lesser degree, since an outright Shakaito victory was never on the cards) as their British counterparts in June 1970.

It may turn out that the Liberal-Democrats have done no more than temporarily deflect what appeared to be a definite, although extremely slow, trend towards the Left in the voting habits of the Japanese. But it is worth considering for a moment the grounds on which Sato Eisaku and his party were able to appeal so successfully to the electorate at the end of 1969. Mention has been made already of the satisfaction over Okinawa. This, however, was only one factor, although doubtless the most significant. At least two other issues were of great importance. One was the general economic record, for which the Government naturally claimed credit. By 1969, as we have seen, *kogai*, pollution of the environment, had caused much popular dissatisfaction. Nevertheless, since the Liberal Democrats, no less than other parties, promised to deal energetically with the problem, it would be difficult to argue that *kogai* constituted *at that time* an electoral liability so far as the Government party was concerned. On the

[1] *Orient/West* (Tokyo) Vol. 7, No. 5, May 1962, p. 12.

other hand, this basic question of pollution, so closely linked with economic growth, may prove to be a decisive issue at the next general election.

The other issue, prominent and important in 1969, was that of 'law and order'. Between the spring of 1968 and the autumn of the following year student turbulence closed, for periods varying from a few days to several months, most of the institutions of higher learning in Japan. Beyond doubt the starkest example of this discord was provided by Tokyo University, when for two days in January 1969 more than eight thousand police fought the student defenders of the Yasuda Hall. The precincts of *Todai* became a battlefield, on which by some miracle nobody was actually killed.

But it was the disorders in the streets in the autumn, before the Prime Minister's visit to America, that caused the greatest public concern. On 'International Anti-War Day', 21 October 1969, the myrmidons of the revolutionary student federation, Zenkyoto, fought the riot police up and down the central districts of Tokyo, Osaka, Nagoya, Sapporo, and Fukuoka. The disturbances in Shinjuku, Tokyo, were particularly savage, and there seems to have been some expectation that the demonstrators might over-whelm the police. Mishima Yukio evidently believed that 'International Anti-War Day' provided the Self-Defence Forces (Jieitai) with an ideal opportunity for intervening and, having done so, for insisting on constitutional revision. He was in Shinjuku on 'Anti-War Day'. It was with bitter dismay that he realized that the police could deal with the crisis without calling in the Jieitai. He made much of this in his last manifesto a year later. ('It was a painful sorrow to me that the Shinjuku "Demo" misfired.') But during the previous twelve months the mobile police squads (Kidotai) had vastly increased their efficiency. Compared with the situation in 1960, when the Kishi Govern-ment felt unable to face the risks of the Eisenhower visit, the strength of the police, in terms of numbers and of skill in riot control, had improved beyond measure.

Thus, the 'Anti-War Day' disturbances, and those of 17 November 1969 (the night before Sato's departure from Tokyo Airport), played into the Government's hands, in two ways. In what has become overwhelmingly a bourgeois society the people at large, frightened by the spectre of anarchy, were badly scared by the unrest and were correspondingly responsive to the firm way in which it was put down.

If the Government is so fortunate in the next general election as to have to its credit a successful record in dealing with pollution, a passable record in foreign affairs (notably in economic relations with the United States), and a fair record in maintaining internal peace and order, there is every likelihood that its majority in the Diet will be further enlarged. In that event revision of the Constitution will become practical politics by the second half of this decade.

There are, of course, two hurdles to be surmounted by those who advocate revision. First, there is the need to secure a two-thirds majority in both Houses of the Diet. This may be feasible before 1975. The second hurdle is the national referendum.

It is here, in the all-important if elusive and imponderable sphere of general public feeling, that the later effects of the Mishima Incident may be revealed. The Incident has focused altogether new and dramatic attention on the Jieitai. Their reputation in the eyes of the people has greatly improved since the 1950s, as opinion polls over the years have shown. Probably this is thanks to their good work at times of natural calamity, such as the really damaging typhoons that seem to occur almost every year. Yet the Jieitai still feel themselves to be 'illegitimate children'.[1] It is alleged that some of the younger officers, graduates of the Defence Academy, resent the principle of civilian control and are convinced that they are the tools of politicians riding high on the hedonism and prosperity of the

---

[1] This label, uncomplimentary though it is, represents an advance on 'rubbish bin' (*gomi-bako*), the title given to the Force by Tsuji Masanobu in conversation with the writer in 1954.

'Showa Genroku age'.[1] Mishima's appeal, for the Jieitai to become a legitimate *kokugun* (national army), provoked a general debate. Moreover, his suicide turned the tables morally on those who had jeered on the parade ground at Ichigaya. It made them seem, to some degree at least, poor-spirited, even cowardly. This is not healthy for the morale of a force unsure of its precise legal, not to say social and political, standing.

The next two or three years may show how far public opinion moved in 1971, in the aftermath of the Mishima Incident, towards a recognition that the Jieitai must be put on a new, legitimate, footing, which can only be achieved through constitutional revision. It will be surprising if opinion polls by the close of 1971 fail to register a considerable swing of sentiment in favour of a revision of Article 9 of the Constitution, even if there is no marked trend in support of the amendment of other clauses, such as those relating to the status and functions of the Emperor.

It is noteworthy that not one of the attempted domestic *coups* and acts of political terrorism that have occurred during the past hundred years has been successful, in the sense of producing an immediate, dramatic, change in national policy. Indeed, the last effective *coup d'état* in Japan was that of 3 January 1868, when Saigo Takamori's troops seized the gates of the Kyoto Imperial Palace as a prelude to the Meiji Restoration. Failure rewarded all later attempts to upset the *status quo*—Eto's rising, Saigo's rebellion, the mutiny of February 1936, the insurrection of 14 August 1945. The Mukden Incident of September 1941 certainly succeeded. But it took place on the continent, not in the homeland. In Japan at least, terrorism impresses the public more than the government. But in the interests of harmony (*chowa*) the government in course of time listens to the voice of the people. And this, in the past at any rate, has tended to be coloured more by sentiment than reason.

The Government, then, may have cause to wait with some

---

[1] Aochi Shin, 'Jieitai wa kudeta no kibakuzai ni naru ka?' ('Can the Self-Defence Force become the detonator of a *coup d'état*?'), *Shukan Yomiuri*, 12 December 1970, p. 33.

confidence for popular sentiment to harden in favour of constitutional revision. Success in dealing with past disorders, such as those of 1969, must hearten the authorities when they think about the bitter protests and violence that will surely explode if revision is pushed through the Diet. Once the two-thirds majority is achieved and the prospect of an affirmative vote in a referendum seems secure, the timing of revision will depend on external factors, such as the likely reactions of Communist China and the Soviet Union.

Much will depend on whether myth replaces reality in the popular mind, so far as the Mishima Affair is concerned. There has been no shortage of warnings by critics, editors, scholars, and other commentators on this score. One of the most serious failures of the post-war parliamentary structure in Japan has been its lack of inspirational appeal. It cannot be maintained, alas, that the title Daigishi, Member of the Diet, has become notably more glamorous and honourable than it was forty years ago, on the eve of Japan's 'dark valley', the terrifying decade of the thirties. The last twenty-five years have promoted individualism and enhanced the consciousness of democratic freedom, but they have failed, in large measure, to consolidate the prestige of the Diet as the supreme organ of the state. If boredom rather than interest is the common attitude to parliamentary government, there is created in the national psyche an empty space crying out to be filled by a popular myth.

Therein lies the true danger of the suicide at Ichigaya. An essentially individual and conceivably insane act could rather easily become a symbolic gesture in the heroic tradition of Oshio Heihachiro.[1] Thus it could serve to promote that turn towards

---

[1] Oshio, leader of the Osaka rising of 1837, was a devotee of *Oyomei-gaku*, the Neo-Confucian school of Wang Yang-ming (1472–1529). Its principle of the unity of knowledge and action (to be demonstrated by the autonomous and, if necessary, rebellious individual) was a central part of Mishima's own credo. At least one Japanese periodical has grouped Mishima with Saigo, Yoshida Shoin, and Oshio, linking the four together as outstanding inheritors of the *Oyomei* tradition (*Sande Mainichi*, 13 December 1970, p. 28).

extremism which sanity and common sense have for twenty-five years so firmly rejected.

The danger is not lessened by the fact that in Japan patriotism of the most ardent and irrational type is the last refuge of the revolutionary. If Mishima is to have his emulators they will step forward from the New Left rather than the Old Right. In the long run this kind of terrorism is more deadly, because more sinister, than the fiercest street 'demos'. At certain historical moments it seems to awaken a popular response which even the cherished ideal of peace and stability, *chowa*, is hard pressed to contain.

CHAPTER VI

POLITICAL DIRECTIONS IN INDEPENDENT INDIA

W. F. CRAWLEY

The aftermath of partition

Any assessment of the political development of India over the past twenty and more years must start with the fact of partition. This last act of British policy in India created two states, both new, but with a difference. Pakistan was obviously a new entity consisting of a historically unprecedented combination of the Muslim majority areas of North-Western India and Bengal. The Dominion of India carried on the name and as much as possible of the historical continuity of the British Raj. For that reason the partition became for Pakistan the central fact of its political existence. The act which had brought the State into being carried with it the central political and administrative problems with which the new State was faced, and which determined the course of its political development.

For India, on the other hand, the numerous other problems which presented themselves in the wake of independence very quickly came to overshadow the fact of partition itself. This was partly because partition had come as a defeat, accepted reluctantly and treated as something to be forgotten as quickly as possible in the process of building up the positive structure of the new nation. For Pakistan, partition was the fulfilment of a political aim, though in a much diminished form. It represented a positive achievement, the creation of an independent homeland for the Indian Muslims, despite the weakness and chaos which threatened it at the beginning. Beside this achievement, the fact that its territory corresponded only to a small part of the original idea, and, more disturbingly, that the creation of Pakistan suddenly left forty million Muslims inside India without a communal political organization to represent them, and with little prospect of exercising the strong influence on Indian politics that the Muslims had been able to do in undivided India, could be seen as minor drawbacks.

The loss of leadership and political direction of the Muslims who remained in India after partition was a gain to the Congress government and to Nehru's hopes of creating a state with a strong central government which would be able to give a unified direction to the politics of independent India.

But it was not only the emasculation of the Muslim challenge that created the new conditions under which the politics of India would operate. It was also the transformation of the politics of the two provinces which had borne the brunt of the partition, Punjab and Bengal.

To Punjabis of all communities independence was a cataclysmic event. If the full consequences of partition had been foreseen by those who made the decisions or by the people who were to suffer because of them, it is inconceivable that they would have been considered an acceptable price to pay. For the new government of Pakistan the refugee problem created by the disruption and terrorism that accompanied the partition of the Punjab nearly succeeded in overwhelming the untried administration. The government of India was faced with an equally vast problem of resettlement, but in the new India the divided Punjab had become a peripheral and truncated province whose problems never threatened the stability of the government in Delhi. In both Pakistan and India the very brutality of the surgery generated the momentum to tackle the refugee problem. The exodus of Muslims and Hindus and Sikhs from their lands on the wrong side of the border left vacant land for redistribution to those who had been dispossessed. If the exchange of population had been accomplished amicably it might have been a neat solution, but no such solution had been possible because without the mass fear of the communal slaughter no one would have been persuaded to leave his home.

The case was somewhat different in Bengal. A slaughter equal in intensity to that of the Punjab had been foreshadowed in the communal riots in Calcutta of 1946. At partition there was every reason to fear a mass exchange of populations and mutual killing. The extraordinary and charismatic intervention of Gandhi prevented this. There was no immediate flood of refugees. Yet this lack of violence meant that the fact of partition was not driven home so inescapably, and the refugee problem was not tackled with the same drastic urgency as in the Punjab. The steady trickle of Hindu refugees from East Pakistan continued to flow into Calcutta. In 1950 the stream of refugees and the grievances of the Hindus of East Pakistan caused riots in West Bengal and much belligerent pressure from Bengal on the Central Government to take retaliatory action against Pakistan.

Yet Bengal, like the Punjab, had now been thrust to the periphery of Indian politics. Throughout the Nehru era no Bengali leader was able to exercise a powerful independent influence on the central government, and Bengali attitudes did not sway those of India as they once had. Under a period of uninterrupted Congress government the leaders of the Bengal Congress Party were able to establish a greater measure of provincial autonomy than many other states whose industrial and economic position was not so strong, but neither during nor after Nehru's time has any Bengali Congressman established himself as a national figure. Bengalis have distinguished themselves in opposition. The most notable was Syama Prasad Mukherjee, founder of the Jan Sangh, a party that stood for non-secular Hindu values and positive nationalism, particularly in relation to Pakistan. Mukherjee more than anyone else came near to assuming the mantle of the great Bengali politicians such as C. R. Das and Subhash Chandra Bose before his death cut short what might have become a strong regional challenge. Subsequently the challenge of Bengal to the central government has come from the Communist-dominated United Fronts. However, its own internal disunity has prevented even the strong Bengal Communist Party from presenting an effective front on the all-India political stage. Despite the pointers given by the Congress governments of West Bengal to the process of 'federalization', or the assertion of provincial power against that of the central government, it is on the whole remarkable that Bengal and Bengalis have not played a more prominent role in the development of Indian politics since independence. Much of the reason for this can be traced back to the sea-change brought about within Bengal and in the relations of Bengal to the rest of India by the fact of partition.

In India as a whole, unlike Pakistan, the dominant problems in the process of consolidation of the state in the years following independence were not those of the partitioned provinces. If India had lost territory in the division of Punjab and Bengal it had also inherited a vast and geographically coherent area, which, with the integration of the former princely states into the Union for the first time, brought under one government (as distinct from 'paramount power') a continuous sweep of territory from the Himalayas to Cape Comorin. There was a pressing need to reorganize this territory in a form more suited to the exercise of a democratic and parliamentary form of government, not to mention the administrative impossibility of preserving as separate units the plethora of small principalities, or, at the other end of the scale, a huge multilingual province such as Hyderabad. The task was to occupy not only the framers of the Constitution but also the central government itself for much of the next ten years. There has been no wholly satisfactory solution, and even today the pressures to subdivide in one area or another have not been played out. The Congress as a party had earlier committed itself to the reorganization of the States broadly along the lines of linguistic areas, but considerable practical and political difficulties made it necessary to proceed with caution. The Constitution of 1950 was framed and enacted before this problem of linguistic states was properly tackled, and it is a tribute to the resilience and adaptability of the Constitution that it was able to survive the great upheaval of redrawing the map of the Indian States along linguistic lines without significant modification.

The reason why the problem of the reorganization of the States could be temporarily shelved in the early years of independence was the still more urgent need for national consolidation and territorial defence. It is in this light that the successive crises over Kashmir and Hyderabad must be seen. In the Punjabi civil war which had accompanied the establishment of Pakistan the operation of regular troops had been totally ineffective either as a means of defining territory or of restoring order. The boundary between the two new states was handed down *ex cathedra* by Lord Radcliffe in the absence of agreement among the parties to the dispute. The Kashmir confrontation, on the other hand, presented an opportunity for the Indian army to intervene swiftly and effectively to defend national interests.

Similarly the police action in Hyderabad established the capability of the Government to act positively to prevent further damage to the prospects of national and territorial consolidation. For both the new governments their initiatives over Kashmir and Hyderabad marked the point at which they took full responsibility out of the hands of the retiring imperial government and exercised it according to a different set of objectives in accordance with their appreciation of their own national interests.

The theoretical freedom of choice given to each of the Princes to accede to one or other of the Dominions was regarded by the governments of both India and Pakistan as a convenient fiction to enable the Princes to make the right choice, dictated by the geographical position and communal composition of the peoples of the states. In most cases the choice was exercised in the only practicable way. In the few borderline cases, however, this tremendous power suddenly given to men who for a hundred years had been in no position to make any independent judgement regarding the foreign relations of their states, and who were virtually condemned under the new dispensation to lapse into a new and more profound political obscurity once they had made their choice, proved a fatal responsibility. Any ruler for whom the choice might be in doubt found himself wooed, cajoled and threatened by governments that had little respect for the kind of authority which he represented. Pakistan was slightly better placed to woo, as its government had inherited no strong ideological commitment to an attack on feudalism. The Congress in India, on the other hand, had never bothered to conceal its view that the princes were an anachronism and that the sooner their remaining powers were abolished the better.

In practice neither government accepted in full the communal guidelines. Jinnah offered the Maharaja of Jodhpur, a Hindu ruler of a predominantly Hindu state, the right to dictate his own terms and accede to Pakistan, as well as actively encouraging the Muslim ruler of Junagadh to accede with his Hindu majority state to Pakistan. The Maharaja of Jodhpur eventually refused Jinnah's offer, and the Nawab of Junagadh was prevented from deviating from the norm by Indian troops.[1]

In the case of Hyderabad the Nizam hoped to the last to be able to maintain himself independent of India and was actively encouraged and aided by Pakistan to this end. Yet the incorporation of Hyderabad into the Indian Union was clearly essential to the self-respect of a government which was ideologically opposed to the survival of feudal dynasties, and which did not accept the right of any of them, however big, to regain a sovereignty that under the British Raj had been strictly curtailed. As Hyderabad was an enclave of Muslim power in an area with an overwhelming Hindu majority, it was even less likely that the Government of India would allow the Nizam to make the wrong decision.

The forcible annexation of Hyderabad in September 1948 might indeed have been a very much more risky and bloody

[1] V. P. Menon, *The Story of the Integration of the Indian States* (1956), pp. 112–13, 135

operation than in fact it was. As it turned out, the operation was well timed and well executed. The irregular forces under a demoralized Hyderabad Government were no match for the Indian army and barely offered any resistance. The success and bloodlessness of the move generally justified it as a bold and constructive piece of statesmanship. The shocked foreign reaction was based on little more than a sedulously cultivated myth that the new India was in some way, unique to itself, committed to the principle of non-violence. That this idea should be laid to rest was all to the good, as it helped to define in the eyes of the world and of India itself the character of the state which had owed so much to Gandhi.

In comparison with Hyderabad or Junagadh the merits of the Indian claim to Kashmir were much more dubious. As in Hyderabad, the continued vacillation of the Maharaja in choosing to which state he would accede, coupled with his own hopes of retaining some form of independence of both of them, created a situation in which both states were prepared to intervene militarily to forestall armed action by the other. However, as Kashmir, unlike Hyderabad, was adjacent to the territory of both India and Pakistan, open intervention would have amounted to a declaration of war.

By backing the tribal invasion with arms and expertise the Pakistan Government attempted to force the issue and bring down the Dogra Government and its ramshackle army with the pretext of a popular uprising, in the hope that authority would collapse and the state fall by popular acclaim to Pakistan before the Indian army had time to intervene.

The gamble brought only limited returns. The tribesmen forfeited much sympathy by their undisciplined marauding, and the Indian Government reacted with a swiftness which no one had believed possible. The Maharaja signed the instrument of accession to India, thus establishing the incontrovertible legal basis on which the Indian right to Kashmir has ever since been based. A massive airlift of troops was sent immediately to

Kashmir, which both checked the invasion and secured Indian military control over half Kashmir, including the all-important Kashmir Valley. Though United Nations mediation was eventually successful in arranging and policing a cease-fire, none of the subsequent attempts to arrange a plebiscite in which the Kashmiris might have had an opportunity of either endorsing the accession to India or choosing to accede to Pakistan met with any success. The plebiscite condition had been attached as an informal undertaking by Nehru at the time of accession. It specified no legally binding procedure, and India consistently refused to allow a plebiscite while a large part of Kashmir was under Pakistani occupation in defiance of the legality conferred by the Maharaja's signature to the instrument of accession.

India's hand was strengthened by the endorsement of the accession by the one undisputed leader of Kashmir, Sheikh Abdullah. That Abdullah subsequently retracted this and showed signs of wanting to establish a Kashmir independent of both India and Pakistan has understandably been discounted by the Indian Government. The plebiscite offer no longer stands, even in theory, and the Indian Government has steadily consolidated its position and drawn Kashmir closer into the framework of the Indian constitution. The Chinese-Indian war of 1962 might have produced a compromise acceptable to both sides, but the Pakistani attempt of 1965 to solve the Kashmir problem by armed action misfired. The cease-fire line has become a *de facto* boundary.

Federalism and the Constitution

With the advent of independence the Congress Party was given a free hand to devise the type of constitution it considered most suitable, unencumbered by the problems of communal weightage and adjustment to the Princes which had dogged the drafting of the Government of India Act of 1935. The common participation in the nationalist movement had forged a unity which transcended the powerful regional political bases of the Congress organization. It was, however, a paradox that the man on whom all the aspirations of the independence movement had been centred, and who more than any other was in a position to wield undisputed authority throughout India, should have been the firmest advocate of decentralization and a return to the self-sufficient village economy of a remote past.

These ideas of Gandhi's were to exercise little influence on the formation of the Constitution of the Republic. It was rather the authority which Gandhi had represented at the centre of the Congress movement which provided the model for the form of government that India was to adopt. It is commonly said that in the framing of the Constitution it was the ideas of the modernist Nehru that prevailed against those of Gandhi. Certainly Nehru insisted that substantial powers must be retained by the central government in order that the country should not be progressively weakened and balkanized. The impressive achievement of Sardar Patel in integrating the Princely States into the Union, and the general revulsion against further weakening of the country after the shock of partition, reinforced this view. Partition might itself have been avoided at one stage if Nehru and the Congress had been prepared to accept a loose federation of the constituent provinces instead of the centralized pattern of administration established under the British Raj, but the price had been too high. It was not likely now that a weak central government would prove acceptable after the trauma of partition had removed the main argument for it.

This may have been contrary to Gandhi's ideals, but it was a logical development in the transition from national movement to national government that the supreme authority which Gandhi had represented in his own person in the old Congress movement should be somehow recreated in the new legal framework of the government. If Gandhi was not there to exercise it, Nehru was.

Moreover, the Congress, in spite of its regional power bases, was committed to an ideology of government socialist and reformist in character. The commitment was not so intense as to prevent a wide divergence of interpretation among its adherents.

171

But the emphasis is perhaps symbolized in the fact that the chairman of the Drafting Committee for the Constituent Assembly was not a regional party boss but a leader of the millions of designated backward classes or 'untouchables' and a determined opponent of linguistic states, Dr Ambedkar. It was a reminder that central authority was to be used to establish the concern for all-India responsibilities for social improvement, and that this would override the pressures for regional autonomy and decentralization.

The Constitution, enacted on 26 January 1950, was thus federal in form, but avoided the use of the term 'federation'. Though it brought the Republic into being, it owed much to the 1935 Government of India Act and it made no outright assault on the pattern of administration established before independence. In this way it was remarkably conservative. The most notable feature of the Constitution was the provision for wide-ranging emergency powers vested in the President (acting on the advice of the Prime Minister and Cabinet) to take over all authority in any of the constituent States of the Union, and rule directly through the administrative services for a period, while preparations were being made for new elections in that State.

By borrowing a device from the Irish Constitution of 1937, and incorporating a chapter into the text entitled the Directive Principles of State Policy, the drafters of the Constitution were able to make some provision for giving expression to the ideals of the Congress movement. The Directive Principles have no legal sanction but serve as guidelines for future legislatures in formulating the laws of the State. They stand beside the legally enforceable Fundamental Rights, and include those parts of the Gandhian vision that were not immediately compatible with the overall objective of creating a modernizing and centralized State, as well as social welfare aims which in a complex and not wealthy society could not be achieved overnight. Thus the protection of cattle and prohibition of alcoholic liquor stand beside the right to work, free education and furtherance of world peace.

It is not to underestimate the importance of the legal and

constitutional framework to say that much of the debate over the centralizing features of the Constitution has in some ways proved to be beside the point. The arguments as to whether the Constitution should properly be called a unitary one with federal features, or a federal one with strong unitary characteristics, whether the Indian Union is a true federation or a 'quasi-federation', are semantically sophisticated but do not shed much light on the manner in which the Indian political system works. The distribution of powers in the Constitution could not be laid down definitively by the document itself, detailed and relevant as it is. The definition of the powers of the States in relation to the central government has depended as much on the internal political alignments in particular States, and the nature of the relationship with the centre in party terms, whether inside the Congress Party, or with an opposition party that has gained power in one or other of the States. It has also depended on the relative economic strength of the State, with a State such as West Bengal, which has been comparatively highly industrialized, in a much stronger position as a net contributor to central funds than a relatively backward and poor State such as Madhya Pradesh. The power of the central government further has to be measured not merely against the constitutional authority of the States' governments but against the depth of popular feeling behind the State government in any confrontation with the centre. The process of reorganization of provincial boundaries and the creation of new units has in turn spawned a number of powerful regional movements, which as minorities in larger existing units had as yet no constitutional powers, yet whose demands were too strongly backed to be ignored.

The constitutional framework, then, is such that it has been possible for far-reaching changes to be made in the political organization of India without upsetting the basic pattern. The most important of these changes have been the result of regional pressure, and in particular the readjustment caused by the demand for the creation of linguistic States.

It would, however, be a mistake to regard the 'federalizing process' as a purely centrifugal phenomenon. Though new States have been created out of a strong sense of regional and linguistic identity, their formation has brought them into a new relationship with the central government in which the pulls and advantages of full participation in the concerns of the central government have played an important part. Much of the success of internal policies in the new States has depended on successful exploitation of the relationship with the centre. The demand for funds, subsidies, new industries financed out of central funds, the scapegoat of the Central Reserve Police in maintaining law and order, and the ability to shift the blame for the failure of policies on to the central government, have all proved valuable weapons in the battle for political survival. The centre in turn has used its influence to manipulate the shifting factional alliances within the State Congress parties. Some State governors in situations of political instability have looked more to the centre than to the Chief Ministers or potential Chief Ministers of the States over which they preside, and in such circumstances the degree of central support has been a decisive factor in the survival of a State government.

So up to now it may be said that the regional challenge has been more successful in forcing the Government's hand over specific demands of regional reorganization than in presenting a permanent check on the power of the central government. While the limitations of central authority have been very clearly exposed, this does not approach the regional fragmentation that one school of Indian political prophets has foreseen.

The restructuring of the political boundaries of the States was the most controversial and difficult problem faced by the Government of India in the first decade of independence and it has even in 1970 not been wholly resolved. The first official body to consider the question, the Dar Commission, which reported to the Constituent Assembly in 1948, came out firmly against the adoption of the principle of linguistic States, on the grounds that it was likely to lead to fragmentation and administrative ineffi-ciency. This was despite the fact that the principle of linguistic areas had long been a part of the Congress political creed. The Constitution therefore took no account of the principle in formulating the outlines of the structure of the national State. On the other hand, a Congress Committee consisting of Nehru, Sardar Patel, and Pattabhi Sitaramayya, which also considered the question in 1948, showed a greater sensitivity to the strong political feelings involved than the Dar Commission (which had been primarily concerned with the administrative consequences) and was more equivocal in its attitude. Though it did not endorse the principle of linguistic states, it was prepared to consider the possibility in some cases.

The subsequent agitation among the Telugu-speaking people of Madras, Hyderabad and Mysore for a separate Andhra Pradesh to be carved out of those provinces probably owed nothing of its intensity to this very qualified encouragement. The Govern-ment were not prepared to grant the demand by negotiation, aware that it would be likely to open up other similar demands in other parts of the country. However, the death in 1952 of Potti Sriramulu while fasting in the cause of Andhra Pradesh led to rioting and violence before which the Government were forced to give way. The concession pointed the way to a more general reshuffle of boundaries, and the States Reorganization Commission was quickly appointed to go into the whole question once again, this time from an obviously sympathetic standpoint.

The fact that it was in the power of the Government to under-take without constitutional amendment this kind of fundamental reconsideration of the whole structure of the State suggests in one way the total strength of the central government. The very existence and boundaries of the constituent States were to be determined by the centre. They were in no sense autonomous. Yet it was clear then and subsequently that the strength of the demand for the creation of linguistic States might be greater than the Government would be able to resist. Nehru was at the time of the concession of the demand for Andhra at the height of his personal authority, and he was not attracted to the idea of a general reorganization on linguistic lines. However, neither then nor later, when the States Reorganization Commission failed to endorse the claim that Bombay should be divided into Marathi-speaking and Gujarati-speaking states, was this reluctance decisive. In the face of strong popular feeling neither the authority of Nehru nor that of the central government counted for anything. The S R C brought into being a Malayalam-speaking Kerala state and an expanded Kannada-speaking Mysore. Their solution to the claims of Marathi, to create a Marathi-speaking Vidarbha state without dismembering Bombay, satisfied no one. It took another four years' agitation before the centre accepted the demand for the splitting of Bombay along linguistic lines, and Gujarat and Maharashtra were brought into being. There remained Assam, from which Nagaland was separated in 1963, and which was further subdivided in 1972 to meet minority demands.

The concessions here had little to do with the policy of forming linguistic States and belong more to the politics of India's frontier. Frontier policy was a special form of diplomacy that for a long time after independence the Indian Government and Nehru in particular believed to be obsolete. The North-West Frontier was no longer an Indian responsibility, and it took the shock of the conflict with China in 1962 to arouse the Indian Government to the importance of a positive policy in the highly sensitive border areas. The formation of a state of Nagaland was an attempt to secure political stability among a dissident minority well placed to receive assistance from a hostile foreign power.

The linguistic demand was raised once more in the cause of Punjabi. This was the last of the major regional languages to have no exclusive State of its own, as the partitioned East Punjab was divided between Hindi and Punjabi speakers. There were good reasons for resisting the demand for Punjabi Suba. Though the demand was ostensibly based on the rights of Punjabi as a language, behind the linguistic demand lay the communal militancy of the Sikhs. The claim could not be treated fully on its merits, since following the partition Punjab had acquired the position of a border State, and it was doubly dangerous to make any concessions to an incipient separatism. Nevertheless, when the agitation reached its peak in 1966, reluctant as the Government was to yield to the blackmail of threatened self-immolation by the Sikh leader Sant Fateh Singh, it judged the situation too dangerous to take the risk of his carrying out the threat.

Though Mrs Gandhi was then in a much weaker position personally than her father had been at any time when faced with similar demands, the authority of the central government in the face of this strong regional agitation was neither more nor less. The decision to give way, with which she was careful to associate her potential rivals in the Cabinet, cannot be ascribed in any way to the weakness of her own political position. The Government was aware that ultimately the Sant represented a moderating voice in Sikh politics. A confrontation might have restored the credit of the aged extremist Master Tara Singh. Tara Singh's own earlier bid to force the Government's hand over the question of Punjabi Suba by a fast unto death had ended in an ignominious retreat. He and his followers had once looked forward to a totally independent Sikhistan, and their cause would inevitably have been strengthened by the communal rioting which would have followed the public immolation of prominent Sikh leaders.

With the creation of Punjab and Haryana out of the Indian half of divided Punjab the movement for linguistic States seemed to have reached its end, though not the demand for the creation of new States on other grounds. The demand for the creation of Telengana out of Andhra Pradesh is not a linguistic one, but an amalgam of the economic grievances of a backward geographical area and a less prosperous community, that feels deprived of job opportunities and subject to discrimination in the allocation of resources within the administrative unit of which it is now a part. Perhaps because it does not have the emotive issue of language behind it, the movement lacks the radicalism of the earlier movements that have thrived in that region, firstly the Communist rebellion soon after independence, and then the agitation for a Telegu-speaking State which brought Andhra itself into being.

The Communists in this case oppose the creation of Telengana, fearing that a movement to isolate the areas formerly in the domain of the Nizam of Hyderabad from the rest of Andhra would only give renewed power to the privileged classes. The separatists are mostly Congressmen, and after a sustained agitation in 1968 and 1969, which seriously disrupted life in the region and which was successful in rousing popular feeling over the issue, they achieved at least attention for their grievances and promises of safeguards for employment and other opportunities in the Telengana region. From the end of 1969 the factional quarrels that imparted much of the intransigence to the campaign were transformed by the open split in the Congress Party. For the time being at least the demand for a separate State was checked. But in the 1971 elections the Telengana Praja Samiti succeeded in withstanding the national trend in favour of Mrs Gandhi's Congress Party. This electoral verdict has lent further credibility to the demands of the Telengana separatists.

It is noteworthy that the assertions of regional linguistic and cultural identity expressed in the demand for linguistic States have come as much from inside the Congress Party as from outside. An important development of the last ten years in Indian politics has, however, been the exploration of possibilities beyond the demand for linguistic States. The 1967 elections brought to power in Madras for the first time a party that has founded its whole *raison d'être* on the assertion of regional particularism. The phenomenal successes of the Dravida Munetra Kazagham (DMK) seemed to foreshadow a completely new direction for Indian politics, in a system where one party would no longer be dominant, and where State politics would be controlled by purely regional parties with no all-India affiliations. Such a judgement would have been premature, and with the experience of four years in which the politics of Tamilnadu have been dominated by the DMK it is possible to assess the impact of the change on the politics of India as a whole, and to ask what effect this new type of regionalism has had on the country.

Regionalism and the South

The *guru* of the Dravidian cause, E. V. Ramaswami Naicker, based his influence on the twin appeal of cultural separatism and the social advancement of the non-Brahmin Tamils. The political aspirations of the movement appeared only late, at the time of partition, when the demand was raised for a separate Dravidasthan to preserve the South from the domination of the Hindi language and a Brahmanical culture centred on the North. Yet Naicker's Dravida Kazagham, founded in 1944 to give new life to the declining pro-British Justice Party, which had been severely defeated in the 1937 elections, always remained more of a cultural than a political movement. In 1949 the Dravida Munetra Kazagham broke away from the parent body as a group which aimed to embody the same objectives and ideals in a primarily political form.

This transition was the equivalent of that which the Congress had to undergo, from an independence movement to the party of government, with the difference that the DMK was not for many years to achieve political power. It carried with it the same loss of a united purpose and the need to broaden its objectives and alliances. With a Congress Government in Madras throughout the 1950s, under Kamaraj as Chief Minister, the Congress itself became the vehicle of the non-Brahmin and Tamil cultural aspirations on which the DMK had founded its appeal. The Congress and the DMK were competing for power among the same groups. Kamaraj had built his political base among the backward classes and succeeded in transforming the image of the Congress as a Brahmin-dominated organization. The Nadars, Kamaraj's own people, were not among his early supporters, but his ascendancy in Congress from 1937 onwards brought many of the Nadar community into the Congress fold. Naicker himself was impressed with Kamaraj, so that in 1961 he endorsed him as his 'political heir' in preference to C. N. Annadurai and the leaders of the DMK.[1]

The DMK, then, had to rely for its impact on its stand on broader economic questions and a general attack on the supposed domination of the Brahmin-Bania business community in Madras. Overt separatism was declared unconstitutional (by the 16th amendment of 1963). The DMK has depended less on that kind of appeal than on extending its originally largely urban organization into the villages. It has exploited economic grievances in taking a stand to the left of the Congress, and in making the most of the emotive issue of language. It has marshalled the widespread opposition to the policy of the central government on the role of Hindi as a link language to replace English, both in the dealings of the central government with the States and in the educational curriculum as a whole.

The DMK has made much of the language issue, both in opposition and in government, so that Hindi has now been pushed to the background in Tamilnadu schools. Before the central government showed ill-advised haste in promoting the national language and in attempting to keep to the original deadline set in the Constitution, whereby Hindi should have replaced English as the link language by 1965, Hindi had been making steady and acceptable progress in the South. The anti-Hindi agitation arrested and reversed this progress even before the DMK came to power.

But as a separatist movement based on a concept of a distinct Dravidian culture the Dravidian movement suffered the same fragmentation as the political structure of India as a whole. The linguistic States redrew the map of the South as much as of any part of India, and the areas of Malayalam, Kannada, and Telugu speech have no part of what has become a highly successful

---

[1] *Link*, 28 May 1961, quoted in R. Hardgrave, *The Dravidian Movement* (1965), p. 76.

sectional Tamil movement. The concept of Dravidasthan, as opposed to that of Tamilnad, has not proved a viable one.

In office the DMK, like the Congress governments and the Communist governments or Communist-dominated United Fronts of Kerala and West Bengal, has been subject to the same stresses of unfulfilled expectations that are likely to erode the authority of any government. Signs that the massive support that the DMK gained in 1967 might not be so whole-hearted, particularly among students, were partly responsible for the DMK government's decision in February 1971 to dissolve the State Assembly a year before its term. The decision proved well-judged and the DMK was re-elected with a convincing majority. Domestic problems have taken precedence over all others and the DMK has proved quite capable of cooperating with the central government in a way that gives much less trouble than many of the States which are under Congress governments. Since the split in the Congress Party Mrs Gandhi has been less embarrassed by the central relationship with the Government of Tamilnadu, in that the defeated Tamilnadu Congress machine built up by Kamaraj is now in the other camp, and the alliance of the ruling Congress with the DMK representatives in the central parliament on the basis of a progressive and Leftist political programme proved very useful to the survival of Mrs Gandhi's government. The DMK has in turn looked to central subvention to underwrite the cost of radical and expensive policies, notably that of heavy food subsidies.

The DMK continues to press a strong cultural revivalism, which, as we have seen, is a policy not exclusive to purely regional parties, and has been less accommodating in allowing the encouragement of the study of other non-Tamil aspects of Indian culture and language. Its existence and policies have perhaps served more than anything else to show up the regional characteristics of a party such as the Jan Sangh. This has projected an image of Hindu nationalism loosely associated with a right-wing ideology, but in reality it has an appeal confined almost entirely to the North, and in particular the Hindi-speaking belt.

The two parties have many similarities, each emerging as the political wing of a cultural and revivalist movement. Yet there are few parts of India where political attitudes are formed normally on an assertion of Hindu values as such, as opposed to Muslim. In the South there is only one area, in the former Malabar districts of Kerala, where the Muslim Moplah community are locally sufficiently numerous to make an impact in politics on a communal basis, and there the Jan Sangh have made some headway.

In the Gujarat textile city of Ahmedabad there has been a progressive loss of confidence in the Congress among Muslim mill-workers since 1965, and there has been some local revival of Muslim communal organizations, paralleled on a local basis in other North Indian towns. The Jan Sangh have been able to exploit the reaction to this, and their activities, along with those of their 'cultural' and para-military parent, the RSS (Rashtriya Swayamsevak Sangh), did much to foster the vicious communal riots in Ahmedabad of September 1969.[1]

Elsewhere in the irreproachably Hindu South the Jan Sangh has represented everything to which the people are most opposed in their concept of the nation. Even more the Hindu and regional chauvinism of the Shiv Sena, a Maharashtran organization more militantly provocative even than the RSS, has been specifically directed at the Tamils of Bombay. In truth the Jan Sangh is much more of a regional party than a right-wing party, whether one understands the phrase in terms of economic ideology or of a communal and traditionalist orientation.

The experience of the DMK suggests firstly that it is perfectly possible for a regional party to cooperate fully with the central government within the framework of the existing Constitution. It also shows that the regional appeal is an insufficient basis in itself to support a political party and that it must provide competi-

---

[1] Cf. Ghanshyam Shah, 'Communal riots in Gujarat: Report of a preliminary investigation', *Economic and Political Weekly* (Bombay), January 1970, pp. 187–200.

tive and attractive policies on the economic front. Thirdly a regional party like any other will be judged on its performance. There is no evidence to suggest that it will retain a peculiar and unassailable voter loyalty. Finally a successful regional party may form an important element in the power equation of the central government.

While it may be assumed that any such party would stress the right to the highest degree of provincial autonomy and freedom from the interference of the central government in the internal affairs of the States, the parliamentary balance after the split in the Congress Party showed that minority parties may hold the balance of power. The considerations which weigh in exercising this power are inevitably more than regional. There were in 1971 two purely regional parties in power in the States. Besides the DMK there was the Punjab Government of the regional-cum-communal Sikh party, the Akali Dal. Before the 1971 elections there were consultations between the two parties with a view to coordinating the attitude of regional parties in the central legislature. Such consultation could well have an important bearing on the future development of national politics. The particular issue is how far regional aspirations are likely to link up with the polarization of politics along ideological lines, which many observers feel is the dominant trend in Indian politics, especially at the national level, since the death of Nehru. Some of the talk of polarization arises from an analysis of actual political developments. Some more originates in projections of theoretical models of the development of a modern party system. The question is nevertheless extremely relevant for the past and the future of Indian politics.

Polarization and the parties

The Congress both before and after independence has been a seed-bed of minority groupings. Some of them, drawn together by commitment to a common social programme, have been able

183

to remain within the Congress organization and retain a measure of group identity and influence. Thus the Congress Socialists remained within the party until a tightening of party discipline in 1948 made it necessary for them to break away and form a separate Socialist party. Other groupings, particularly within State Congress parties, have owed more to factional or caste loyalties to give them identity than to their ideological colour, and have from time to time broken away from the parent party to try their fortunes in the shifting sands of State coalition politics, armed as often as not with a programme as flexible and adaptable as that of the Congress itself. This kind of breakaway has contributed no more to the process of polarization than the increasingly frequent and opportunistic defections which began to characterize the unstable coalitions in those States where the Congress had lost its dominating position, or where the Congress itself was divided into warring factions.

The Socialist separation from the Congress (first the Congress Socialist Party, then Kripalani's Kisan Mazdoor Party, which after the 1952 elections merged to form the Praja Socialist Party), was an invitation to what would now be called polarization which the Congress Party as a whole did not accept. Nehru made efforts to bring the PSP back into the Congress, and extensive discussions were held in 1953 to that end. Nehru himself shared many of the Socialists' objectives and was aiming to steer the whole Congress organization in that direction. Thus after the failure of the talks with the PSP the Congress Party within a short time incorporated into its declared programme several of the points which the PSP had put to the Congress as conditions of their rejoining the Party. Meanwhile, despite Nehru's personal convictions, the Congress continued to play host to a wide range of political ideology ranging through conservative, traditionalist, capitalist, Gandhian, and socialist.

The adoption in 1955 at the Avadi session of the Congress of the objective of a 'socialistic pattern of society' did not shake this coalition. Though the objective was much discussed and commented on, and though it became a basic text of Congress policy, it was a far cry from the implementation of specific socialist and radical measures. The conservatives wisely reserved their energies for resisting such specific proposals rather than general statements of intent. It was only in 1959, after the Nagpur session of the Congress had adopted resolutions of a radical nature on agrarian policy, that the first avowedly conservative party, the Swatantra Party, was formed to provide a right-wing opposition to the Congress. However the Swatantra was no more successful than the Socialists had been in drawing away from the Congress substantial numbers of those who were in sympathy with their political standpoint. One still had to look inside the Congress Party as much as to opposition parties for significant conflicts of political ideology.

In this ideological confrontation the Communist Party occupied a rather special place. In principles and organization it owed less to an imitation of, or reaction to, the Congress than any other major political party. Yet its international affiliations and avowed acceptance of a Marxist programme and a Soviet model of political tactics and organization have moulded its character less than might be expected. This is partly due to a conscious realization that a successful Communist movement could not depend solely on outside assistance and direction, but must strike firm indigenous political roots. Even more compelling has been the need to use methods similar to those of the Congress and other competing parties in building up a political base. This has meant that the Communist Party was never able to establish the firm discipline and unequivocal ideological commitment that have characterized the European Communist parties. The Communist Party, like the other all-India parties, suffered from internal divisions arising from the caste and regional preoccupations of its political strongholds. The strong support for the Communists among the Ezhava caste in Kerala is natural from a community which is both numerous and traditionally underprivileged. In Andhra, however, the backing of the Kamma caste, which is relatively wealthy and owns considerable amounts of land, is less easy to explain along economic or class lines.

This is not to suggest that caste groupings are in most cases, or even usually, the determining factor in political alignments. The Kamma-Reddy caste rivalry in Andhra does not provide a complete explanation of the politics of that State, as the running factional quarrels between the two camps of the divided Congress Party (and earlier within the Congress Party) have shown. In these the chief protagonists were former Chief Minister Brahmananda Reddi, supported by Mrs Gandhi, and Sanjiva Reddy, the former speaker of the Lok Sabha and defeated presidential candidate (in 1969), who was then aligned with Mrs Gandhi's opponents in the Organization Congress. In Kerala the Communist Party has had a strong appeal, among other reasons because the leaders of the Communist Party were also the leaders of the nationalist movement in the area before independence. In the Telengana region also the Communist-led insurrection of 1948, before the formation of Andhra Pradesh, was a movement which grew out of genuine peasant grievances. Many of these were reflected in the agitation of 1968–9, a demand which the Andhra Communists then opposed.

But a group such as the Naxalites, which relies on active revolutionary tactics, has not been able to extend its rural political base outside a few isolated pockets in West Bengal, Andhra, and the sub-montane regions of Uttar Pradesh.[1] The Naxalites have made their impact more as urban guerrillas, especially in Calcutta, where their activities have added to the violence and general instability of West Bengal politics. In most parts of India the Communist parties have had to contend with the headstart which the Congress, or ex-Congress factions, have gained among the agricultural classes and the small farmers in particular. The promise of thorough-going land reforms serves only to antagonize electorally influential groups.

[1] Cf. Gautam Appa, 'The Naxalites', *New Left Review*, No. 61, May–June 1970, pp. 34–41.

Recent studies have shown that, while political parties have provided a medium for caste aspirations, the modernizing effect of bringing caste into modern politics has been more striking than any tendency to narrow the objectives of the political parties into sectarian channels. Even the plague of factionalism, whether at State level or at village level in the factions among the dominant caste, has perhaps performed a service in helping to integrate the lower castes into Indian political life. Few factions or parties can win elections on the basis of the support of one caste, and their appeal has to cut across caste lines.[1]

The question of the ideological adherence to Moscow or Peking, on which the Indian Communist Party split, though it was of great importance to the intelligentsia of the Party leadership, does not therefore represent the substance of the dissensions within the Party. Nor does the question figure very much today in attracting their political support. The Communists face a common problem with the regional parties in that their supporters are no more permanently committed to them than are the voters of other parties. In the 1962 elections the Communists suffered heavy losses in Calcutta and the suburbs because their organization took the area too much for granted. The Communist-dominated United Fronts in West Bengal have been given more trouble by their own supporters and extremists than by the opposition. The Kerala elections of September 1970 showed that they can still lose massive support to the Congress, as they did in the elections of 1960 after their first three-year spell in government. The revival of the fortunes of Mrs Gandhi's Congress Party in West Bengal in 1971 confirmed this.

Meanwhile the Congress divided into two parties and the hopes of polarization were given a new boost. Mrs Gandhi's wing of the Congress set about cultivating a more Leftist image, without rashly abandoning the political accommodations neces-

---

[1] Cf. M. S. A. Rao, 'Urbanisation in a Delhi Village', *Economic and Political Weekly*, 15 October 1966, pp. 369–70, and Paul Brass, *Factional Politics in an Indian State* (1965), p. 67.

sary to the survival of a major all-India party. Bold measures such as the nationalization of Indian-owned banks and the abolition of the Princes' privy purses aimed at proclaiming the new orientation. But before 1971, as leader of a minority party at the centre she depended on the support of the 'Right' Communists (the CPI), the Socialists and other regional parties. In return the Congress in Kerala gave its support to a coalition led by the CPI. This kind of cooperation continues to play its part in the politics of the States, though in the central parliament Mrs Gandhi's overwhelming victory has made it unnecessary. Where no party has a clear majority, a Congress-dominated coalition must depend on such flexibility.

It is too much to expect that ideological commitment will quickly replace political juggling or the ubiquitous 'brokerage' system on which parties depend for reaching out to a mass base. This is not due to something inherently different in the Asian processes of political choice in comparison with the Western. Few European or American political parties are purely ideological and it is not likely that India will produce a greater degree of polarization than other political systems. Experience has shown, however, that in India programmes and ideologies are an important element, which has a strong influence on the traditional and regional groupings and the inter-party and inter-factional alliances that play a big role in the Indian political system.

Prospect

Perhaps the most significant aspect of Indian political development is not that India has sustained through two decades a formal structure of political democracy despite the internal strains to which it has been subject. It is rather that within that formal structure there has evolved a living political organization which has affected in some way or other almost every level of society. The participation of groups and individuals in the political process generated by the independence movement has been continued in the adaptation of the movement to governing power. Many of the elements of this evolution are not necessarily characteristic only of a democracy and would be likely to survive and develop even under a different political system. In the South Asian context at least there are no social origins which are peculiar to a democracy or to a form of autocratic government. Because some of the most important changes are due to a fundamental process of modernization, either India or Pakistan might pass from one system of government to another and back again without arresting this process.

As it is, the relative stability of the Indian political system has allowed this process to be studied and observed more openly than in Pakistan. The two states have faced very similar problems, notably those arising from the need to adjust to the competing claims of region and language and the struggle for economic power. Despite the differences of religion the social structure has more points of contact than of divergence. The problems that beset Pakistan in 1970 after twelve years of virtual military rule were similar to those of India after twenty-three years of democracy, but in India the problems have been continuously faced and in many ways successfully met, whereas in Pakistan their suppression made them burst out with greater intensity in the disorder which ended the rule of Ayub Khan.

Some of the boldest and most original of the Indian experiments in government, from the ventures in centralized planning to the implementation of democratic decentralization in the programmes for community development and Panchayati Raj, are not integral to the form of parliamentary democracy as laid down in the Constitution, and draw their inspiration from Soviet, or, in the case of Panchayati Raj, Gandhian, models. These parts of the Indian political system might well flourish also in a different, not necessarily democratic, power structure.

Behind them lies the bureaucracy. The old 'steel frame' has been profoundly modified both by the democratic system and the expanded social aims of the Government. It has continued to serve as a main channel for the aspirations of the graduates of a greatly enlarged educational system. It has been affected by the same demands that have shaped politics, by linguistic and regional preferences, and the reservation of jobs for castes and communities designated as backward. But it has retained an essential and influential role in political life.

The Indian democracy has developed on many different levels and on some of them it has been more successful than on others. It has borrowed from foreign models, but by adaptation has made them indigenous. There is a continuous adjustment of traditional institutions and loyalties to a more modern role. While its stability cannot be taken for granted, it has built up a fund of political experience on which to draw. In a crisis there might be changes, but it is certain that this experience would not be swept aside.

CHAPTER VII

PAKISTAN'S EXPERIMENTS
IN DEMOCRACY

H. KHUHRO

Pakistan came into existence on 14 August 1947 as a result of the partition of the subcontinent of India on the grounds of religious and cultural differences between Hindus and Muslims. Historical accident had placed the Muslim community predominantly in two parts of India, the north-east and the north-west of the subcontinent. Thus Pakistan found itself divided into two parts, separated from each other by a thousand miles of Indian territory, able to communicate only across northern India or by a long sea voyage round the peninsula. In addition, therefore, to the usual problems of developing countries, Pakistan inherited some unique problems of its own.

Pakistan came into being in the face of bitter Hindu hostility and the general expectation that it would soon collapse. It managed to survive, however, and emerged with a viable economy and a remarkable rate of growth for an underdeveloped country. Politically, however, Pakistan has not been so successful. The results of this failure have been a chronic political instability, a vain search for a constitution and finally a tragic civil war ending with the dissolution of the country within twenty-four years of its creation. With the benefit of hindsight it will be argued that dissolution was implicit in the birth of this unique and 'unnatural' state with its people widely separated geographically and culturally. Such a fate was not however obvious to the people of Pakistan in either the East or the West and political life was deeply imbued with the belief in the continued existence of the country. Nevertheless separation became inevitable through the policies of the groups who wielded power during most of Pakistan's history. It is reasonable to suppose through a study of these policies and their effects that the tragedy of Pakistan was man made and not historically inevitable.

The first two decades of Pakistan's existence fall more or less neatly into two periods. For the first ten years it had a parliamentary form of government inherited from the Government of India Act of 1935 and the Independence Act of 1947. After 27 October 1958, an authoritarian form of government was imposed on the country by General Ayub Khan backed by the army, although this was camouflaged in its later stages by a form of democratic constitution. In March 1969, Ayub Khan resigned after a wave of popular unrest in the country, handing the country over to a new martial-law regime. The Commander-in-Chief, General Yahya Khan, formed a caretaker government to govern the country until elections could be held and a new constitution formed by the elected representatives of the people. The expected transfer of power to a National Assembly did not take place. Faced with a Bengali majority in the country and seeing the threat that was posed to its power under such a government the army chose to use force to crush East Pakistan in order to continue its own predominance. Then followed bloody repression, guerrilla warfare, Indian invasion and separation and independence of East Pakistan.

The chaotic events of the twenty-four years of Pakistan's existence are not meaningless or arbitrary. A closer examination of the events and of Pakistan society and politics reveals a pattern of groups and interests competing and combining to achieve supremacy. This contest is not yet over. By an examination of social and political factors it is possible to identify these groups and to assess their present position and their chances of success or failure in the future continuing contest.

These groups or interests broadly defined fall into two categories: politicians, i.e., those who want some form of parliamentary government or a constitution by compromise; and secondly, the 'anti-politicians', i.e., the civil servants and the army who would prefer an authoritarian type of government with little interference from politicians, themselves exercising the authority. These broad divisions perhaps oversimplify the issues involved. Many other groups either coincide with or cut across these divisions, the most important of these being the provincial or linguistic divisions. In addition to identifying interest groups, any meaningful discussion of post-independence events in Pakistan must take into account the factors that made up the Pakistan movement and the events leading up to independence. These factors will help to explain the problems that Pakistan inherited and the way politics in Pakistan developed. If the hopes and ideals that were involved in the struggle for Pakistan are explained and the expectations aroused by the vision of an 'Islamic' state stated clearly, then it will be possible to assess how far these hopes and ideals were actually achieved and how far they fell short of expectation in reality. It will also be possible to explain the disillusion and frustration which followed the creation of Pakistan.

Together with the intellectual and spiritual problems of the independence movement, Pakistan also inherited the political set-up of the pre-partition days. The pattern of Pakistan's politics after independence was a continuation of Muslim and Muslim League politics before independence and reflected the stage of maturity which had been reached by 1947. It is necessary, therefore, to recapitulate the state of Muslim politics in the forties to see how these appear in the Pakistani context.

Up to 1936, Muslim participation in the Indian independence movement had been the nationalist demand for freedom with the addition of safeguards for the Muslim minority. Some time after the Act of 1935 had come into partial operation—between 1936 and 1940—the demand for Pakistan crystallized and became part of the official programme of the Muslim League. But even after the Lahore Resolution of 1940 it was widely believed, and it was a belief shared by most Muslim Leaguers themselves, that this demand was merely a bargaining counter to force the Congress and the British Government to see the seriousness of the Muslim situation. Although it is still a matter for debate as to when the Pakistan demand became the serious demand of the Muslim League, the most likely date is after the failure of the Cabinet Mission plan of 1945. The idea of Pakistan therefore had a fairly short period in which to mature before it was swept into the highly charged atmosphere of the months immediately preceding partition. The fact that exhaustive discussion and analysis of the idea had not taken place, and that it was presented to the people in the form of a nebulous ideal, meant that Pakistan meant all things to all men. Inevitably, therefore, debate regarding the nature of the state in Pakistan was particularly heated after independence and still continues unresolved, adding to the dissension within the country.

The Muslim League itself had not begun to be properly organized on a nationwide mass scale until the late thirties, after the disillusionment with the Congress policy towards the Muslim League and the experience of Congress ministries in power in the provinces. Until this time Muslim provincial politicians had worked through parties organized on provincial lines and serving the interests of the community on a provincial basis.[1] These politicians were men of experience and had worked in district local boards and provincial legislatures. They had organized their parties and had been fighting elections since the establishment of Ripon's local self-government in the 1880s and the establishment of Dyarchy in 1919. By the late thirties, parliamentary practice was well established in the provinces.

Provincial Muslim politicians had not been closely associated with the Muslim League. The last national movement they had participated in had been the Khilafat movement, and that had left bitter memories. Many senior politicians had attended Muslim

---

[1] Elections were regularly held, though on a restricted franchise.

League sessions in the past and were loosely members of that organization, but this had formed the fringe of their activity. It was only after Congress had been successful in the elections of 1936 and had formed the ministries that Muslims found detrimental to their interests that they were forced to work for a national organization that would act for their interests and force the Congress into a less arrogant and more conciliatory attitude. Consequently the most important Muslim politicians threw their support behind the Muslim League. Even in cases like the Punjab, where the provincial political party was very strong,[1] leaders like Sir Sikander Hayat found it expedient to ally themselves with an organization with such a strong appeal to the Muslim masses over the heads of the provincial leaders.

As the Muslim League gathered strength, through the work of the provincial leaders at the grassroots level and through Mr Jinnah at the national level, a pattern of organization emerged. A part of Mr Jinnah's success as leader was his way of dealing with the Congress and the British Government and his success in making them accept the Muslim League as the sole representative of Muslim opinion in the subcontinent. The other aspect of his triumph was his success in convincing the provincial leaders that he was indispensable to them and to the safety of the Muslim cause. They supported him because they believed that he was the only man who could be a match for the subtle and wily Congress leadership which had 'corrupted' such men as Maulana Azad. Jinnah was incorruptible. As a price for his leadership Mr Jinnah demanded virtually unquestioning obedience. Although debate was allowed in the Working Committee, decisions were those of Mr Jinnah. This became more and more the case as time went on and the freedom movement gathered strength and Mr Jinnah's personal popularity increased. The Council, in theory the decision-making body, became merely a loyal rubber-stamping body. This pattern was inherited by Pakistan where, at the provincial level, there was genuine

[1] I.e. the Punjab Unionist Party.

195

leadership and a working parliamentary system but at the centre the tradition was authoritarian. After Mr Jinnah there was no worthy or disinterested leadership to try and bridge the gap between the centre and the provinces. The idea persisted among politicians that the proper sphere for political activity was the province and that the centre could look after itself. Thus power there fell into the hands of 'anti-politicians' almost by default. Provincial leaders failed to realize that the approach to national politics after independence needed to be changed and that it was essential to establish a share in the decision-making at the centre. They nominated second-rate men to the central cabinet posts and the result was that the civil servants in power at the centre—the anti-politicians—were easily able to out-manoeuvre these men, and with the strongest levers of power at the centre provincial politicians were powerless to prevent their growing authoritarianism.

Coincidentally, the anti-politicians at the centre were mainly a Punjab group. The major factor in Indo-Pakistani politics is the existence of different provincial and linguistic nationalities. These nationalities antedate British rule. The Raj had maintained provincial boundaries with minor modifications, and when self-government was gradually introduced it was based on the provincial divisions. Although the question of the rights and autonomy of the provinces was temporarily obscured by the struggle to achieve Pakistan, it was taken for granted that provincial autonomy would be the basis of any constitution that might be framed in Pakistan. The Lahore Resolution itself went so far as to talk of 'independent states' forming Pakistan, meaning perhaps a federal arrangement with wide powers for the provinces.[1] Pakistan comprised five major provinces and a number of states. The two largest provinces were East Bengal

---

[1] The Lahore Resolution states: 'That geographically contiguous units are demarcated into regions which should be so constituted . . . that the areas in which Muslims are numerically in a majority, as in the north western and eastern zones of India, should be grouped to constitute "independent states" in which the constituent units shall be autonomous and sovereign.'

and West Punjab. East Bengal was the largest province in terms of population, with a population equal to the whole of West Pakistan. It could dominate any legislature elected on the basis of adult franchise. But the most 'advanced' province in terms of education, representation in the services, both civil and military, and with the most enterprising farmers, was the Punjab. One of the major problems of *realpolitik* that had to be solved by the constitution was the balance of power between West Punjab and East Bengal. Politicians struggled with this question for ten years but it was the decisive and unconstitutional action of the anti-politicians that settled the question by the formation of 'One Unit' in West Pakistan and the achievement of 'parity' between the East and West wings of the country in the matter of representation in the Assembly.

The two pieces of legislation, 'One Unit' and 'Parity', did not succeed in solving permanently the question of provincial rivalries. If anything, the fears of the smaller provinces about Punjabi domination were increased, fears which became reality in the working of 'One Unit'. The bitterness of Bengal was increased still further by the language controversy.[1] The final *coup*, which established the predominance of the anti-politicians' group, was the military takeover under Ayub Khan with the connivance of President Iskander Mirza.

The ten years of authoritarian rule under Ayub Khan proved decisively that the basic realities of Pakistan's socio-political structure could not be suppressed for long by any regime, no matter how strong. The provincial demands for autonomy, for a share in the decision-making processes, for a fair share in the jobs and services, had in the end to be conceded. These feelings were strong enough to bring down Ayub Khan's carefully constructed, but inflexible, power structure in March 1969.

On independence Mr Jinnah took over as Governor-General

[1] The question was whether Urdu or Bengali should be the national language. Bengal's bitterness was increased by the tactlessness of many political leaders, including Khwaja Nazimuddin, himself from Bengal, who insisted that Urdu should be adopted as the national language.

of Pakistan. It was not to be expected that, long used to exercising absolute authority, he would restrict himself to the constitutional role assigned to the head of the state in a parliamentary system. And although he was a lawyer by training, Mr Jinnah did act as the effective head of the cabinet during his Governor-Generalship. In fact, his powers went even further than those of a Prime Minister in such a constitution. Jinnah did not hesitate to impose his will in any situation where he met opposition, even if this meant going against accepted constitutional and parliamentary behaviour. For instance, when he decided to separate Karachi from Sind and create a federal area, the Government and the Legislative Assembly of Sind refused the suggestion. Instead of accepting this decision, which Sind was perfectly entitled to make, he dismissed the Chief Minister and appointed another, more amenable, man. Such instances of interference and high-handedness in provincial politics set a precedent which was to be followed all too faithfully by his successors.

Jinnah died in 1948 and was succeeded by Khwaja Nazimuddin, an East Pakistani politician, as Governor-General, while Liaquat Ali Khan continued as Prime Minister. As Nazimuddin was not a particularly forceful personality, Liaquat Ali was now able to exercise his legitimate powers as Prime Minister. He did not, however, confine himself to the exercise only of legitimate powers but on various occasions brought pressure to bear on persons and made undue use of his position as Prime Minister to influence events—as, for example, by his interference in provincial elections in the Punjab. Liaquat Ali was responsible for the enactment of the instrument of coercion known as PRODA (Public Representative Officers Disqualification Act). The purpose of this Act was to remove by disqualification any politician who was troublesome to the Prime Minister and the central leadership. After Jinnah, nevertheless, Liaquat Ali was the only national figure in a position to settle many national issues and obtain agreement from the different provinces on sensitive issues such as the national language and the constitution. At this stage it was possible and fairly simple to get such an agreement, as the post-independence euphoria had not entirely vanished. He made no serious effort to obtain concensus, however, and it may be claimed that he deliberately used delaying tactics, using as an excuse the necessity for obtaining agreement on the Islamic basis of the constitution. That this was hardly a real issue was proved by the ease with which the Objectives Resolution was passed, although it was very little more than a number of pious resolutions and did not include any real concessions to the demands of the Ulema.[1] Again and again Islam was to prove a convenient escape route for a political leader in search of delay.

Liaquat Ali Khan was assassinated on 16 October 1951 at Rawalpindi. Immediately after his death, secret negotiations between a number of Central Government executives—prominent among whom were Ghulam Mohammed, the Finance Minister, Chaudhri Mohammed Ali, the Secretary-General, and Mushataq Ahmed Gurmani—decided on the composition of the next government. This government was formed with Ghulam Mohammed as Governor-General and Khwaja Nazimuddin as Prime Minister. The cabinet included Chaudhri Mohammed Ali. The *fait accompli* was then presented to the country and was accepted without any objection to the unconstitutional method used. There seemed to be no realization of the danger of this precedent, and the acceptance no doubt encouraged further and bolder unconstitutional actions.

Khwaja Nazimuddin himself proved a weak Prime Minister without noticeable political acumen. He failed to get support from provincial leaders and interfered in provincial politics. He took an uncompromising attitude on Urdu as the national language, although this was a touchy issue in Bengal and Nazimuddin was himself a Bengali politician. He interfered in Sind, was put in a difficult position by the Ahmadiyya riots in the Punjab and had to dismiss the Punjab government. He was also

[1] Objectives Resolution—C.A.P. Debates, Vol. V, No. 5 (12 March 1949). For a discussion in detail of this Resolution, see L. Binder, *Religion and Politics in Pakistan*, 1961.

faced with a general food shortage in the country. The impression grew of a weak and thoroughly inefficient government. Taking advantage of this feeling, the Governor-General suddenly dismissed the Prime Minister in April 1953, a blatantly unconstitutional action which he was able to carry off with remarkable ease. Nazimuddin put up a very feeble and ineffectual resistance. He tried unsuccessfully to contact the Queen in England to get her to declare the action of the Governor-General unconstitutional and illegal, as theoretically he was Her Majesty's agent, but he made no other serious attempt to fight the constitutional issue, merely giving a statement to the press explaining his viewpoint. His contention was that the Governor-General's action was unconstitutional and that the discretionary powers of the Governor-General and his exercise of individual judgement had ceased to have effect with the enforcement of the Indian Independence Act of 1947.

The new Government in a note to the press said in rebuttal of this that the Council of Ministers was not a Cabinet as in the British constitutional practice. Although the Governor-General was required by constitutional provisions of 1947 to be 'aided and advised' by this body, it was to be chosen and summoned by him and to hold office during his pleasure. If the Governor-General decided to withhold his pleasure 'in the interest of public order and tranquillity of the realm or in any emergency', the ministry ceased to hold office. Confusion, the note claimed, arose through 'undue emphasis on certain conventions' as they were known to British constitutional practice, and the confusion got 'worse confounded' when these conventions were 'read into the text of the existing constitution of Pakistan as though these were a part of it'. The Governor-General's action in dismissing the Nazimuddin cabinet was sanctioned by the provisions of Section 10 of the Government of India Act 1935, as adapted, '. . . and was implicit in the entire constitutional set-up envisaged by that Act'.[1] Nazimuddin did not follow up with a reply and

[1] *Pakistan Times*, 19 April 1953.

the constitutional issue was not conjoined. The press was full of acclamation for the Governor-General's action. The statement of the Government was clearly in contradiction to the democratic spirit in which the Independence Act had so far been understood and was obviously a casuistic justification for the coup. Mohammed Ali of Bogra from East Pakistan, who until then had been the Ambassador in Washington, was appointed the new Prime Minister. The reaction in Washington was reported to be favourable to the new government and aid was promised in the shape of food grain to help tide over Pakistan's food shortage.

The *coup* of 17 April revealed clearly the state of power politics in Pakistan. The façade of parliamentary government was beginning to crack and it was seen that power was in the hands of a group of senior executives from the Punjab who had passed beyond the ranks of civil servants into a decision-making inner circle. The ruling groups in Pakistan at this time consisted in lesser or greater degree of the following: the West Pakistan landed aristocracy, the East Pakistan middle class politicians, the army, the civil service, and the rising class of industrialists. The first two groups had been active in the Pakistan movement and had become the working politicians after independence. It was clear, however, that power was falling increasingly into the hands of the third and fourth groups, the army and the civil service, at the expense of the politicians. The industrialist class was as yet too small to wield much influence. The long-term aims of the inner circle of decision-makers were to reveal themselves gradually. These were to ensure a strong central executive unhampered by political influence from the provinces and to ensure a balance in representation in the central legislature between East and West Pakistan with West Pakistan being firmly under Punjab dominance.

With Mohammed Ali of Bogra as figurehead Prime Minister and some of the key members of the Punjab coterie in the Cabinet—as, for instance, Chaudhri Mohammed Ali—the clique was now in a strong position, but it still had to crush the independence of the provinces and render them subservient. This was a process which had begun under Nazimuddin who, under the influence of Ghulam Mohammed, had continually interfered in the politics of Sind and the Punjab. Ghulam Mohammed and, after him, Iskander Mirza, continued this practice and with the help of PRODA undermined almost completely the independence of provincial politicians.

In East Pakistan, however, the central clique could not so easily control the politicians, particularly the opposition. Here opposition to the Muslim League government had been growing, especially after Nazimuddin's tactless handling of the language question and the failure of the League government to provide reassurance against the threat of West Pakistani domination. Opposition parties led by Fazlul Haque and Suhrawardy, fighting elections on a platform of maximum provincial autonomy, were able to defeat the Muslim League party in March 1954. The United Front got approximately 220 seats out of 239 Muslim seats and the Muslim League got only 9.

This spectacular defeat of the Muslim League caused a crisis at the centre. The United Front would have to form a government in East Pakistan, the Constituent Assembly would have to change its composition to include the new representatives of East Pakistan, and the central cabinet itself would have to do the same. In fact, Bogra's own position might prove untenable, since at least nominally he was Prime Minister by virtue of being a Muslim League member from East Pakistan. Apart from these effects, the results of the East Pakistan elections had caused a political ferment in West Pakistan and a demand for new elections there. The central government with its palace politics and penchant for arranging matters without reference to the Constituent Assembly or the electorate was duly alarmed. Threatened with the collapse of its carefully constructed power structure, the central clique kept its nerve and acted with firmness and determination to resist any changes that might take away its predominance. It was made clear at any early stage that no change would be made in the central Cabinet or in the Constituent Assembly. The Muslim League members of the Constituent Assembly were asked not to resign and it was obvious that the *status quo* would be maintained.[1] At the same time central government, offering the carrot after the stick, promised to push the Constitution through quickly and to hold the elections by May 1955.

Unfortunately for the newly elected United Front, the central government was able to exploit the differences between the various groups within it. The situation was made worse by Fazlul Haque's pronouncements in Calcutta which cast doubts on his loyalty to Pakistan. It was with some difficulty, therefore, that the United Front formed a government in Dacca on 13 May 1954. On 15 May, a serious riot occurred among workers of a jute mill when about 300 workers were killed and a thousand wounded.[2] Fazlul Haque was reported to have made more disloyal statements and this gave the central government the excuse it needed to act. On 30 May, the Fazlul Haque ministry was dismissed and Governor's rule was imposed on East Pakistan. Iskander Mirza was appointed, and since he was well known as a 'tough man' it was clear that no nonsense would be tolerated. Thus the central government was able to avert immediate danger to its power, but in doing so delivered a heavy blow to democracy in Pakistan.

By now the anti-politician clique at the centre had worked out the strategy that would help it to achieve its aim. This strategy consisted of the enforcement of the principle of parity between the East and West wings in any legislature and of bringing West Pakistan into line with the Punjab through merging the administration of the different provinces and creating the so-called One Unit in West Pakistan. The idea of One Unit had been heard of some time earlier, but the smaller provinces had been hostile. It was now revived by the central government with the Punjab

[1] *Pakistan Times*, Lahore, 27 March 1954, and other press reports.
[2] *Pakistan Times*, 15 May 1954.

group in a much stronger position. Opinion in the provinces was still hostile, but the strength of the centre and the disagreements of the provincial politicians made it a feasible proposition.

The Constituent Assembly was engaged in its work of drawing up a constitution when at this point a rift appeared between it and the Governor-General. Some of the members of the Assembly felt that the Governor-General would probably use PRODA against them, if they did not do something to forestall him. They managed to get the support of the Prime Minister, who had been hitherto a faithful 'yes-man' of the Governor-General, but who now wanted to establish some solid support for himself. Timing their action so that the Governor-General was out of the way on holiday, the group in the Assembly repealed PRODA with the proviso that those under current disqualification or proceedings would not benefit from the repeal.[1] At the same time, a number of amendments to constitutional provisions were introduced, designed to curtail the powers of the Governor-General. Thus war was openly declared between the Constituent Assembly and the Governor-General. The *coup* against the growing power of the Governor-General was not expected to be unopposed, and everyone waited for Ghulam Mohammed's reaction. The Prime Minister meanwhile left for an official visit abroad. Ghulam Mohammed bided his time and carefully planned his counter-*coup*. He wooed the politicians who were out of power and discriminated against under the recent repeal of PRODA, quashing the PRODA disqualification of Khunro and Daultana. He made overtures to East Pakistani politicians, especially Suhrawardy. The United Front, bitter at being excluded from power, had already demanded the dissolution of the Constituent Assembly. Ghulam Mohammed now approached Suhrawardy and others with the promise of office. Suhrawardy and other United Front leaders issued statements demanding the dissolution of the

---

[1] Khuhro in Sino was the most prominent politician under disqualification. This provision was made to exclude him and Daultana (from the Punjab) against whom proceedings were under way.

Assembly. A political crisis seemed imminent. Bogra cancelled a visit to Canada and came home. Accompanied by Iskander Mirza and General Ayub Khan, he was driven straight from the airport to Government House. Here Bogra was persuaded to sign a statement recommending the dissolution of the Constituent Assembly. Ghulam Mohammed had staged his boldest *coup*.[1]

The next morning a proclamation was issued from Government House to the effect that the Governor-General, 'having considered the political crisis with which the country was faced', had come to the conclusion that the constitutional machinery had broken down. He had therefore declared a state of emergency in the country, dissolved the Constituent Assembly and invited Bogra to form a new cabinet.[2] By this *coup* one of the two principal institutions set up by the Independence Act of 1947 was dissolved by the Governor-General. Such action had not been conceived as a part of the Governor-General's functions, and was contrary to the spirit of the Independence Act.

No successor Assembly was offered as consolation and for some time government was carried on merely by the executive.

The dissolution of the Assembly marked the complete triumph of the central clique. All obstacles now appeared to have been removed from their path in their pursuit of a constitution and method of government in which they would reign supreme. But this *coup* had been helped along by the dissensions among the West Pakistan politicians and the East Pakistan politicians' willingness to compromise democratic principles in order to achieve a share in power. The membership of the new cabinet revealed the source of real power. Chaudhri Mohammed Ali remained in charge of Finance and in addition took over Economic Affairs, Refugees and Rehabilitation and Kashmir Affairs. Iskander Mirza resigned as Governor of East Pakistan and

[1] Ayub Khan claims that Ghulam Mohammed suggested to him that he should take over the government and declare martial law, but that he refused. It is clear, however, that Ghulam Mohammed must have acted with the support of the Commander-in-Chief Ayub and the strong man Iskander Mirza, a close friend of Ayub Khan.

[2] *Dawn*, 25 October 1954.

became Minister of the Interior. General Ayub became Defence Minister while remaining Commander-in-Chief. Bogra remained Premier, but more than ever a puppet figure. Political nonentities were taken from Sind and the Frontier province.[1] The West Pakistani clique which dominated the centre consisted of Ghulam Mohammed, Chaudhri Mohammed Ali, General Ayub, and M. A. Gurmani, who was shortly to become Governor of the Punjab. These were the anti-politicians who were shaping the politics and government of Pakistan. They had no background of activity in the Muslim League or any other political party and had belonged to the executive services—civil or military. They had a contempt for, and dislike of, politicians and were advocates of a 'controlled' or 'guided' democracy.[2] The group nevertheless did not hesitate to play politics and established connections with politicians and influenced them as they found it necessary to their purpose.

The *coup* of October 1953 had been engineered with the implicit support of the East Pakistan United Front leaders. Suhrawardy's party, consisting of 65 per cent of the United Front, had practically promised cooperation. Suhrawardy, however, delayed joining the Cabinet, as he wanted a clear understanding that democratic rule would be restored to East Pakistan and that power would be fairly shared at the centre, but in the end he joined the Cabinet as Minister for Law and Constitutional Affairs in December 1954, without a clear commitment from the centre on either point. The alliance between the central clique, which had risen to power by means of palace intrigue, and the East Pakistan United Front, whose strength lay in their electoral support and democratic processes, was in itself unnatural and could not last long. It survived for as long as it did because it appeared that Suhrawardy was content to play along with the anti-politicians in their creation of a strong centralized govern-

---

[1] Dr Khan Sahib, the brother of Ghaffar Khan, a personal friend of Iskander Mirza, was taken from NWFP and Ghulam Ali Talpur from Sind.

[2] Iskander Mirza, reported in *Dawn*, 31 October 1954.

ment with a unified West Pakistan and as little concession as possible to democratic and federal principles. Occasionally he paid lip service to free elections and democracy, but otherwise was willing to be an instrument of legislation to create their system.

Just at this point, however, when the power of the central executive seemed supreme, events took—superficially at least—a sharp turn. On 27 March 1955 the Governor-General promulgated an 'Emergency Powers Ordinance', assuming powers to make provisions for framing the constitution of Pakistan and to constitute the province of West Pakistan on a specified date, to validate laws which had not received the Governor-General's assent, and to authenticate the central government's annual budget. It was announced that One Unit would come into being by May 1955. The Governor-General had, as one paper commented, 'virtually assumed the powers of an absolute ruler'.[1] In April the Federal Court of Pakistan gave a ruling that the Governor-General's promulgation of the 'Emergency Powers Ordinance' was *ultra vires*, as was also his assumption of powers to make constitutional provisions. For a while the Government was confused as to the method to be used to deal with this complication, but soon found a way round it. It was announced that a constitutional convention would be summoned consisting of sixty members, thirty from East and thirty from West Pakistan. The Convention would sit for six months and would frame a constitution. In deference to a further Federal Court ruling, it was decided that all the members of the Convention would be elected and it would be called a Constituent Assembly. It would appear, therefore, that parliamentary institutions were to be restored. But this was not entirely a genuine restoration. It was at best a device to provide a parliamentary cover for the power of the central clique. At all events, the Constituent Assembly was summoned, members being elected by the already-sitting provincial assemblies, and the work of constitution-making was

[1] *Pakistan Times*, editorial comment, 31 March 1955.

begun again under the leadership of the Law Minister, Mr Suhrawardy.

For some time now the basic incompatibility between Suhrawardy and the central clique had been becoming apparent. Suhrawardy's position was growing increasingly weak as he failed to obtain any significant concessions from the centre in the shape of restoration of democracy in East Pakistan, with an Awami League government in power, or any of the other demands that East Pakistan had put forward. On the other hand, the central government flirted quite openly with Suhrawardy's opponents. His position was further weakened when Fazlul Haque's group obtained a majority of the seats from East Pakistan in the new Constituent Assembly with sixteen members as opposed to the Awami League's twelve.

At this point changes were introduced in the composition of the central government. Ghulam Mohammed, now totally paralyzed and almost completely insane, was removed, and Iskander Mirza became Governor-General. These decisions were taken by the inner clique as usual. A new cabinet was formed, taking into account the new political realities. Bogra, no longer needed, was dropped. Chaudhri Mohammed Ali was chosen leader of the Muslim League party, the largest group in the Assembly, with thirty members out of a total of sixty. He was also able to obtain the support of the Fazlul Haque group. Suhrawardy was thus eliminated. Chaudhri Mohammed Ali formed his government with Fazlul Haque as Minister of the Interior. The basis of the new coalition was reported to be agreement on three points: One Unit in West Pakistan, 'parity of representation' between the two wings of the country in the new constitution, and a distribution of power between the centre and the provinces by majority vote in joint sessions of the parliamentary sections of the government parties.

The second Constituent Assembly met in July 1955. Under the leadership of Chaudhri Mohammed Ali the constitution was completed on 26 February 1956 according to the wishes of the central anti-politician group, with a strong centre and powers shared between the President and the Assembly. Under this constitution Pakistan became a republic on 23 March 1956. Iskander Mirza was elected President by the Constituent Assembly and Fazlul Haque became Governor of East Pakistan.

In spite of all the hurdles crossed, the path still did not prove to be clear for elections and a smooth transfer to a parliamentary democracy. With the inauguration of the Republic and the new constitution, attention had turned towards the elections that were expected to be held shortly; the different parties began to assess their strength and to manoeuvre for the most favourable electoral positions. In view of the political realities in Pakistan, the best chance of winning an election lay with the party that was in power at the time of the election. The struggle between parties and factions to achieve office or, failing that, to find a popular public platform, became fierce as the time for elections drew nearer. In East Pakistan the struggle took the shape of a contest between Fazlul Haque's Krishak Sramik and the Awami League. In West Pakistan the contest was between the Muslim League and a new party sponsored by the central clique, the Republican Party, which had been brought into being by Iskander Mirza, Gurmani, and others in order to keep a better hold on provincial politics.

In an effort to strengthen its position the Muslim League group in the West Pakistan Assembly revolted against Dr Khan Sahib, the Chief Minister nominated by the centre, and demanded a Chief Minister from the Muslim League itself. It looked now as if all the hard-won power of the anti-politicians was being threatened. Ministries changed at the centre and in the provinces, and everyone waited for the elections fixed for early 1959 to settle the issue.

At this stage the most powerful man of the central clique was undoubtedly Iskander Mirza. His overriding concern was to ensure that he would remain in power as President. Without any elected political party or politician with public backing to thwart his designs, he had been able to exercise supreme power. He was afraid that this would not last after the elections, especially if Suhrawardy came in. With his background as a 'political officer' on the Frontier, Iskander Mirza was a past-master at intrigue and divide-and-rule tactics. But he was aware that he was personally unpopular and might be jettisoned by the politicians. All these years he had carefully cultivated a friendship with Ayub Khan, a useful man to know. Mirza tried to get a definite commitment from politicians that they would support him as presidential candidate, but was not satisfied with their promises. He had been playing around with the idea of a *coup* with army backing for some time, and towards the end of September and early October he decided that the time had come.[1] The election date was set and Mirza saw no certain future for himself in a parliamentary democracy with a constitutional President. He carefully encouraged the appearance of instability and chaos in the country and then, taking advantage of the set scene, he and Ayub Khan declared martial law in October 1958.[2]

The promulgation of martial law was the culmination of the centralizing and authoritarian tendencies in Pakistan politics. The forces of decentralization and parliamentary government had been defeated for the time being and the central group of anti-politicians had tried to establish control through constitutional means in the 1956 constitution, but any constitution and parliamentary form of government inevitably meant compromise, checks and balances, and curbs on the power of the central executive. Periodical elections introduced at least some element of uncertainty, and this Iskander Mirza was not able to accept. He took advantage of the predominant position that had been

---

[1] Persistent rumours attributed such a plan to Mirza throughout 1957 and 1958. In July 1958, Ayub Khan informed M. A. Khuhro, the then Defence Minister, that Mirza had suggested to him that he should stage a military coup.

[2] Mirza encouraged the appearance of disintegration and chaos in the country. For instance, he encouraged the Khan of Kalat, ruler of a Baluchistan state, to declare independence. The Khan foolishly believed him and prepared for independence, whereupon, instead of the matter being tackled with tact and diplomacy, troops were ordered into Kalat at the suggestion of Mirza and the Khan was arrested.

acquired by the office of the President as the head of the central executive to exercise supreme power. When he felt uncertain of his re-election, he convinced Ayub Khan that the introduction of martial law was his patriotic duty. Ayub, with his own ambitions, fell in with the plan, and martial law was promulgated.

Now there could no longer be any questioning of central authority. Eventual restoration of democracy was promised— but this would be a 'guided democracy'. As Ayub Khan put it, 'Let me announce in unequivocal terms that our ultimate aim is to restore democracy but of the type that people can understand and work'.[1]

The ascendancy of the central executive meant in practical terms the ascendancy of the Punjab. Ayub Khan himself was a Pathan from the Hazara District adjoining the Punjab. Martial law, however, brought in the mainly Punjab army and civil service as the real rulers of the country. The army, the nominal ruler, had to rely heavily on the civil service, which thus became the real ruler. Mirza lasted as President for about three weeks and was then exiled from the country. After his departure, Ayub Khan took over as head of state. He ruled for ten years with almost dictatorial powers and the army firmly behind him. With his promotion of free enterprise and lavish concessions he was able to win the support of the industrialists. Only two elements in the power structure of Pakistan were potentially hostile, the politicians who were mainly the landowning classes in West Pakistan[2] and the middle class professionals in East Pakistan.

These groups who had been out-manoeuvred were, of course, partly Punjabi. But for the Punjab the blow was softened because, although the landowning class had been deprived of power, the situation was easier for the professional middle classes of the Punjab who had relatives and friends in the civil or

---

[1] Ayub Khan, broadcast to the nation on Radio Pakistan, 8 October 1968.

[2] Nawab Kalabagh was a notable exception. He was Governor of West Pakistan for several years and served Ayub well in crushing all opposition and keeping the province well in hand. In East Pakistan this collaborating part was played by Nomen Khan, a small-town lawyer and minor politician.

military services. Claiming to be a Pathan himself, Ayub Khan made special efforts to win over the Frontier Province by special concessions. Pathans were given jobs in the armed forces and the civil service. Emigration to industrial centres such as Karachi was encouraged and industries were set up in the Frontier Province. As a result, some of the hostility in the Frontier was blunted. But Ayub was not able to win popularity in the rest of the country. East Pakistan, deprived of a voice in decision-making at all levels, could not be reconciled to the regime, no matter what the bribe. Baluchistan was in open rebellion from the early sixties. Sind, the favourite hunting-ground of Ayub, was bitter against One Unit and against Punjabi official tyranny.

The lack of forums where grievances could be aired made for a feeling of great frustration. The ten years of the Ayub regime served to rouse nationalist feelings in the provinces to an unprecedented height. As long as there was a semblance of parliamentary government, grievances could be aired in the assemblies, ministers were available for reassurance, there was always the prospect of the distribution of patronage, and the bureaucratic red tape could sometimes be cut through the intervention of ministers and members of legislative assemblies. All that was now at an end. Newspapers were censored and sycophantic. Officialdom was arrogant and mainly Punjabi. Outside the Punjab all classes of people united in a growing dislike of the regime. Obviously some men were bought over with favours or offices, but these could not make any significant difference to the general antagonism to the regime.

The regime itself was fully aware of the sources from which opposition might be expected.[1] Landowners were, of course, vulnerable to government pressure, relying as they did on allocation of water from irrigation canals and the favour or otherwise of the district officials. But they had long since had a taste of political power. Since the late nineteenth century they had been associated with democratic processes, elections in some

[1] M. Ayub Khan, *Friends, Not Masters*, p. 209, OUP, 1967.

form, and local self-government, which had developed into considerable power under the Act of 1935. It was to be expected that their resentment at being deprived of any share in power would show itself in hostility to the regime. The logical step for the martial law regime was therefore to try to break the political power of the landowners. The instrument used to achieve this was Land Reform. Appropriately enough, Land Reform was the first item on Ayub's list and a Land Reforms Commission was set up on 31 October 1958. In fact, the land reforms were unable to accomplish their purpose fully and were a failure as far as the object of creating an independent landed middle class was concerned. The biggest landholdings were broken up, but the ceiling of 500 acres encouraged many landowners to adopt modern methods of cultivation and thus created a class of progressive landowners in West Pakistan. At the same time, Ayub tried to reconcile East and West Pakistani politicians by a mixture of coercion and flattery.

In 1959, Ayub Khan inaugurated the system of 'Basic Democracies' which was to be another device to curtail the political power of the landowning class. Basic Democracies were local village councils empowered to organize sanitation, local road-building, etc. The real aim of setting up the councils was to allow the peasantry and the small farmer to take over some of the functions of the local large landowner and form a centre of authority independent of him. In East Pakistan also the Basic Democracies served to create certain vested interests which would support the Ayub regime.

In theory, Ayub could have ruled indefinitely with the support of the army and the civil service. But although it might be possible to rule West Pakistan in this fashion, it was impossible to rule East Pakistan for very long under a regime regarded as one of West Pakistan imperialism.

Ayub himself wanted to widen the basis of his support. He had experienced popular acclaim in the early days of martial law and this had given him a taste for popularity. But he could not long retain popularity as a martial law administrator, and had to appear to restore people's rights. Hence the necessity for a constitution. There was also pressure from outside, especially from the United States, which was providing economic and military aid and did not want to appear to be supporting a military regime indefinitely. In March 1962, therefore, Ayub announced a new constitution which he described as 'a blending of democracy with discipline—the two prerequisites to running a free society with stable government and sound administration'.[1]

The 1962 Constitution, which introduced the Presidential system, was carefully worked out to make the electorate as amenable as possible to government wishes. The National Assembly was to be elected by an elaborate process of indirect elections. Thus, 80,000 locally elected Basic Democrats were to act as an electoral college for the provincial assemblies, the National Assembly and the Presidency.

The restriction of the franchise to 80,000 voters in a population of over 100,000,000 was obviously meant to make the electorate manageable. It would be responsive to pressure in West Pakistan and easily corrupted in East Pakistan.

The provincial and national assemblies had powers of legislation, but the President retained powers of revision and veto. The Assembly could discuss the Budget, but did not have the power to reject it. Ministers were appointed by the President and were responsible to him and not to the National Assembly. Critics of the new constitution claimed that it had the appearance, but not the reality, of democracy.

Ayub Khan tried for a while to run the National Assembly without any political parties, but it became obvious that party discipline was necessary to make the Assembly function properly. Ayub toyed with the idea of a single-party state, but finally decided to allow free organization of political parties. He revived the Muslim League as a vehicle for himself and was able to get a

---

[1] Ayub Khan, broadcast on Radio Pakistan, 1 March 1962.

substantial membership for the party in West Pakistan.[1] He had already taken the precaution of disqualifying from political life all those politicians who could possibly form an effective opposition[2] and, if powerless to do more, would be a considerable nuisance within the Assembly. He had thus only to deal with second-rank men. Elections were held under the new constitution in 1964 and 1965 and proved a shock for the President. Elections were held for both the provincial and national assemblies. The Government obtained majorities in the national as well as the provincial assemblies, but important politicians not under EBDO were returned, forming a small, but formidable, opposition, especially in the National Assembly. The biggest shock for Ayub was, however, in his own election. So far he had firmly believed in his own popularity among the masses and was convinced that they regarded him as their saviour. The extent of the opposition and the bitterness of the campaign against him proved a traumatic experience he never forgot or forgave.

The opposition parties hurriedly pulled themselves together and combined to fight the elections. The Combined Opposition Parties (or COP) persuaded Miss Jinnah, the sister of Mr M. A. Jinnah, to be their candidate for the presidency. In Miss Jinnah they had a national figure who had consistently opposed the authoritarian regime of Ayub and had issued outspoken statements demanding a return to democracy. Her dedication was undoubted and her popularity nationwide. Such was the power of her appeal and her suitability for candidature that even the Jamaate Islami, the orthodox Muslim party which was on principle opposed to a woman as head of state, accepted her and issued a *Fatwa*[3] to say that under exceptional circumstances it was permissible to elect a woman.

The election campaign became an opportunity for the airing

---

[1] Ayub Khan, *op. cit.*, p. 232.

[2] Important politicians were disqualified under EBDO (Elective Bodies (Disqualification) Ordinance) of 1959.

[3] *Fatwa*—a decision on matters of religious importance by a body of men competent to give such a decision, i.e. a body of Ulema.

of grievances and pent-up frustrations. Miss Jinnah attracted huge crowds wherever she went, the press gave her great coverage,[1] and for a time it looked as if free political activity had returned to the country. Politicians campaigned vigorously and were able to arouse considerable enthusiasm.

But this upsurge alarmed Ayub Khan. Huge amounts were taken as subscriptions from industrialists to help his campaign. Efforts were made to bring the press in line, though this could not be done satisfactorily until after the elections. As the elections drew nearer and the tension grew greater, the Government grew increasingly uneasy at the possibility of an adverse vote. Money was used freely to bribe Basic Democrats, especially in East Pakistan. Mr Z. A. Bhutto, the Foreign Minister, was sent to East Pakistan where Maulana Bhashani was 'persuaded' to withdraw support from Miss Jinnah. Official pressure was brought to bear on the landowners of West Pakistan.[2] As a final threat it was rumoured that if the vote went against Ayub Khan, martial law would be reimposed. As elections were taking place, the army took up positions in the major towns where the opposition was expected to make the greatest gains. In fact, the election victory of Ayub Khan was never in any doubt. The restricted franchise of 80,000 voters made it very easy for the Government to manage the electoral college with a mixture of bribery and coercion—most of the former in the East, and most of the latter in the West.

The astonishing thing about the elections was, first, the enthusiasm of the opposition, which knew from the beginning that it was fighting for a lost cause. Secondly, the fact that Miss Jinnah was able to carry both Karachi and Dacca and a substantial number of votes in Lahore and in Sind. This was in spite of the fact that her electoral platform was avowedly the abolition of the Basic Democracies system and the restoration of a universal

---

[1] Ayub notes this in his book—with some bitterness. Ayub Khan, *op. cit.*, pp. 235–6.
[2] These facts were revealed in the press after the fall of Ayub, though they were an open secret in Pakistan before then.

adult franchise and the parliamentary system. The wonder was that Miss Jinnah got as many votes as she did in a system built for Ayub's victory. The opposition to Ayub as revealed in the 1964–5 elections came from various sections of Pakistan society. The refugee population of Karachi and Sind was solidly behind Miss Jinnah, and this meant most of the professional middle classes outside the Punjab—and some even in the Punjab—the old politicians' class and the rural areas still under their influence and the whole anti-one-unit population of West Pakistan. In East Pakistan the ex-politicians, which meant most of the middle class, the lawyers, and what may be loosely termed the intelligentsia, were against Ayub. This basic opposition to Ayub had gaps. There were those like Bhashani who were won over and the Basic Democrats who had a vested interest in the continuation of the Ayub regime.

Shocked and disillusioned by the extent of the hostility to him in the country, Ayub took certain actions and adopted certain policies which led to his ultimate downfall in March 1969.

There is a school of thought which feels that Ayub could not retain power because he was too 'soft'. This claim may be true. It is possible that if he had been more ruthless, less concerned with popularity, more open in his use of coercion and an outright military dictator, he could have ruled Pakistan indefinitely. This is, however, in the realm of speculation and one must concern oneself with what actually happened.

Ayub emerged from the 1965 elections firmly convinced that he had won because of the devoted work of the civil service. There was, of course, the army in the background and the Nawab of Kalabagh, the Governor of West Pakistan, who was unequalled in his election management methods, but it was the solid support of the civil service that had ensured victory in most districts. The Muslim League party, which had been assembled under his leadership, had proved ineffective as a vote-catching or popularizing organization. This conviction determined Ayub Khan's thinking from 1965 onwards. He came increasingly to

REFORM AND REVOLUTION IN ASIA

rely on the advice of the civil service and to regard the Muslim League as merely a vehicle for discipline of the members of national and provincial assemblies. Ministers of his cabinet were a mixture of non-officials and ex-officials, but with one or two exceptions they were mere ciphers,[1] with very little voice in policy-making, and were meant merely to be public relations officers for the Government. Ayub rendered the Muslim League utterly powerless and without influence by leaving all the patronage in the hands of state officials and treating the members of his party with more or less open contempt. He thus cut off a channel of contact with public opinion in the country.

Another possible channel of contact between the Government and the people was the press. At the time of the elections the press had had almost complete freedom and, although it had not dared to criticize the regime directly, it had given full coverage to opposition speeches and campaigns. Immediately after the election, however, the Government put an effective stop to all overt and covert criticism of its policy in the press. A National Press Trust was created, which bought a number of independent newspapers and turned them into government papers.[2] Censorship was imposed for a while and was later removed only in return for sureties to be provided by all newspapers. A deliberate attempt was made to cultivate a personality cult for Ayub Khan, and Ayub Khan's autobiography was to be written. A major campaign was undertaken to 'sell' Ayub Khan to the country according to the latest advertising methods of western countries. This was officialdom's answer to the opposition that had shown itself during the election, and Ayub Khan fell in readily with the programme.

In September 1965, the short Indo-Pakistan war broke out

[1] The Nawab of Kalabagh, Governor of West Pakistan, when confronted with a dispute between a Minister and Secretary of a department, informed the Minister that his function was only that of a post box between the Secretary and the Governor (or President).

[2] The owner of the *Pakistan Times*, an independent socialist newspaper, was forced to sell the newspaper, which was first bought by an industrialist and later by the Press Trust.

following Pakistani action in Kashmir. There can be no doubt that an important consideration that sent Ayub into this venture was a desire to win permanent fame and popularity in Pakistan's history as the Liberator of Kashmir. When seen against the essential moderation of his nature and actions so far, this action shows clearly the extent of Ayub's desperation and disillusionment after the elections. That Ayub was not normally a trigger-happy general is proved by his restraint during the Indo-Chinese war of 1962.

The war was ended with the Tashkent Declaration, which was by any calculation a remarkable diplomatic achievement. But the reaction in Pakistan was utterly hostile and indignant. Ayub's all-too-effective propaganda machine had led the country to believe that it was on the eve of a brilliant victory and now it felt that by the Tashkent agreement it had been deprived of this victory. The people of Pakistan had been united during the war as never before except during the original struggle for independence. Now they were to be robbed of the triumph they had been told was theirs. All the disillusion and disappointment rebounded on Ayub Khan's head. This time it was the Punjab that was the most bitter and most disappointed. The armed forces blamed Ayub for their own shortcomings—the Punjab had suffered most during the war and its people now blamed Ayub for their vain sacrifice. East Pakistan realized, as it had never done hitherto, how vulnerable it was to Indian attack, and indeed, had it not been for China, surely they would have been attacked and overrun.

Ayub had sown the wind and now he was to reap the whirlwind. From the end of the 1965 war the tensions in the country grew rapidly. Luck, which had held so long for Ayub, seemed now to have deserted him. Throughout 1966 and 1967 it became gradually apparent that his government had lost confidence in itself. Ayub's most trusted men were dismissed. First to go was Bhutto, the Foreign Minister, sacrificed after the fiasco of the war, soon to be followed by the supremely useful Nawab of

Kalabagh. The new Governor of West Pakistan was the former Commander-in-Chief, Musa, a competent, if not inspired, military officer, but a thoroughly inept choice for the difficult post of Governor. In early 1968, Ayub Khan fell ill, and was cut off from public affairs for several months. During this period administration was in the hands of a group of favourite civil servants who ran the day-to-day administration, but were unable to take any major policy decisions. Unrest in the country grew and was exacerbated by the celebration of the tenth anniversary of the military takeover as the beginning of the 'Decade of Reforms', which was regarded by most people as adding insult to injury, in the midst of rising prices and artificial shortages created by profiteers. At this point the Ayub regime made some completely miscalculated moves. A conspiracy case was instituted against Mujibur Rahman, the East Pakistani leader, who was already in jail, and a number of minor civil servants and others. This case was widely believed to be false and united East Pakistan behind Mujibur Rahman.

Meanwhile in West Pakistan the government was making clumsy attempts to frame charges of corruption against Mr Bhutto, the former Foreign Minister. The well-publicized plans to arrest him forced Mr Bhutto to preempt the government by courting arrest on political grounds. About this time the retired Air Vice-Marshal Asghar Khan, the hero of the 1965 war, who had retired from the air force, took an openly anti-government stand by writing articles and making speeches and helped to create an atmosphere hostile to the government. The public mood was now such that any incident could set off an explosion, and this incident was provided by a minor clash between students and the police near Rawalpindi. Some students were held for allegedly bringing smuggled goods from the Pakistan-Afghanistan border. The students resisted the police efforts to stop them and there was a clash. With this incident the whole carefully woven fabric of Ayub's power was torn apart. There were countrywide demonstrations and strikes and months of riots.

Ayub hesitated, undecided and irresolute. He called in various politicians for consultation, and summoned a Round Table Conference to decide on constitutional changes, but failed to find complete agreement. He consulted the heads of the armed forces on the possibility of abrogating the constitution and ruling with the help of the armed forces. The service chiefs made it clear, however, that if the constitutional rule was to go, Ayub would have to go with it. They were fully aware of Ayub's personal unpopularity and were not willing to accept the liability of his presence in a new martial law regime. After weeks of hesitation Ayub finally resigned on 25 March 1969, and handed the government over to the Commander-in-Chief, General Yahya Khan. Under him martial law was established in the country for the second time.

On taking over the administration of the country, Yahya Khan made certain commitments to the public on behalf of his government. He described the martial law regime as a 'caretaker' regime until a constitutional government was ready to take over. Elections were to be held on the basis of universal adult franchise as soon as arrangements could be completed. A constituent assembly would be elected to frame a new constitution for the country. The new assembly would be allowed 120 days to complete its task. If it failed to do so, it would be dissolved. The President would then present a constitution to the nation for referendum. If the referendum was favourable, fresh elections would be held and democratic rule would be restored. Meanwhile, as public opinion had clearly expressed itself against the One Unit, the President decided that it should be dissolved and the former provinces of West Pakistan be restored by July 1970. This action served to de-fuse one of the hottest political issues in West Pakistan.

Elections were held in December 1970 to both the Constituent Assembly and the provincial legislatures. In East Pakistan, as expected, the Awami League under Shaikh Mujib-u-Rahman, with its platform of maximum autonomy as articulated in the

221

'six points', won an overwhelming majority. In West Pakistan it had been expected that most of the seats would go to the established political party, the Muslim League, which had now split into three main groups. The parties of the 'Right' (notably the Jamaate Islami) and of the 'Left' (i.e. the People's Party of Pakistan led by Z. A. Bhutto, the Foreign Minister in Ayub's cabinet, which had a Left stance), were expected to get a few seats each. The actual results astonished the victors and the vanquished alike. The majority of seats was won by the People's Party, showing that not only had certain social changes occurred in West Pakistan but that the people generally had a growing political awareness and a desire for material betterment. The People's Party had won on its slogan of '*Roti Kapra aur makan*' (Bread, clothing and homes for everyone).

Before any economic reforms could be tried, however, the constitution had to be framed. Here, on the issue of the distribution of powers between the centre and the provinces, there appeared to be a cleavage of attitudes between the two majority parties: the Awami League demanded complete autonomy for the provinces and an 'emasculated' centre, while the People's Party, with its main strength in the Punjab, wanted a fairly strong centre. This polarization of attitudes might have been avoided if any political party had emerged with substantial support from both East and West Pakistan, but it was difficult to escape it with two parties as unbending as the People's Party and the Awami League.

Even at this stage compromise did not appear to be out of reach if the parties could actually meet as a constituent assembly and if an interim government could be formed by the majority party, the Awami League, in coalition with the smaller parties of West Pakistan. The Pakistan People's Party could, in accordance with democratic usage, have formed the Opposition party within the Assembly. Mr Bhutto, the PPP leader, however, refused to be left out of any proposed government and threatened to boycott the National Assembly. The extreme attitude adopted by Mr Bhutto forced the Awami League leader, Shaikh Mujib-u-Rahman, into an intransigent attitude to satisfy public opinion in Bengal. The threat he used was that of separation and independence of East Pakistan unless his conditions were met. At this stage, President Yahya Khan announced the breakdown of talks between himself and the Awami League. He declared Shaikh Mujib-u-Rahman a traitor and outlawed the Awami League. Full martial law was declared once more and all political activity was banned until the situation had returned to 'normal'.

For the time being, therefore, the prospect of a democratic government in Pakistan appeared to be at an end. Why, then, this sudden collapse of what looked like the most promising situation for over a decade? The answer could be the obvious one that the military regime baulked when faced with the prospect of actually handing over power to an uncompromising popular government with support from East Pakistan and the smaller provinces of West Pakistan. Such a government would not hesitate to introduce changes and modifications in the existing arrangements for defence and the civil services. The Awami League leadership had made no secret of its plans. In its actions the army was supported by the PPP with its main strength in the Punjab, the province of the 'haves'.

By using military force to crush political leadership and aspirations of East Pakistan martial law authorities hoped to ensure army dominance and therefore the dominance of the élite which had ruled Pakistan for so long. They had made careful preparations for a short and powerful blow which would achieve their object. In this however they had miscalculated. Military operations had to be prolonged and a guerrilla movement, with aid and comfort from India, sprang up in the country. The scene of destruction looked as if it could continue indefinitely when India decided to intervene. For India East Pakistan posed several problems: the immediate one was the presence of several million refugees on her soil and the other obvious one was the growth of a guerrilla army within the borders of her problem province of West Bengal. The decision to intervene, although fraught with dangerous possibilities, appeared to be the most feasible one at the time. A friendly and grateful Bangladesh ruled by a middle class Awami League would be a masterstroke for her domestic and foreign policies. Consequently towards the end of November 1971, India started an invasion of East Pakistan. War between India and Pakistan widened with Pakistan's air strikes in the west on 3 December and a fortnight later ended with the surrender of the Pakistan army in East Pakistan on 16 December and a ceasefire on the western front on 17 December.

With the birth of Bangladesh Pakistan as conceived and established on 14 August 1947 was finished. The urge for power and dominance of an elite group, 'the anti politicians', had been too strong to be moderated by any considerations for justice and allow the sharing of that power—a condition necessary for the survival of the unique idea of Pakistan as an Islamic nation state in South Asia. The future of the western part of Pakistan now has a question mark against it. Have the anti-politicians of the Punjab learnt anything from their mistakes and will they allow a genuine partnership to grow between the various components of the country? Otherwise, and as is more probable, West Pakistan can survive as an authoritarian state for a time, to dissolve in due course in another bloody struggle to become part of some new pattern of states in the subcontinent of South Asia.

CHAPTER VIII

INDONESIA SINCE INDEPENDENCE

L. PALMIER

Revolution

With the Declaration of Independence on 17 August 1945, at the end of the Japanese occupation of their country, Indonesian nationalists began a four-year-long struggle against the reimposition of Dutch rule. To this external threat were added internal challenges; the new establishment's survival says much for its Japanese nurture. For though the Asian conquerors stayed in Indonesia only some three and a half years, the Indonesian political body they left behind was very different from the one lost by the Dutch in 1942.

In the third decade of this century, in a febrile attempt to keep their colony when all other Western powers in South and South-East Asia were gradually abandoning theirs, the Dutch strengthened the position of the traditional rulers in the islands (those on Java having been incorporated into a Local Government Service), on the assumption that their customary hold on the people would ensure a continuance of the colonial dispensation. Secular nationalists, their activities limited to the urban population, were rendered impotent by legislation, police surveillance, detention and exile. Religious leaders, though they avoided political activity, were carefully watched; their influence in the countryside was too strong to be ignored. Lastly, but perhaps most important, the Netherlands Indies' Army was officered largely by Dutchmen and manned by a small minority group, the Ambonese, who were Christians and thus set apart from most Indonesians.

The Japanese were at heart no less colonialist, and perhaps

more ethnically arrogant, than the Dutch, and at the inception of their rule maintained a distant attitude towards the secular nationalists, while encouraging their rivals, the religious leaders. Late in 1943 they created a federation of Islamic organizations called the Masjumi, and gave its leaders official positions, while permitting them to develop a military arm.

At first the conquerors strengthened the traditional rulers. Many were promoted to more senior positions (though, unlike the Dutch, Japanese were not to be found working under Indonesians). This was part of a policy of weakening the secular nationalists, adopted when the Japanese thought to colonize the Indies. It was abandoned, and indeed reversed, when they concluded that an Allied invasion was possible. Increasingly they gave the nationalists prominence, permitting their most important leader, Sukarno, to deliver speeches of a nationalist character and, for the first time, to address audiences in the countryside. When defeat became imminent, the authorities prepared to transfer power to the nationalists, represented by Sukarno from Java and Hatta from Sumatra. The traditional rulers had been eclipsed.

These three members of the body politic—the Muslim organizations, the traditional rulers, and the nationalists—had in a sense only been remodelled by the Japanese, whose new creation was, without doubt, the Indonesian Army. Its foundations were laid in September 1943, when the Peta or 'Volunteer Army' was established. This was no disinterested gesture. Though Indonesian-officered, it was Japanese-trained, with the object of defending the country against the expected Allied invasion. Already by mid-1945 it numbered some 120,000 men.

What the leaders of all these four social bodies had in common was that they owed their positions to the occupying power, no matter what were the latter's motives. Not surprisingly, therefore, Sukarno and Hatta not only had no objection to receiving their independence from the Japanese, who promised it for 24 August 1945, but resisted great pressure, even including kidnapping, by the anti-Japanese underground to declare independence without waiting for official sanction. Only the intimation by the authorities that the terms of their surrender to the Allies precluded a transfer of power eventually decided the two leaders to make the declaration of independence on their own.

The underground mentioned included principally two organizations: a social-democratic grouping led by Sutan Sjahrir, and a Dutch-financed Communist organization with Amir Sjarifuddin at its head. Neither of these groups achieved much; the Japanese secret police were too efficient. The underground's attempt to force a declaration of independence showed their perception that if the new Indonesian State were to be delivered by the Japanese, their own claims to inclusion in the establishment would lack validity, and their underground efforts would appear only as hindrances to independence. In the event, though they obtained the symbol they wanted, a unilateral declaration of independence, the internal substance eluded them. The influence of neither the democratic socialists nor the Stalinists was deep or lasting.

Until 1948, Sjahrir and Sjarifuddin worked together (the latter had not then revealed his long-standing Stalinist allegiance), and, arguing that the Western powers, in whose orbit Indonesia would in any case remain, would be unwilling to support the independence of a transparently Japanese-created state, sought to have themselves accepted into the establishment. Though they achieved some success at first, and compelled Sukarno to abandon a Presidential Cabinet for a Parliamentary one, the obduracy of the Dutch and pusillanimous attitude of other Western states cut the ground from under their feet.

No more successful was the group round Tan Malaka, a Comintern agent in the 1920s, who had broken with Stalin and founded his own Leninist party. His attempt to wrest leadership from Sukarno in 1946 was suppressed without difficulty. Another challenge was met in 1948, when Musso, a Stalinist who had been resident in Moscow since the failure of a feeble PKI (Communist Party of Indonesia) revolt in 1926, returned breathing fire, was joined by Sjarifuddin, and was caught up with him in a revolt ignited before due time. The body politic rallied behind Sukarno, and both Musso and Sjarifuddin perished.

Meanwhile, of course, the Dutch were exerting themselves to regain mastery over their former subjects. Having limited the Republic to Java and part of Sumatra, they then set up a number of puppet states to cover the remainder of the archipelago, as well as mounting two 'Police Actions', in July 1947 and December 1948, which progressively reduced the area under Republican control. The latter indeed captured the Indonesian Cabinet as well as President Sukarno and Vice-President Hatta. But the Indonesian Army wisely avoided direct fighting and restricted itself to guerrilla tactics, making Dutch control both uncertain and unprofitable. The United Nations Security Council condemned the Dutch attack, and for fear that in the chaotic conditions obtaining in the Republic the leadership would be seized by Tan Malaka's followers or the Stalinists, the United States threatened to cut off Marshall Aid from the war-devastated Netherlands if the Dutch did not recognize Indonesian independence; they complied. However, they insisted on retaining Western New Guinea (Irian Barat in Indonesian); the Republican negotiators, fearing that an extension of the struggle might consolidate the Dutch-created states on the one hand, while encouraging the extremists in the Republic on the other, agreed without demur. Paradoxically, it was the negotiators from those same states who objected to the Dutch retention, which was to cause considerable trouble in the future. But their doubts were not allowed to hinder the negotiations, and on 27 December 1949 the Netherlands surrendered sovereignty over the whole territory of her former Indies, always with the exception of Western New Guinea.

Oligarchy

The new sovereign United States of Indonesia was made up of the Republic and the Dutch-created states. This federal constitution was one possible answer to the question which has continually bedevilled Indonesia's politics, namely the distribution of power between its peoples; in practical terms, this means between the Javanese and the others. The former, whose homelands are Central and East Java, are the largest single ethnic group, though just in a minority in the population as a whole. They are also the most evolved of the Indonesian peoples, in the sense of having the most complex culture and the highest standard of education. Accordingly, they almost monopolize the state services. (They are less noted for creativity and leadership; contributions in these fields have been made predominantly by the Batak and Minangkabau, both in Sumatra.) Unfortunately, however, the Javanese homelands are permanently depressed areas, and do not produce enough even to feed the Javanese; the shortage has to be met by the proceeds of the exports produced by the other Indonesian peoples.

Clearly, then, political stability requires that an accommodation be reached between the educated, but poor, Javanese, and the more productive, if less advanced, other peoples of Indonesia. The federal constitution offered one possible point of balance (which is not to say that the Dutch states were created with these considerations in mind). However, it was not a solution that the Javanese were prepared to accept. Not only did it mean that they were compelled to share power, but the establishment of 'states' carried the risk that one or more of the component peoples might secede; indeed the Ambonese tried to do so. The Javanese were well aware that the enthusiasm for their Republic was somewhat muted outside their homelands; the Dutch had not found it difficult to recruit participants for the states they had set up. If matters went far enough, the Javanese might be left with an indigent rump state limited to their own people. This danger they were determined to avoid. Accordingly, adroitly using the federal constitution's Dutch authorship to condemn it (one should perhaps mention that, in contrast, the Indonesian legal system remains basically Dutch to this day),

229

Sukarno and his followers, the guardians of the Javanese interest, applied a variety of pressures, including the naval bombardment of Amboina, to impose a unitary constitution over the whole territory of the new state, and on 15 August 1950 the country became known as the Republic of Indonesia. In effect, the original Javanese Republic had expanded to cover the whole of the previous Netherlands Indies, always excluding Western New Guinea.

The dismantling of the federal constitution, however, made the situation even more unstable. Now those who provided the resources for government were excluded from power (even, be it noted, in their own areas); this was held almost exclusively by those who disposed of the resources. The new unitary constitution, by including provisions for decentralization, held out hopes that a better balance of power would be sought; but to the present day, despite much pressure from the non-Javanese peoples, nothing of significance has been done. The natural consequence, implicit in the constitution, which was not only unitary but also highly centralized, was that the majority of Indonesian peoples have been exploited for the benefit of the Javanese.[1]

As in many other, even very rich,[2] countries of the world, Indonesian social bonds are mainly of an ethnic character, and are of course reflected in political associations. In the unitary state, as in the previous Republic, the pillars of the establishment were the secular nationalist PNI (Partai Nasional Indonesia) and the Masjumi. The PSI, Sjahrir's Socialist Party, was fading into impotence; the PKI (Communists) had not yet recovered from its abortive 1948 revolt. However, the expansion of Republican control over the whole of Indonesia had brought about a radical change in the nature of the support for these parties, and con-

---

[1] Paauw, D. W., in McVey, *Indonesia*, 1963, p. 169, 170.
[2] Cf. *Violence in America: Historical and Comparative Perspectives*, a report by the U.S. National Commission on the Causes and Prevention of Violence, 1970.

sequently in the balance between them. The PNI remained the party of government officials, limited to the island of Java (including the Sundanese in the west). On the other hand, the Masjumi, as ever a federation of Muslim organizations, derived its support from all the Indonesian peoples, and no longer represented mainly Javanese interests. These were embodied in one of the Masjumi's most important constituents, the Nahdatul Ulama, or Muslim Scholars, which represented the orthodox (i.e. not Modernist) religious teachers of Central and East Java.

That it was an Islamic, and not a secular, party which appealed to the non-Javanese peoples of Indonesia is perhaps understandable. Just as Islam had been the banner under which had fought many who, at different times and places and for different reasons, had resisted colonial rule, so also it now seemed to perform the same function for the peoples of Indonesia who objected to the Javanese dispensation. This trend had already begun in 1948, when the Darul Islam (Home of Islam) movement struck firm root among the Sundanese of West Java and began a struggle against the Republic which was to last many years. Its purported aim, and that of similar movements which sprang up among several other peoples later, was an Islamic state. But this is to be read as meaning, primarily, a state in which the Javanese would not be dominant; it did not mean one in which the Javanese Nahdatul Ulama, however Muslim, would have the key role.

From the start, it was obvious that government by consent in the unitary state would depend on an accommodation between the Javanese and the other peoples. In the political field, this meant between the PNI and the Masjumi, and, at the head of the state, between Sukarno, who drew his support mainly from the Javanese, and Hatta, who originated from the Minangkabau people of Central Sumatra and was regarded by the non-Javanese as a guardian of their interests.

The struggle against the re-imposition of Dutch rule had repressed any differences that arose within the establishment.

With the external threat removed, the main protagonists began to fall out with one another, their animosities exacerbated by preparations for the country's first parliamentary elections. The PNI in particular looked forward to them with foreboding; it could not hope to rival the Masjumi's organizations with their committed membership across the archipelago. President Sukarno, too, whose popularity outside Java was not unlimited, knew that he had no future in the Islamic state to which the Masjumi was committed, nor could he accept loss of control by the Javanese establishment of which he was the head. This is not to say that self-interest was the sole motive of the Javanese and their representatives, such as Sukarno and the PNI. Undoubtedly, there was also an implicit faith in nationalism, the nation being defined as synonymous with the inhabitants of the previous Dutch colony, and a consequent determination to keep Indonesia whole, if not united. It is also clear that the Javanese leaders generally considered the other peoples too backward and too divided to take an effective part in government, as well as suspect because of their support for the Dutch-created states. They therefore felt that it was in the best interests of the country for them to retain their dominant position.

Thus one had on the one side a single, determined people, who had fought and won independence and who were in no mood, even had their circumstances been less desperate, to share power; on the other several peoples, resentful of the fact that they had little say in the disposal of the resources they created, but divided among themselves by mutual animosities at least as great as their dislike of the Javanese. The outcome was foreseeable.

Shadows of coming trouble were already cast in 1952. From the beginning, Sukarno had set his face against the Masjumi. and, through his influence with the PNI, intrigued against it. In that year the Nahdatul Ulama, already known for corruption, was lured by the promise of Cabinet posts to withdraw from the Masjumi. This halved the latter's popular support, and excluded it from influence over the Javanese; by the same token it sharpened the division between them and the other peoples, so that there was now no party which could claim to represent both.

Equally ominous were the events set in train by a Ministry of Defence proposal to reduce the hypertrophic army by disbanding its less efficient members. Many of them would have been the Javanese ex-guerrillas supporting Sukarno, and he saw the plan as an attempt by members of Sjahrir's Socialist Party, several of them from Sumatra, who held senior positions at the Ministry, to weaken his influence. He arranged for his supporters in Parliament to oppose the measure, but in reply senior officers, the most prominent being Colonel (as he then was) Nasution, organized a 'popular' demonstration in Djakarta on 17 October of that year, demanding that Parliament be dismissed and elections held, while training field guns on the Presidential Palace. Sukarno bluffed the demonstrators into waiting until he had ascertained the wishes of the people outside Djakarta; with the time gained he intrigued in the Army itself so as to upset a number of regional commanders opposed to him and so re-established the position.

The importance of the 17 October Affair, as it came to be called, lay in its consequences for the attitudes of both the Army Command and the President. The former acquired the conviction, reinforced by increasing government incompetence, that the parliamentary form of constitution was enfeebling its professional capacity, and should be replaced. The Army's conception by the Japanese out of the occupation should perhaps not be forgotten. Sukarno, for his part, attempted to insure against a repetition of the Affair by intriguing within the Armed Forces to place his supporters in critical positions. But also he sought to foster an organization which would rival the Army in both its discipline and its popular ramifications.

As it happened, the PKI was now willing and able to play the required role. Its new leader, Dipa Nusantara Aidit, had escaped detention at the time of the 1948 revolt and had travelled in Communist China and North Vietnam, returning to Indonesia in 1950. He took over the leadership of the party in the following year, and in 1952 reversed its previous policy and declared his loyalty to Sukarno. The President was not slow in appreciating the advantages of encouraging the growth of the PKI. He was not, however, the only one; the PNI also, fearing electoral doom, saw profit in cooperation with the Communists against the Masjumi. Between them Sukarno and the leaders of the PNI ensured that government officials did not obstruct the PKI's expansion in the countryside; despite this, however, its appeal remained virtually limited to the Javanese.

The result of these manoevures was seen in the Cabinet that took office in August 1953, led by Ali Sastroamidjojo. It was based on the PNI, included the Nahdatul Ulama, was supported by Sukarno and the PKI, and excluded the Masjumi. Javanese domination of government was now obvious, and painful, to the other peoples. The Atjehnese, a people of North Sumatra long known for their independent, even rebellious, character, rose in revolt early in the Cabinet's life, using Darul Islam as their rallying cry, and were pacified after long months only when the government accepted a limitation on its powers in their territory. This did not deter the Cabinet from greater administrative centralization than ever before, while favouring Djakarta specifically and Java generally in public expenditure. Its most extravagant gesture was the holding of the Asian-African Conference at Bandung in West Java. This too was a straw in the wind; the country was to know many other exotic spectaculars provided to distract attention from internal problems.

The Cabinet devoted its considerable powers of patronage to buy political support for itself, and to weaken that of the Masjumi; elections had been appointed for 1955. Despite its notoriety, therefore, it enjoyed the support of both the President and the PKI, and remained in office for two years, longer than any of its predecessors. Sukarno also used it to build up a personal following among the military, and it was precisely when one of his men, the Defence Minister, attempted to force a Chief of Staff on the Army that the Cabinet finally rotted away. Its electoral work, however, lived after it, and the results of the 1955 elections gave the PNI alone more votes than the Masjumi, while the PKI emerged as a considerable force, so that the three Javanese parties (PNI, Nahdatul Ulama, and PKI) together were in a considerable majority over the Masjumi. Whereas 86 per cent of the Javanese votes had been cast for the PNI, Nahdatul Ulama, and PKI (the Masjumi picking up most of the remainder), the other peoples had spread their votes among several parties (not excluding those favoured by the Javanese), though the Masjumi emerged as the only one they strongly supported.

Using the contrived election results as an argument, Sukarno now moved a step further in his strategy. He demanded that the third Javanese party, the PKI, as one of the four largest, be included in the Cabinet. He met with a refusal; even the PNI saw the PKI as a good servant but a bad friend. But this was the only point on which the non-Communist parties agreed; their distrust of one another prevented effective government. Patronage and corruption continued on a large scale, while the inflation, never altogether absent since 1942, began to run out of control. All this of course was grist to the mill for the PKI, which tried to direct popular discontent against the Masjumi. It correctly saw that party as its most formidable opponent.

While the government in Djakarta were favouring their close friends, they neglected the more distant non-Javanese peoples, and also refused to delegate sufficient powers to permit them to improve matters. Conditions had consequently worsened to the point that, for example, wheeled traffic was no longer possible on the roads in certain rubber-growing areas of Sumatra. Nor was it only the civilian population that suffered; military units in the other islands (usually drawn from the people among whom they were garrisoned) found themselves without money to pay their men or rice to feed them. Naturally enough, by mid-1956 regional commanders were financing their units, as well as helping to develop their territories, by selling copra and rubber direct to Singapore and the Philippines.

The Javanese leaders, of course, had no intention of permitting this *de facto* decentralization to continue, and their attitude put a stop to any movement towards democracy. If the demands of the non-Javanese were to be successfully resisted, popular representation would have to go. Sukarno in particular had never liked the parliamentary form of government forced on him by Sjahrir in 1945; he now seized his opportunity to scuttle it. On his return from a tour of the United States, Western Europe, the Soviet Union, Eastern Europe and China, he used the Chinese example to advocate the abolition of political parties and the adoption of a 'guided democracy'; he was too modest to name the guide. Hatta thereupon resigned his office of Vice-President on 1 December 1956. His going was a clear sign to the non-Javanese peoples that their interests were no longer considered at the centre. Later that month joint military and civilian councils took over North, Central and South Sumatra, announcing that they no longer recognized the Cabinet in Djakarta. (However, a counter-*coup* supported by Javanese estate workers reversed the situation in North Sumatra.)

These developments placed the Masjumi in an impossible situation. The elections had cast it, more than ever before, in the role of representative of the non-Javanese, but it held a minor role in the Cabinet, and was therefore unable to improve the conditions of its supporters. It had been under great pressure for some time to go into opposition; the Sumatran revolts settled the matter, and on 9 January 1957 the Masjumi withdrew from the Cabinet, which now represented only the Javanese.

Sukarno's *riposte* was to propose once again a Cabinet which would include all the major groups in Parliament, including the PKI. In addition there would be a National Council, which would include representation from every section of the Indonesian people—occupational, religious, social, cultural, as well as the chiefs of the Armed Forces and of the Police, the Attorney

General, and the most important government ministers. Sukarno would be chairman, and its task would be to supply the Cabinet with 'advice', wanted or not. These proposals were accepted by the Javanese parties; the Masjumi, who would have held office without power, rejected them. Their view was echoed by more non-Javanese; in the first week of March 1957 joint civilian and military councils took over the administration in Celebes and Indonesian Borneo. Unable to cope, the Cabinet declared martial law and resigned. This edict, while it merely confirmed the powers that the rebellious military commanders outside Java had already seized, put all others on the same footing, thus considerably enhancing the Army's position in the country as a whole.

Again in the formation of the new Cabinet Sukarno tried to introduce the PKI; again he failed, and was eventually able only to form a Cabinet of 'experts' which included a couple of fellow-travellers. The Cabinet was of course strongly supported by all the Javanese parties, including the PKI; it was entirely Sukarno's instrument, and marked the decay of Parliament. The National Council was established in May; appointment of its members was a Presidential prerogative, and Sukarno ensured that it had a very solid majority of Javanese representatives in its 'functional groups'.

In mid-1957 provincial elections were held in Java; the PKI emerged as the largest single party, capturing 27·5 per cent of the total vote. However, this was mainly at the expense of the PNI; the Muslim parties' supporters were not seduced.[1] This continuing Communist growth alarmed the other three large parties sufficiently to induce them to talk about a common front, but none emerged. The gulf between the Masjumi and the Javanese parties was far greater than any common political interest in opposing Communism, and Sukarno of course had no interest in encouraging opposition to the PKI.

Matters moved rapidly to a crisis. The dissident councils now retained most of their foreign exchange earnings, effectively

[1] Hindley 1966, pp. 224, 225.

putting the squeeze on the government at Djakarta, while they demanded that Hatta be given an effective voice in government. National conferences of military and civilian leaders were organized in September 1957 in an attempt to reconcile the two national figures. The President, however, was determined on autocratic rule, and refused to accommodate Hatta. Then an attack was made on Sukarno, apparently organized by a Colonel Lubis who was in close contact with the dissident army leaders, and all hopes of reconciliation evaported.

Repression at home is often relieved by diversion abroad. Over the years Sukarno had been keeping the claim to Western New Guinea on the simmer. Now he brought it forward as a major weapon in his strategy, considerably helped by the fact that the Dutch retention of the territory had neither justice nor logic on its side. When the United Nations in December 1957 refused to pass a motion which would have effectively demanded that the Netherlands surrender the territory to Indonesia, Sukarno launched an hysterical campaign intended to frighten out of the country the 46,000 Dutch citizens still resident (most of them Eurasians who knew no other home), accompanied by a seizure of Dutch property, implemented at Sukarno's request by the PKI-controlled Trades Union Confederation, SOBSI. The economic chaos thus threatened alarmed even the Government, and it ordered the Army to take over the expropriated enterprises from the unions. Thus to some extent Sukarno's stratagem miscarried. A vital part of the economy was now controlled not by the PKI, but by the Army, increasing its independence of civilian political authority.

The mindless sponsored hooliganism was critized by Masjumi leaders; in exchange they found themselves intimidated by 'youth' groups under Sukarno's influence, with their arrest imminent. They took refuge in Padang, the chief town of the Minangkabau people in Central Sumatra, and the home of one of the first dissident councils. In February 1958 they and the rebellious military commanders of Sumatra and Celebes issued an ultimatum demanding a change of government and the exclusion of the PKI from it, with Sukarno returning to a purely constitutional role. When the Cabinet rejected their demands, the rebels proclaimed a Revolutionary Government. Unfortunately for them, the divisions and jealousies among the non-Javanese peoples precluded adequate support; the only peoples who took up arms were the Minangkabau, the Bataks of North Sumatra, and the Minahassans of North Celebes. These were later joined by the Atjehnese of North Sumatra, and formed links with a Makassarese 'Darul Islam' movement in South Celebes. But even these allies did not see eye to eye; the Christian Batak group, for instance, did not want the Islamic state favoured by the Muslim Bataks.

The Revolutionary Government's stand was not matched by the level of training of its Minangkabau soldiers, who simply ran away when the Djakarta government sent Javanese troops in to Central Sumatra. The Minahassan troops showed much more fight, but even there government troops had taken all major towns by July 1958, though guerrilla activity continued for another two and a half years. British and American supplies had been furnished to the rebels, but with their defeat the flow stopped.

Autocracy
In the political field the Javanese were now firmly in the saddle, and the opposition had been crushed. The Masjumi, because of the involvement of some of its members in the unsuccessful rebellion, was discredited. The PKI, on the other hand, extended its influence in the wake of the Javanese victory. For Sukarmo the time seemed opportune to impose his political ideas on the country.

The final steps began in July 1959. The Constituent Assembly, elected shortly after the Parliament in 1955, was on the point of reaching a decision in favour of a bicameral constitution with an Upper House to ensure regional representation. This was precisely what Sukarno did not want; he intervened and asked the Assembly to accept the original constitution of 1945, which had prescribed a strong Presidential cabinet. The Assembly refused, and he sent it home. He then decreed the 1945 Constitution, and named the National Council as the Supreme Advisory Council provided for in that document. Such steps as had been taken towards decentralization were abruptly cancelled and Javanese officials and teachers were despatched in increasing numbers to the other peoples (among whom they lived often in complete ostracism).

In March 1960 the elected, if corrupt, Parliament was replaced by a 'Mutual Help' chamber. Not only were the Masjumi and Sjahrir's PSI, the two parties most identified with the other peoples, excluded, but the elected representatives were treated as if they were simply a professional group and allotted half the seats in the new Parliament. No votes were to be taken in it, either; in case of disagreement Sukarno himself would decide.

As supreme body a Provisional People's Consultative Assembly was created. Parliament was included as a 'functional group'. The Assembly met for the first time in November and December 1960, and took two decisions. The first was to confer the title of 'Great Leader of the Revolution' on Sukarno; the other to form a National Front to whip up enthusiasm for the claim to Western New Guinea.

Local assemblies were now established on the same formula as the Parliament, and the new political structure was complete. This system of impotent and unrepresentative debating chambers was called 'Guided Democracy'. It was designed to stifle all dissent and expressed the idea that Sukarno knew what was best for the country. As a final touch, he decreed that only eight political parties were to exist; the Masjumi and PSI were not among them.

The President then turned his attention to the minds of the masses. He produced a number of slogans, including MANIPOL, USDEK, and NEKAD, which all Indonesians were required to absorb. The first stood for the Political Manifesto in which

Sukarno had set out his concept of 'Guided Democracy'. USDEK represented the initial letters of five statements of principle in the manifesto, namely: return to the 1945 constitution, Indonesian socialism, guided democracy, guided economy, Indonesian identity. Similarly, NEKAD summarized the goals of maintaining the unitary form of the republic, socialism, security, religion, and loyalty to democratic principles [sic]. An increasingly oppressive form of thought control was based on these slogans. All holders of public office were judged by their loyalty to them, and denunciations became commonplace. The newspapers simply echoed official views, and no serious intellectual discussion was possible. Democrats of long standing such as Sjahrir, or Mochtar Lubis, editor of the leading Indonesian newspaper, were imprisoned without trial. In all fields, but academic and administrative especially, incompetent demagogues used the slogans to unseat the efficient. The bureaucracy, more than ever before, became not so much a centralized administration as a number of private empires, reminiscent of the German Nazi structure. Happily, this process itself imposed some limitation on the effectiveness of thought control.

The structure of tyranny was supported by a cultivated xenophobia, which did not scruple to attack the Chinese community long resident in the country. Numbering only some 3 per cent of the population, their thrift and industry over the centuries had given them a strategic position in the country's economy. The legal structure of the Netherlands Indies, little changed since, had compelled them to remain a distinct minority, although those with the longest history in the country, especially those in Java, have probably at least as much Indonesian as Chinese blood in their veins. In brief, as a group they are both distinctive and better off than the Indonesians surrounding them, and therefore natural objects of a latent hostility.

Relatively few Chinese have been permitted to acquire Indonesian citizenship. Most of the others are considered stateless, as they do not follow Communist China, and Indonesia does not recognize the Kuomintang government in Taiwan. It was these who suffered first. Late in 1958, on the assertion that the Kuomintang government had helped the rebellion, many were arrested, all Kuomintang organizations were banned, and schools and business connected with them were placed under government control.

Less than a year later it was the turn of the small minority of Communist Chinese. In September 1959 the government decreed that all foreign (i.e. Chinese) traders were to move out of rural areas and to sell their businesses to Indonesian citizens or co-operatives. Those affected did not take it lying down, and a number of incidents occurred which involved the Chinese Embassy. Though the Peking government protested, it eventually had to accept the decree.

As was admitted at the time, the attacks on the Chinese were modelled on those against the Dutch. They both created an external focus for hostility and sized property which could be used to provide jobs and coax political support.

The Army, meanwhile, had its own concerns. One of the most important was the ending, by force or persuasion, of the various disorders to which the country had been subject ever since attaining its independence, and even before. The Army had indeed, long maintained, that only the interference of politicians had prevented it from settling, for example, the Darul Islam movement among the Sundanese of West Java. Now, with the country under martial law, it was not accountable to the politicians for the method it used to 'restore security', as the phrase has it.

In its task the Army was considerably helped by being re-equipped, in considerable measure as a direct result of the rebellion. The arms supplied to the rebels by Britain and the United States had done little more than provide a plausible excuse for Sukarno to turn to the Russians and the 'neutralists' for help. Only too glad to encourage anti-Western sentiments, Russia and Czechoslovakia provided weapons in large quantities.

Smaller amounts came from Yugoslavia, India, and Egypt as tokens of 'anti-imperialism'. Even the United States, when the rebels had clearly lost, agreed to supply light military equipment.

However, force was not the principal means used by the Army to end the 1958 rebellion, led largely by its own defecting officers. Secret negotiations were conducted with each rebel group, and the terms of reconciliation differed. Broadly speaking, however, they ensured that there was no 'surrender' and consequent loss of face; the rebels simply 'returned to the Republic', taking an oath of allegiance to the Chief of Staff and to the President. In North Celebes, for example, the Minahassans who had fought so long were simply left in charge of their area after taking the oath, while the Javanese troops withdrew. The implication was clear enough; rebellion against the politicians who ran the country was not treason in military eyes. In fact, many of the rebels laid down their arms only because they were convinced that the Army Command was as opposed to Communism as they were. By the end of 1961, most of these rebels had been once again incorporated into the Indonesian Army. Settlement of the lesser, though longer-festering, disorders did not delay. The most determined rebels of all, the Darul Islam Sundanese, eventually surrendered in mid-1962.

In this process of pacification the Indonesian Army was becoming a state within a state. Its administration of expropriated Dutch enterprises, as well as direct trade by some of its outlying units, had given it a certain degree of economic independence, while the state of martial law gave it political powers. It used its new position in a way that Sukarno and his supporters did not like. Where their only remedy for discontent among the non-Javanese had been outright repression, the Army Staff tempered force with concilation. This was not entirely good nature. The civilians had no choice but to accept the dictates of the government at Djakarta, enforced by the police, who in turn were dependent on it. The local military units, on the other hand, as the Atjehnese and Minahassans had shown, were capable of long and determined resistance if they thought themselves unjustly treated. Conciliation was therefore necessary if the Army was not to weaken itself by internecine warfare. But by pursuing this policy the Army was adopting a decentralization which combined on the one hand a certain degree of local independence, even including the tolerance of direct foreign trade, with on the other an insistence on complete loyalty to the Army Command, who saw themselves as custodians of the Indonesian nation. Pressure of circumstances had therefore compelled the Army to go some way in reforming the political structure at its most critical point, that of the military underpinning. While Sukarno and his supporters, especially the PKI, were demanding the suppression and punishment of the rebels, the Army was quietly composing differences. Success greeted their policy where it had shunned the politicians' for many years, and the Army leaders' confidence in their ability to handle affairs of state was correspondingly increased.

The country's turmoils were doing little to improve its economic situation, and so arrest the continuous improverishment to which the ordinary Indonesian has been subject for several decades. Yet what was required was well known: diversification of exports, investment in agriculture, and encouragement of manufacture. For nearly 80 per cent of Indonesian foreign exchange was produced by exports of two commodities, rubber and tin, making the country more vulnerable to the vagaries of the world market than it had been as a Dutch colony. The proportions of manufacturing industry both in the national product and in the working population employed had declined as compared with the pre-war period. Similarly with foodstuffs: though the country was largely agricultural, food production had not kept pace with the growth of population, and the country had to purchase abroad some 10 per cent of its requirements, costing up to $150 million a year.

The regime made a gesture by publishing in 1960 an Eight-Year Development Plan (1961–9). Its largely symbolic purpose was shown by the fact that the number of its chapters, volumes, and pages was made identical with the date of the proclamation of independence. In retrospect, it was principally important for a belated recognition that Indonesian development depended on foreign capital. This modified the government's hostility to it, and generated the idea of 'production sharing', whereby foreign investment was regarded as a redeemable loan, repayable in shares of output.

The Plan was doomed from the start. Implementing it would have meant reducing the amount devoted to 'defence', but the campaign for Western New Guinea was politically more important to Sukarno than the improvement of his people's welfare. So in 1961 some 40 per cent of the budget went on military expenditure, the inflation continued apace, and the Plan was forgotten.

Sukarno made one last attempt to enlist Western support in April 1960, when he visited the United States and the Soviet Union. The former refused to change her neutral stand on the issue, and Sukarno then put pressure on the Dutch. Their legation in Djakarta was stormed, Dutch shipping was banned from Indonesian waters, and diplomatic relations were broken off. It became clear that Sukarno had decided on armed aggression. Submarines, cruisers, and other warships arrived from Yugoslavia and Poland. Army leaders formed part of a delegation to Moscow in January 1961 which obtained Soviet support for Indonesia's claim and arms worth some $400 million.

A year later the crisis came. In January 1962 Indonesian torpedo boats tried to enter Western New Guinea territorial waters and were fired upon. This created a war scare in Djakarta, which the regime used to advantage by incarcerating several leaders of the dissolved Masjumi and PSI parties. Sukarno ordered general mobilization in February. Since the country was already under martial law, this measure was perhaps intended more to impress foreign correspondents than to move Indonesians.

Just as in 1949, so now thirteen years later the United States came to the rescue, and both the Netherlands and Indonesia agreed to hold preliminary talks with an American mediator. They dragged on for several months, against a background of more Russian arms sales to Indonesia. Finally in June both sides agreed to negotiate on the basis of a plan which provided that administrative authority in Western New Guinea be transferred to the United Nations in the first instance. Indonesia did not stop her war preparations, and dropped a few hundred paratroops into the forlorn jungles of the territory, with little evident result. A formal agreement was signed on 15 August, the United Nations assumed control on 1 October, and Indonesia took over six months later. Diplomatic contacts were resumed with the Netherlands, and over the next few years relations between the two countries improved considerably. Indonesia undertook to hold a plebiscite before the end of 1969 to enable the Papuans of Western New Guinea to decide its future status. The extent of the freedom they would have in making this decision was shown by the fact that, shortly after assuming control, Indonesia closed the territory, nobody being allowed in or out without a special permit.

Acquisition of the territory was of course a great victory for the regime. It had eluded the more democratically minded politicians who had sought to steer a middle course between the democracies and the communist states; now an authoritarian regime with communist support had successfully extended Indonesia's boundaries to coincide with those of the former Netherlands Indies, thus establishing beyond all doubt her claim to be considered the successor state.

This triumph established the regime more firmly than before, but did not remove the need for an external enemy. Towards the end of 1962, just after the Dutch had handed over Western New Guinea to the United Nations, Sukarno broadcast a call for help for a revolt which had broken out in the British protectorate of Brunei. He thus confounded those, like ex-Vice-President Hatta Mohammed Hatta, who had argued that once Western

New Guinea was incorporated in Indonesia politics would cease to be irrational, and confirmed those who had long asserted that the claim for Western New Guinea, however just, was a diversionary tactic. For his broadcast was the beginning of a long-sustained opposition to the plan to form a Federation of Malaysia from Malaya, Singapore and the British Borneo territories. Acrimonious exchanges with the Malayan Prime Minister, Tunku Abdul Rahman, followed; they became worse when the agreement creating Malaysia was signed in London on 8 July 1963. However, Sukarno, the Tunku, and President Macapagal of the Philippines met in Manila from 30 July to 5 August and decided to ask for and accept the results of a United Nations investigation into the question whether the people in British North Borneo and Sarawak wanted to join Malaysia. But when the United Nations confirmed that this was indeed their wish, Sukarno refused to believe it and did not recognize Malaysia when it came into existence on 16 September.

Malaysia therefore broke off diplomatic relations with Indonesia, and in Djakarta the usual hooligan mobs burnt the British Embassy and destroyed British property; they were answered in kind by their counterparts in Kuala Lumpur. British subjects and other foreigners were moved out of Indonesia. Following what was now an established Indonesian routine, PKI labour unions seized British firms, which were then taken over by the government, and in this fashion nearly all were expropriated.

Indonesia began hostilities with economic sanctions against Malaysia, which provided a convenient excuse for stipulating that the produce of the non-Javanese peoples pass through government hands, and be not exported direct, thus reducing their independence. Indonesian troops, working in collusion with Communist Chinese in Sarawak, carried out ever larger raids across the border, but to no great purpose.

These activities brought to an end the Western world's one-sided courtship of Sukarno, and increased its help to Malaysia. The United States stopped all aid to Indonesia; so did Britain,

Australia and New Zealand. France refused to supply arms. Australia introduced conscription for the first time while at peace, and sent her soldiers to join the British, New Zealand and Malaysian forces in resisting Indonesian incursions, while the Royal Navy assembled a large armada in Malaysian waters to prevent sea-borne landings.

The cost of Indonesian belligerence was reflected in consumer prices. The index for nineteen foodstuffs on the free market in Djakarta, taking 1953 as the base year, stood at 1,287 by the first quarter of 1962; by December 1963 it had soared to 4,674. Sukarno's response to the plight of his people was to continue to play politics. His sabre-rattling had contributed to a great increase in Army power, and more than ever he feared becoming its captive. Reasoning that the Army command's animosity towards the PKI would always make the latter dependent on him for protection, he had continued to encourage its growth so as to provide a balance which he could manipulate. In consequence, the PKI had burgeoned into the largest party; at the end of June 1963 it claimed to have three million members, in addition to some fourteen million in various of its 'fronts'. The death of the then Prime Minister, Djuanda, in November 1963 provided Sukarno with an opportunity to place his thumb on the scales. He appointed himself Prime Minister (as well as President), and reshuffled the Cabinet so as to downgrade Nasution and the Army with him. Meanwhile he continued with his incantation that Malaysia must be crushed, dutifully echoed by the PKI. Peacemaking efforts by both the United States and the Philippines proved fruitless. Then, after Mr Mikoyan, the Soviet Deputy Prime Minister, visited Indonesia in July 1964 and reaffirmed Soviet support for Indonesian hostilities against Malaysia, Indonesian guerrillas began to land by sea and air on the Malayan peninsula proper. They achieved little, being quickly captured with the help of the local people. But Sukarno took advantage of the crisis to reshuffle the Cabinet again and appoint to it the Deputy Chairman of the PKI, Nyoto. He had thus, after many years, finally achieved his aim of including the Communists in the government.

The PKI was emphatically pro-Chinese, and Sukarno turned to hew the same line. The United States had provided Indonesia with some $666 million in aid between 1949 and 1964 but in his Independence Day speech in August of the latter year Sukarno attacked her and four months later the regular treatment began. At his instigation PKI hooligans sacked the libraries of the United States Information Service in both Djakarta and Surabaya, the country's largest port. Thereafter they made the American Embassy and consulates the targets of regular demonstrations, purportedly against the American rescue of civilians in the Congo. American rubber and oil companies were placed under government control. American films were banned; PKI unions deprived American residents of water and electricity.

The President's new foreign policy, however, was hardly distinguished by success. Sukarno failed to gain support for it at the Cairo 'Non-Aligned' Conference in October 1964. In December a majority of members of the Security Council deplored Indonesian hostilities, only to be frustrated by a Russian veto. The condemnation put Sukarno into a political tantrum. In January 1965 he ordered the withdrawl of his country from the United Nations; to whose existence, perhaps, Indonesia owes its own. The pretext was Malaysia's election to the Security Council, an arrangement made a year earlier without Indonesian objection. Sukarno's action was of course strongly supported by Communist China when the Foreign Minister, Subandrio, visited Peking the same month. Chou En-lai even suggested that a 'revolutionary' United Nations might be set up in competition with the original body, and Sukarno obliged with the new 'concept' of 'New Emerging Forces' or NEFO. This was intended to include all the poor nations of the world, who in his opinion gained nothing from working with the West, and would be better advised to turn their backs on it. He deliberately, and for the first time, abandoned non-alignment, which had been the basis of all previous Indonesian foreign policy, on the ground that it was out of date so long as the Old Established Forces (OLDEFOS) were not crushed. This part of his new foreign policy was no more successful than the others. He found his only friends now were the Communist states of Asia: China, North Vietnam, and North Korea.

Courting of Communists abroad was matched by support of them at home. In January 1965 Sukarno declared that he would have no objection if Indonesia became Communist. To please the PKI, he suppressed the Murba Party, which kept alive Tan Malaka's independent Leninism. Clearly, Marxism was not enough; it had to be of the PKI variety. The PNI, now totally dependent on Sukarno for its existence, was compelled to declare its adherence to the ideology in November 1964, and gradually to rid itself of its most anti-Communist leaders.

In this atmosphere, fear and foreboding beset all non-Communists in Indonesia. The PKI, of course, was much encouraged. The President had proscribed its most determined enemy, the Masjumi, several of whose leaders were in jail. Now the PKI turned against the Nahdatul Ulama, which had not been noted for its anti-Communist ardour. The national leaders were too valuable to Sukarno for his NASAKOM (Nationalist-Religious-Communist) window-dressing, so the PKI set its members on to attack the local dignitaries, on the pretext that it was taking a land reform law into its own hands. This was to cost it very dearly.

Unfortunately for Sukarno, he could never dominate the Army. As we have seen, his policies had necessarily involved strengthening the Army as well as increasing its independence of him; it was not to be cajoled into welcoming his Communist friends. At most, it reluctantly accepted that Communist organizers were to give indoctrination courses in all the armed forces; like most preachers, they do not seem to have had much effect except where the ground was already fertile. The two most important formations to be influenced were the Air Force, which was motivated as much by jealousy of the Army as by conversion to Marxism, and the Diponegoro Division of Central Java, which became known for its sympathy to the equally Javanese PKI.

Sukarno's failure on the Malaysian front in no way abated his ranting against 'imperialist encirclement' and 'nekolim' (neo-colonialist-imperialism). Aidit, chairman of the PKI, took up the theme and urged that to fight both these threats it was important to arm the workers and peasants. This was not dissimilar to the attempt made more than a decade earlier by Sukarno's man in the then Cabinet, Iwa Kusumasumantri, to arm the PKI 'ex-servicemen', a scheme which collapsed on Army opposition. Sukarno now agreed publicly with Aidit's suggestion and went further; he hinted at the introduction of a system of political commissars within the Armed Forces. This would of course have meant giving control over them to their arch-enemies and Sukarno's friends, the PKI.

The Army's opposition to these schemes was well known. Sukarno announced that he would consider the matter and decide whether or not to order the Army to arm the peasants and workers. Rumours (which proved unfounded) then began to spread of a sudden and fatal deterioration in Sukarno's health, and of the consequent imminence of the long-expected trial of strength between the Army and the PKI. Though warned of the danger in which they stood, the Army commanders took no special precautions. It would seem that their awareness of their strength and independence had perhaps made them overconfident. In consequence, on the night of 30 September 1965 six generals were murdered, and the radio station and the Post, Telegraph and Telephone Office in Djakarta were occupied, while the Presidential Palace (whose principal occupant had taken refuge in the Air Force base outside the capital) was ringed by a group calling themselves the '30 September Movement'. They declared they had acted in support of the President against the Army General Staff. The leaders and most of the participants in the conspiracy were all uniformed men, principally from

Javanese Divisions, but included also the Air Force Commander Omar Dhani. There is also evidence of connivance by certain PKI men, including Aidit, and by the President himself. This bloody but amateurish attempt at a *coup* was snuffed out overnight by Major-General (as he was then) Suharto, commander of the Strategic Army Reserve, whom the conspirators had not considered bullet-worthy.

The generals had been taken from their homes to a place where the PKI Youth and Women were being trained by the Air Force, and here those still alive were tortured and despatched by members of the Women's Organization. When the generals' bodies were recovered from the dried well into which they had been cast, a wave of anti-Communist hysteria seized the country. For the next six months, alleged Communists in Muslim Atjeh, Christian North Sumatra, Hindu Bali, and Muslim Central and East Java were meekly led to execution, at the hands of those they had injured in the past, in what was said to be hundreds of thousands (though few if any reliable witnesses have seen a sufficient number of bodies to substantiate this estimate). The largest number of murders were committed in Central and East Java and in Bali. In the former, the arrival at a village of an Army unit searching for Communists was a signal for Muslim youths to take the knife into their own hands and despatch their enemies. In Bali, however, the killings began spontaneously and the Army had to despatch units there to restore order. Communists denounced one another to the authorities, and Aidit himself met his end in this way at the hands of an Army patrol in November. It would seem that the PKI had not acquired a hold on the affections of the people at large as great as that, for example, of the Darul Islam in West Java, whom the Sundanese shielded from military harassment for many years.

Sukarno's recent policies had perhaps indicated that his political sense, once fairly reliable, was weakening. With the failure of the conspiracy, it appears to have deserted him entirely He seems to have been unable to grasp that the PKI had been crushed and that he had to come to terms with their conquerors, the Army, while a considerable part of public opinion still supported him. Like a witch-doctor who knew only one set of incantations, he continued to voice his support for the PKI, to mouth the old slogans of 'Nasakom' and 'anti-nekolim'. But these were prayers to gods that had died, and he only convinced many that his own hands were at least pink with the blood of his generals.

And now it emerged plain for all to see that despite, or perhaps because of, his 'progressive' posture Sukarno had lost the support of the younger generation. Its principal representatives grouped themselves into 'Action Fronts', of which the first and most important was KAMI, which spoke for Indonesian students. In January it demanded with demonstrations the dissolution of the PKI and more efficient government. Again Sukarno displayed an astonishing lack of political acumen and simply turned on the old routine. He formed a new cabinet which excluded General Nasution (one target of the conspirators, whose bullets had found his daughter and his aide instead) and consisted largely of his old cronies, many of whom supported the PKI. KAMI was banned and the University of Indonesia closed. Then, and only then, did certain Army elements decide that the joke had gone on for too long. Troops of the Strategic Command and of the Para-commando Regiment advanced on the Palace. Sukarno fled to Bogor, forty miles south of Djakarta. There on 11 March 1966 three generals persuaded him to sign an order authorizing Suharto (who had been appointed Chief of Staff of the Army after the failure of the September coup) to take all measures necessary to restore order and protect him. It was the end, in fact if not in form, of the Sukarno regime.

Reform

With power in its hands, the Army lost no time in promulgating a formal ban on the PKI and on the dissemination of Marxism and Leninism. In contrast, the press was released from its

Sukarno shackles, and for the first time in many years it was possible for the ordinary Indonesian to read honest newspapers.

PKI sympathizers were rooted out from military and civilian posts. The Cabinet was reshuffled; fifteen ministers including Subandrio, as well as Omar Dhani, the Air Force chief, were arrested. Sukarno's political prisoners emerged into the sunlight; a stroke had already discharged the most eminent of them, Sjahrir, to exile in Switzerland, where he lived only long enough to know that his gaoler's power was broken.

The PNI, Sukarno's other support, was compelled to replace its entire national committee. A similar 'cleansing' operation was carried out on the Provisional People's Consultative Congress, or MPRS, which reconvened at the end of June 1966 with General Nasution as Chairman and busied itself dismantling the structure of the Sukarno state. Suharto was named assembler of a new cabinet and successor to Sukarno in case of incapacity. The President was ordered to account for his stewardship, in particular during the abortive coup of 30 September.

The proceedings at the trials of Subandrio and Omar Dhani implied that Sukarno had known more than he cared to admit of the conspiracy. When in January 1967 he presented his report, its contents and tone were insulting, and lent force to the demands that he be put on trial. Suharto, however, reckoning with the many supporters of Sukarno still in the country and in the Army especially among the Javanese, refused to do anything which would alienate them. The MPRS at its meeting in March 1967 accepted this argument, but appointed Suharto Acting President, while leaving Sukarno with the empty title. Even this was taken away from him and given to Suharto a year later. Sukarno was left to follow the life of a restricted private citizen in Bogor; he died of natural causes in mid-1970, and was given a state funeral. His earlier services to the nationalist cause had not been obliterated by his later vagaries.

The government of the 'New Order', as it styled itself, was effectively Suharto, assisted by twenty-two ministers as well as by a personal staff of senior army officers and a team of civilian advisers. Parliament, though purged of sympathizers with Sukarno's 'Old Order' and stiffened with military representatives, had very limited powers.

The new regime's principal tasks were to establish order in the country, resuscitate the economy, and restore international confidence. The first was seen as basically a matter of rooting out all supporters of the PKI and of Sukarno. Despite the great number of those killed, and the arrest of 200,000 suspects, the PKI had not been totally eliminated; it was reported that two thirds of the members of the Central Committee were still at large. In the first half of 1968 it attempted to secure a 'liberated area' round the small town of Blitar in East Java; members of Muslim organizations, especially the Nahdatul Ulama, were killed in reprisal for the murder of PKI members after the failure of the *coup*. The revolt collapsed when the Army moved 10,000 troops into the area.

Further PKI activity was later reported from Central Java, but after this was suppressed there were no more signs of co-ordinated activity, and the party seemed unable to form a central leadership. Continuous sifting of the detainees had reduced their number by August 1969 to some 45,000, of whom two thirds were considered relatively harmless and due for release in the near future.

On the border with Sarawak in Borneo, a communist-led group known as the PGRS, or Sarawak People's Guerrilla Movement, had under the Sukarno regime been actively assisted by Indonesian forces. Policy was now reversed, and the Movement was quickly brought to a halt by joint operations with Malaysian units. Some 3,500 of its members surrendered in February 1968, and by August it was reported down to only 270.

It was not only opposition to its rule that exercised the Army, but also disloyalty within its own ranks and those of the other state services. The Javanese Diponegoro Division's purge began immediately after the failure of the September conspiracy, and may not have been completed at the time of writing. Then in 1968 investigation into the Blitar uprising showed that certain officers in the East Java Division, the Brawidjaja, were involved. Given the Javanese sympathy for Sukarno and the PKI, this was understandable. More surprising, however, was the discovery that the PKI at Blitar had received assistance in training from a colonel in the country's élite division, the Siliwangi, based at Bandung in West Java, which had the reputation of being the most loyal, the best educated, the most highly trained, and the least ethnically based. The enquiry that followed swept out several senior officers including a major-general.

Meanwhile the Air Force, the Navy, the Marine Corps, and the Police were all examined and purged of sympathizers with either the PKI or Sukarno. Encouragement of rivalry between the different branches of the Armed Forces (which in Indonesia include the Police) had been one of the methods which Sukarno had used to establish his position and which had seriously weakened them. Suharto therefore abolished the separate Ministries of the Army, Navy, Air Force, and Police, placing all four services directly under him, and ruled that officers for all these services were to be trained in the same academy.

Many of the military accused of plotting against the new regime were not so much followers of the PKI as supporters of Sukarno. The political party which was most suspect on the latter score, as well as because of its past collaboration with the PKI, was the PNI. The wholesale purge of its central executive, mentioned earlier, split the party. One part declared its loyalty to the new regime; the other, led by the ex-prime Minister Ali Sastroamidjoyo, and a previous Secretary-General and fellow-traveller, Surachman, went underground. The latter was killed in the course of the Army's operations against the PKI's Blitar uprising.

The local branches of the party did not escape overhaul. Some were dissolved; Army Commanders took over the leadership of others; yet others were ordered to get rid of pro-Sukarno members. Even after this thoroughgoing 'cleansing', however, in non-Javanese areas strong objection was made to the continued existence, or revival, of this Party's branches. They were seen for what they largely were—political organizations of Javanese civil servants.

Organized Islam presented a different problem. Muslims generally considered themselves among the victors in the struggle with the PKI, and entitled to take the law into their own hands. Instances of persecution of Indonesian Christians were reported, and led President Suharto to a rare personal intervention. The NU's youth groups had played a prominent part in the killing of PKI followers; this evidently purged their Party's collusion with Sukarno's policies. The Masjumi, however, proscribed by Sukarno, remained so. The new regime refused to lift the ban, no doubt to avoid giving the impression that it was encouraging, however retrospectively, rebellion against government. However, the need for urban, Modernist, Muslim representation remained; it would have been unwise to permit the NU, whose political ideas were naive, fanatical, and commercial, to emerge as the only representative of Indonesian Muslims. Eventually Suharto agreed to the formation of a new party to be called Parmusi, or the Party of the Muslims of Indonesia, on condition that none of its office-holders had been leaders of the Masjumi.

The major political preoccupation of the regime, however, was with constitutional reform. The major body in this field, the MPRS, was increased in size (to 828 members) and designated the body to which the President was responsible. It quickly addressed itself to the holding of elections and in 1966, in the first relief at Sukarno's downfall, had resolved that they were to be held by 5 July 1968. Later counsels, however, convinced the members of the MPRS that they should be held three years later. That date remains unchanged at the time of writing. Suharto made it plain that the election rules were to ensure that they neither hampered the country's economic development nor threatened the continuance of the 'New Order'. It was by now well accepted that the Army had a dual military and civilian role, and that it was not going to surrender its overlordship of the country to the political parties.

Elections were to be not only for the People's Consultative Assembly and the Parliament, but also for the regional assemblies; in all of these a substantial proportion would be appointed, not elected. In the MPR (it would then no longer be 'Provisional') they would amount to one third, and in Parliament 100 out of 460.

It was through this machinery of representation that the New Order hoped to go some way to reconciling the conflicts between the peoples of the country. (Nasution observed that over the last twenty years regional discontent had arisen because of inadequate local autonomy and development.) Accordingly, members of the Consultative Assembly were to be elected by provincial electorates; in effect, it was a means of providing for regional representation at the centre of decision, a totally new departure in Indonesian political life.

The number and size of political parties that would emerge from the elections of course depended on the voting system to be adopted. This was still under discussion at the time of writing. An Armed Forces Seminar had concluded that a 'single-member' constituency was the most desirable; but naturally enough the many parties favoured proportional representation as the system that offered them the best life assurance, though its results wherever used hardly justified an expectation of stable government.

At least as important as reforming the country's political structure was the rehabilitation of the economy. It is difficult to exaggerate the task facing the regime. Between 1955 and 1966 exports had fallen by 13 per cent in volume and 26 per cent in value. The principal export was rubber; the trees had not been replanted with high-yield types as in Malaysia, and competition from synthetic had forced down prices. The population had been increasing by about 2·8 per cent per annum; the production of rice limped behind at a rate of only 2·2 per cent p.a. Of the

74 million people in the labour force, some $3\frac{1}{2}$ million were unemployed, 15 million under-employed, and about $1\frac{1}{2}$ million young people entered the job market every year. The inflation had soared to new heights: in 1966 alone prices rose by 860 per cent.

The situation was perhaps epitomized in the fact that Indonesia's maximum export capacity was $550 million, whereas its import bill was $650 million, on the most austere assumptions and without making allowance for any development spending. It was clear that if the economy was to be made viable, new sources of production would have to be developed, and new policies pursued. Perhaps the regime's most important step was the first; it recalled from exile Indonesia's most eminant economist, Sumitro Djoyohadikusumo, who had taken part in the Revolutionary Government of 1958, and appointed him Minister of Trade. The policies that then emerged were radical in being dictated by common sense. They were to seek emergency economic aid for essential requirements, to negotiate a postponement of repayment of the large debts incurred by Sukarno, and to invite foreign investment.

Success was attained in all these endeavours. Indonesia's Western creditors agreed to provide $200 million in 1967, $325 million in 1968, $500 million in 1969, and $600 million in 1970. They also accepted a delay in repayment of the debts, and in 1970 agreed to a scheme whereby the amount owed to them, some $1,300 million, would be repaid free of interest over thirty years. Indonesia's other major creditor was the Soviet Union, to which was owed some $800 million, mainly for arms. Repayments were to have started on 1 April 1969 and cover a 12-year period; the Russians refused to complete their projects in Indonesia until she met her obligations. This she was quite unable to do, and her agreement with her Western creditors in any case precluded favourable treatment for any others. The Soviet Union's attitude to the agreement was that it was in no way binding on her.

To raise the Indonesian economy to a more viable level, however, a Five-Year Plan was drafted, to begin in 1969, and known by its acronym of 'Repelita'. Emphasis lay on agriculture and associated industries and transport. Some 70 per cent of the finance of the Plan was to come from foreign sources, the object being to raise exports to over $900 million by 1973-4; most of these were to be primary products, especially oil.

Where the Sukarno regime had manifested xenophobia, the New Order invited foreign investors to help Indonesian development and passed a Law on Foreign Investment in January 1967. Up to mid-1970 some 172 projects of a value of over $1,000 million had been approved, mostly in mining and forestry.

The fruits of this new approach were not long in appearing. In 1968 rice production exceeded 10 million tons for the first time, largely as a result of the distribution of fertilizer, improved seeds, and pesticides on a large scale. And perhaps the most telling indicator, the price index rose only 115 per cent in 1967; 85 per cent in 1968, and 10 per cent in 1969. Probably for the first time since independence, inflation was under control.

Prices had been one of the constant preoccupations of the Action Fronts, which had become the conscience of the new regime; the extent of corruption in the public service was another. The success achieved in the first case was not matched by progress in the second, though in 1970 a Commission of elder statesmen led by ex-Vice-President Hatta was installed to find ways of reducing corruption. But at bottom this failing stemmed from the low salary level of the civil service, which in turn could be traced to its elephantine size. In 1942 some 50,000 civil servants administered the whole of the Netherlands Indies; in mid-1969 some 480,000 were engaged in the same task in the successor state. Unfortunately, any attempt to reduce their numbers, given the lack of other employment, was fraught with grave political, and even security, risks.

The welcome to foreign investors was part and parcel of Indonesia's new foreign policy, which returned to its traditional neutralism, and swung away from Sukarno's pro-Chinese stand. The Minister responsible was Adam Malik, a life-long member of the Murba party, which had enshrined the ideas of Tan Malaka, and also at one time Ambassador to Moscow.

Indonesia's self-imposed isolation was brought to a rapid end. The United Nations and its various agencies were rejoined, and links with the Western powers re-established, as implied above. This did not mean an enmity to Russia or her protectorates in Eastern Europe; on the contrary, steps were taken to recognize East Germany. It was made clear that, while the PKI was to be suppressed, this did not mean hostility to Communist regimes abroad.

Nearer home, hostilities against Malaysia were brought to an abrupt end, and relations between the two countries improved considerably. Ambassadors were exchanged; the two heads of state visited each other's country. The two countries jointly fought the PGRS, as mentioned above. Malik worked for regional cooperation, and in August 1967 Indonesia became founder-member of the Association of South-East Asian Nations. In September 1968 Malik withdrew Indonesian support from the Philippines' claim to Sabah, and so indicated unmistakably that the days of fishing in troubled waters were over.

Relations with China were in a special category. That Peking had been in touch with the September 1965 conspirators was soon well known. Equally, the Indonesian Chinese Association had been strongly influenced by the PKI, and many Chinese had been massacred after the failure of the conspiracy. Radio Peking had continued to agitate against the government, while the Army had frequently reported the capture of Chinese subversive agents.

The new regime therefore adopted the policy of encouraging the assimilation of Chinese in Indonesia on the one hand, while ensuring that Peking did not meddle in Indonesian affairs. In June 1967 a Cabinet instruction guaranteed protection for all aliens, but decreed that no work permits would be issued for new Chinese immigrants, and no new Chinese schools would be permitted. In October relations with Peking were 'frozen', a state short of diplomatic rupture; that country's citizens, amounting to some 250,000 out of a total of 2,750,000 Chinese in the archipelago, thereby lost the protection of their government. Paradoxically, this appears to have improved relations between Chinese and Indonesians. At the end of the year Chinese religious ceremonies were restricted to the family circle, while Chinese with Indonesian citizenship were invited to change their names. In brief, they were being asked to make themselves indistinguishable from other Indonesians. In April 1969, however, in an evident attempt to obviate the creation of a fifth column, the citizenship agreement reached with Communist China at the Asian-African Conference at Bandung in 1954 was declared invalid. This had the effect of preventing Chinese from automatically assuming Indonesian citizenship, and thus compelled a positive vetting of all applications. A special staff for Chinese affairs was assembled to assist in the assimilation of this minority. This did not mean a state of continued hostility to Peking; in 1970 the regime began exploring the possibility of resuming diplomatic relations on condition that Communist China did not interfere in Indonesian internal politics.

However concerned the New Order was to be friends with all, its nationalism was not to be doubted. In 1969 it was compelled to make good the promise given to the United Nations in 1962 that the inhabitants of Western New Guinea would be permitted to choose between Indonesian rule and independence. Though this was called 'The Act of Free Choice', the regime let it be known to all and sundry that only one result was to be permitted. As the time for choice drew nearer, a number of small-scale uprisings were forcibly put down by Indonesian Army units specially moved in. In due course, the 'Act' produced the required result, and Western New Guinea's formal incorporation into Indonesia was placed beyond doubt. Though the fact that the elections were rigged was patent, no critical voices of consequence in the international community were raised; the rest of the world was apparently only too glad to see Indonesia assume the burden of this barren and backward land. She in turn did not intend to be unduly weighed down by it; indeed Adam Malik in a visit to the territory after the successful conclusion of the 'Act' declared that the Government was in no position to provide much help with development and that the people of the territory would have to rely on their own efforts.

This approach to the problem of Western New Guinea was entirely consistent with the realism that has marked the 'New Order' from the outset. Beginning by snuffing out a bloody conspiracy intended to increase even further Sukarno's autocratic powers, continuing with a refusal to make a martyr of him, Suharto and his colleagues went on to develop a policy unprecedented in its empiricism. A carefully cultivated neutralism in foreign affairs is combined with a watchful encouragement of the foreign investment that the country desperately needs, sober economic plans are allied with constitution-making designed to combine representation with stability. Totally absent—but not missed—is the hysteria which imbued the Sukarno regime and so many other tyrannies, past and present.

The future historian may well conclude that the attack on Indonesia's principal problems of political integration and economic progress, by means other than Sukarno's rhetoric, began only with the 'New Order', though he may perhaps clutch consolation from the thought that the previous seventeen years' dismal experience of independence perhaps served to cast out the devils of political frenzy and economic delusion. Whether the more rational methods of government adopted by the Suharto regime will prove adequate to the task, and whether the Indonesian people will develop sufficient patience to await the harvest of their efforts, only the future can tell. Indonesia's friends can only hope.

BIBLIOGRAPHICAL APPENDIX

Benda, H. J. *The Crescent and the Rising Sun.* The Hague, van Hoeve, 1958.
Feith, H. *The Decline of Constitutional Democracy in Indonesia.* Ithaca, Cornell U.P., 1962.
—— and D. S. Lev. 'The End of the Indonesian Rebellion', *Pacific Affairs*, Vol. XXXVI, No. 1, pp. 32–46.
Hindley, D. *The Communist Party of Indonesia 1951–1968.* Berkeley, University of California Press, 1966.
Hughes, J. *The End of Sukarno.* London, Angus and Robertson, 1968.
Kahin, G. McT. *Nationalism and Revolution in Indonesia.* Ithaca, Cornell U.P., 1952.
—— (ed.). *Major Governments of Asia.* Ithaca, Cornell U.P., 1963.
McVey, Ruth T. *Indonesia.* New Haven, H.R.A.F. Press, 1963.
Palmier, L. H. *Indonesia and the Dutch.* London, Oxford U.P., 1962.
—— *Indonesia.* London, Thames and Hudson, 1965.

CHAPTER IX

CONCLUSION:
ASIA IN THE SEVENTIES

G. F. HUDSON

Modernity and Change

In the nineteenth century and, though to a diminishing degree, through the first half of the twentieth, the general way of life of the peoples of Asia appeared to the West as basically unchanging. In Europe the marriage of a new scientific technology and capitalist finance had brought about an ever-accelerating economic growth with an ever-increasing shift of population from the countryside into the towns and continually changing conditions of life for more and more people; parallel with the economic transformation there had been political reforms and revolutions which had by 1914 everywhere superseded or deeply modified the monarchical and feudal institutions inherited from an earlier age. In North America, a continent of recent European settlement, where great cities were springing up in what had been empty prairie a generation before, the tradition of the past was weaker than in Europe and the spirit of innovation and progress even more potent. In contrast Asia, with the important, but marginal, exception of Japan after 1868, presented a spectacle of massive inertia and immobility. Many of the phenomena of Western economic progress—railways, steamships, telegraphs, electric power stations, banks and insurance companies—were present, but they owed their existence almost entirely to Western initiative, investment and management, whether in territories which had been subjected to Western imperial rule or in those countries which had retained their formal independence. The new modern industrial development of the West was conspicuously absent; the Western imperial powers, whose manufacturers regarded colonial territories as markets for their goods, had no zeal for promoting it in Asia, and whether within or beyond the boundaries of their rule there was a notable lack of the kind of energetic private capitalist enterprise which had flourished in Western Europe for the past three centuries. The landowning classes were not interested and even among merchants and moneylenders there were few who showed any disposition to depart from traditional patterns of finance and commerce. At lower social levels vast masses of mostly illiterate peasants, living by subsistence agriculture, seemed to constitute a great barrier of passive resistance to any fundamental social change. Political forms (with the partial exception of Japan which had a weak parliamentary constitution from 1889) were everywhere authoritarian without elective institutions until well into the twentieth century; the Western powers, in spite of their own democratic systems, governed autocratically in Asia, and in the independent countries absolute monarchy was the rule. An observer of China shortly before the Revolution of 1911 called it 'the last of the great empires of the ancient world', and at the other end of Asia a similar claim could have been made for Turkey in the reign of Abdul Hamid II.

It is a problem for historians to explain why Europe and North America moved so far ahead of Asia in economic development during the eighteenth and nineteenth centuries, but the fact that they did so provides the historical background to current events in Asia. The late-starting industrialization of Asia proceeds in circumstances very different from those characteristic of the period of the rise of modern industry in Europe and North America. In the age of jet aircraft and radio communications, of computers and automation, it is not a question of merely repeating more rapidly the stages of industrial advance since the invention of the steam engine; not only must the tempo of development be much quicker, but there has to be a leap forward to a far more complex and sophisticated economy than that which existed in the West two centuries, or even one century ago, and the social impact of such changes is bound to be correspondingly abrupt and dislocating. Further, the political conditions of this later time are quite different from those under which the system of private capitalist enterprise developed in the West. There are many things that in the West separate the second half of the twentieth century from the early days of industrial capitalism— the spread of parliamentary democracy and the rise of working-class organizations, trade unions and the International Labour Office; the expansion of social services financed from taxation; the Bolshevik Revolution in Russia and the international communist movement. The demand for social justice, the idea of the welfare state, the pressure of rising expectations in the masses of the people now confront a nascent capitalism in an under-developed country no less than they do the bourgeoisie of an advanced industrial nation; the permeation of the intelligentsia by socialist ideology may now precede the emergence of even the most primitive forms of capitalist enterprise. Thus today a rising capitalist class is caught between two fires, from the Right and from the Left; it has to cope not only with a privileged landowning interest, a feudally-minded officialdom and the inertia of an ancient traditional society, but also with pressures for socialist expropriations of property or at least for higher wages, better conditions of work and the provision of social services which in their total effect, in so far as they are enforced, seriously reduce the profitability of its investments.

In such conditions it is inevitable that governments play a much greater part in capital formation and the promotion of economic growth than they did in the classic age of *laissez faire* capitalism. Even where they are committed to reliance on a system of private enterprise for the development of production and trade they cannot confine themselves to the mere provision of a framework of law and order for economic activities or even to policies of tariff protection for infant industries. They must actively stimulate and direct the economic process, make plans for it, initiate particular projects with government funds, control foreign currency exchange so as to ensure needed imports of capital goods and assume responsibilities for national education, health, housing and relief of unemployment such as their predecessors would not even have imagined. For those in government, however, who are not directly involved in the profits of industrial enterprises—and who, if they seek personal profits, have quicker and easier means of extracting them than from long-term business investments—the inspiration for undertaking the arduous task of driving a people onward in the path of economic development cannot itself be merely acquisitive, and even for the business men who have the prospect of making money in the new enterprises the difficulties and risks may be too deterrent to induce adequate activity. In these circumstances the motive power of an idea which cannot be stated in purely economic terms is required to unleash the forces even of a private capitalist economy. In the words of an analyst of economic growth in underdeveloped countries:

'To break through the barriers of stagnation in a backward country, to ignite the imaginations of men and to place their energies in the service of economic development, a stronger medicine is needed than the promise of better allocation of resources or even the lower price of bread. Under such conditions even the business man, even the classical daring and innovating entrepreneur needs a more powerful stimulus than the prospect of high profits. What is needed to remove the mounting routine and prejudice is faith.'[1]

The faith, the impelling idea, is provided by nationalism. This is so throughout Asia, and in the countries which have come

---

[1] A. Gerschenkron, *Economic Backwardness in Historical Perspective* (Cambridge, Mass., 1962), p. 24.

under communist rule as well as in those which give scope to private capital. What has happened in the communist countries, in China, North Korea and North Vietnam, is that a social revolution based on a Marxist-Leninist ideology has been added to a nationalist one. In all countries which became colonies or semi-colonies in the age of Western ascendancy the primary urges have been for emancipation from foreign political and economic control, for national independence and national power. Where the desire of entrepreneurs for profits and the aspirations of the masses for higher standards of living may be insufficient to move the economy into rapid progress, the national idea can provide a great impelling force. A people attaining, or retaining, its political independence must deliver itself from dependence on foreign capital; it must refuse to be simply a producer of primary commodities and a market for the manufactured products of advanced industrial nations; as an equal among the nations of the world it must have at least the outward and visible signs of economic modernity.

The part which can be played by an intense national patriotism in promoting a rapid economic growth was vividly illustrated in the case of Japan, the one Asian country which in the nineteenth century succeeded in escaping from colonial or semi-colonial status under the economic and strategic pressures of the West. The industrialization of Japan in the Meiji era was far from being the result merely of an exceptional degree of business skill and initiative in the Japanese commercial class. Although the economic institutions developed in Japan during the period of feudally controlled isolation played a part in preparation for the subsequent economic progress, the main impulsion for the Meiji Restoration and the reforms that followed came, not from the merchants of Osaka, but from dissident *samurai* determined to preserve the independence of their country in an age of imperialism and make it into a great power equal to the strongest nations of the West. The slogan *fukoku kyohei*, 'rich country, strong army', implied the overriding importance of national power as the purpose of economic activities, and the formula was justified by results; through modernization of the state administration and the creation of a modern industrial economy Japan was able to sustain the military and naval power which brought victory in war over China in 1894 and over Russia ten years later. In some cases the government started industries with public funds and later sold them to private companies—a procedure which often involved corrupt dealings, but nevertheless ensured that the country was provided with the industries in question. The industrialization thus initiated by a group of ultra-nationalist soldiers and statesmen produced not only factories, steamships and railways, but also a strong and self-confident capitalist class which before the end of the nineteenth century had a restricted, but not ineffective, parliament to give voice to its interests. The Meiji leaders insisted on a priority for strategic purposes but had no wish for more socialism than the cause of national power required; the Western economic models of that time were those of private capitalism and it was taken for granted that the private entrepreneur would step in where state promotion left off.

Japan's industrial take-off was about midway in time between that of Western Europe and that of Asia outside Japan. A British economic historian has estimated that 'the industrial production of Japan in 1936–37 was probably nearly twice that of the whole of the rest of Asia excluding the Soviet Union'.[1] A decade later, after the disastrous outcome of eight years of fighting in China and four years of the Pacific War, Japan's economy appeared to be in ruins, but it soon began to recover and its expansion had by 1970 achieved the greatest economic 'miracle' of the age, making Japan into the world's third industrial power. The economy has remained one of private capitalism and the society has become far more essentially bourgeois than before the war; a drastic land reform carried out during the period of the post-war American occupation virtually eliminated the numerous landlord class of pre-war Japan, and the demilitarization, imposed

[1] G. C. Allen, *Japan's Economic Recovery* (1958), p. 6.

by the victors of the Pacific War, but written into the new Japanese constitution and generally accepted by the Japanese people because of the disastrous outcome of the former militarist policies, has removed from Japanese national life both the far-reaching political influence of the armed forces and the heavy taxation required for their maintenance. A modest 'self-defence force' has modified the complete defencelessness contemplated by the constitution, but it is weaker than the military potential of either North or South Korea, absorbs a far lower percentage of the gross national product than is normal among the nations of the world, and has so far remained under the strict control of a democratically elected civilian government. The changes in Japanese life and popular attitudes since the war have been deep and widespread; there has been a drastic reduction of the rural element in Japanese society, a rapid increase in urbanization with its new problems, a great weakening of traditional beliefs and customs, especially in relation to authority in family, school and university, and a general rise in standards of living which has produced an impressive degree of social and political stability, but has not allayed an acute spiritual discontent in wide sections of the younger generation.

In Asia outside Japan industrialization through private enterprise has had great difficulty in getting off the ground for reasons already indicated, and the adverse conditions have been greatly, indeed catastrophically, aggravated by the massive increases of population which have made enormous additions to the numbers of human beings in Asian countries since the beginning of the century. These increases have been due to a branch of modern technology—the control of epidemic diseases through medicine and hygiene—which can operate independently of general economic progress and thus produce great increments of population in stagnant agrarian societies where there is already overcrowding and underemployment on the land. To provide employment for rapidly increasing populations and to assure adequate food supplies when they were already suffering from widespread malnutrition even before the addition of so many extra mouths, a superlatively rapid rate of economic growth is required, but the conditions are unsuited to such advances. In some countries foreign exchange urgently needed for the import of capital goods has to be diverted to purchases of food to avert starvation; where no thoroughgoing land reform has taken place, landed property is often a more attractive investment than harassed industrial enterprises; vast numbers of peasants migrate to the towns, providing cheap labour for industrial development, but impeding it by their sheer mass which creates large-scale unemployment with its consequences of unrest, disorders and demands on already overburdened social services. Calcutta in particular attained in the 1960s an unenviable notoriety for its uncontrollable enlargement, its immense slums and the inability of its municipal administration to cope with the problems created by the continuing influx from the countryside; it was estimated that a quarter of a million homeless people were sleeping in the streets, and when a food ration was introduced as a relief measure they were not eligible for it because they could not give any address in the city as the official regulations required.

The alternative to reliance on government-stimulated private enterprise for economic growth is some form of socialism, and this normally means communism in the sense of state or collective ownership of the means of production and control by a communist party dictatorship, but it can also cover systems such as that in operation under the rule of General Ne Win in Burma; it should not, however, be extended to include such 'socialism' as that of the Indian Congress Party, which maintains a large public sector of the economy while leaving its main development to capitalism. The recent political development of Asia apart from the Soviet Union and Japan has been marked by situations in which all non-communist governments have been challenged by communist movements and have reacted with policies which are partly repressive, but partly also competitive in trying to steal the thunder of social revolution. It is difficult today to find any regime which simply stands on traditional loyalties and beliefs in opposition to all change; the endeavour of the former Sultan of Muscat to do so only led to his deposition by his own son. The modern world cannot be kept out; every country must come to terms with it in one way or another. But there are alternative ways of modernity, and the conflict between the rival political forces is often intense; moreover, antagonisms which are primarily between bourgeois nationalism and communism are complicated by ethnic struggles, such as the civil war in East Pakistan, or by international rivalries, such as those involved in the war in Vietnam. Further the communist movement has itself been split by the ideological rivalry between Moscow and Peking, and the Sino-Soviet power struggle has come to overshadow the entire continent.

Communism in Asia has reached the opposite pole from the conviction of Marx that the socialist revolution would only occur when private capitalism had developed to the limits of its capacity, the rural sector of the economy had been outweighed by the urban, and the industrial proletariat had become the most numerous class in society. The victory of the Chinese Communists from an almost exclusively rural social base provided Asia, and all under-developed countries, with the model of an agarian guerrilla revolution, in which the industrial proletariat plays little or no part and the capitalist stage of economic development is more or less bypassed in a direct transition from a 'feudal' to a socialist economy. The idea of eliminating the capitalist stage is much nearer to the thought of the nineteenth-century Russian Narodniks than to that of Marxism, and comes naturally to a radical intelligentsia emerging in a predominantly agrarian and traditionalist society; in practical terms it means, however, that the revolutionary party, if successful in seizing the state power, does not take over an already industrialized economy, but must itself create one, that is to say, it must perform what for Marx was the historic task and function of capitalism. In circumstances of economic backwardness the problems of growth are fundamentally the same for communist and non-communist states, and in this respect, though not in their politics and ideology, the degree of industrialization is the most important criterion for classifying nations; thus in Asia Japan and the Soviet Union are in one category and India and China in another.

Lenin with his political exploitation of the peasant *jacquerie* in Russia, albeit only as an auxiliary of the urban insurrection, was already halfway between Marx and Mao, and the Bolshevik revolution in Russia, brought about not in the most advanced industrial country of Europe but in a relatively under-developed one, was in contradiction to what orthodox Marxism had previously regarded as the historically pre-ordained sequence of social change. It was, however, just this relative backwardness of Russia which made it so much more liable to a fundamental disruption of the social order than other nations which likewise endured the strains and stresses of the greatest war the world had ever known; a still overwhelmingly rural society torn by deep conflicts over the tenure of land, a small but rapidly growing modern industry, with a working class formed for the most part by a recent uprooting from the villages, a dynastic autocracy modified later and less deeply than in other parts of Europe by parliamentary politics, a sophisticated and iconoclastic intelligentsia almost entirely detached and alienated from practical affairs—these were the conditions in which it was found so easy for a numerically minute, but highly indoctrinated and disciplined, group of revolutionary socialists to dominate and transform the Russian nation—and a number of non-Russian peoples who had been subjected to the rule of the Russian Tsars.

Similar conditions prevail today in many Asian countries which at the end of the Second World War were far less industrialized than Russia had been in 1917. Advanced industrial societies are certainly not immune from revolutionary disturbances and there is no government in the world which is quite secure against communist takeover, but the course of history since 1917 indicates that the countries of advanced industrial development are less vulnerable to revolutionary upheaval than those emerging from conditions classified by Marxism as feudal in the economic and political circumstances of the twentieth century. However, the uncertainty and instability characteristic of these countries is conducive not only to revolutions, as exemplified in China and Vietnam, but also to counter-revolutions, as demonstrated by the events of the last decade in Indonesia. Moreover, the rift between Peking and Moscow has the effect, as long as it lasts, of thwarting the solidarity of the communist world in support of revolutionary movements which Marxist-Leninist principles assume. In the following pages an attempt is made to assess trends in Asia in the contemporary period by a survey of individual countries grouped according to the three main types of political system prevailing there—democracy, communism and military dictatorship.

Democracy in Asia

The two great examples of parliamentary democracy in Asia are Japan and India—two countries which in other respects afford the most striking contrasts. Japan has entered the seventies as an ethnically cohesive insular nation with a predominantly urban population, a highly developed modern industry, almost full employment, and a widespread affluence; India is a federation of more than a dozen different linguistic nationalities, with long, dangerous land frontiers, a population and economy still predominantly agrarian, a developing but inadequate modern industry, massive unemployment, and large pockets of extreme poverty. From this comparison it is reasonable to infer that parliamentary democracy in Japan has better prospects than it has in India, and certainly at the time of writing it seems that Japan is less beset than India by troubles that might drive the body politic towards some kind of authoritarian solution. On the other hand, it must be borne in mind that the Japanese nation as a whole in the recent past accepted very willingly a violent chauvinist military regime centred on a cult of a divine monarchy and that their present democratic constitution was in effect imposed by a foreign military occupation after a disastrous defeat in war; unlike the old 'emperor system' or the Meiji Constitution of 1889, it was not made in Japan. In contrast Indian democracy was part and parcel of the struggle for national independence; if the colonial power itself originally provided the model for it, it was established as the form of the state created by Gandhi and Nehru and is today led by Nehru's daughter.

The politics of Japan since the recovery of full national sovereignty by the San Fransciso Peace Treaty of 1952 have conformed to a pattern which still prevails, though it shows some signs of changing. It is a pattern in which the moderate Right (the Liberal Democratic Party) holds power with an absolute parliamentary majority, the extreme Right, roughly identical with the ultra-nationalist and anti-democratic groups aiming at a restoration of the pre-war political system, is in almost total political eclipse, the parliamentary Left is divided between several political parties, and the extreme revolutionary Left, from which the orthodox Communists are now excluded, enjoys widespread support among students but hardly any among workers or peasants. The ruling Liberal Democratic Party stands squarely behind the capitalist economic order which has achieved such spectacular successes in industrial growth over the past two decades; on the other hand, it publicly accepts—with whatever mental reservations—the existing democratic constitution and has observed its provisions in practice, so that it can fairly be claimed that post-war Japan has become a genuinely free country, with freedom of speech, freedom for political opposition and free elections. In foreign policy the Liberal Democrats have stood for maintenance of the Security Pact with the United States, whereby Japan is protected by the American 'nuclear umbrella', the American armed forces continue to have the use of certain bases in Japan, and Japan provides a small 'self-defence force' as an element of the alliance.

The Left in Japanese politics comprises the Socialist and Communist parties; the Democratic Socialist party, which was formed by a right-wing secession from the Socialists; the Komeito, which was formed as the political counterpart of the Buddhist revivalist organization known as the Soga Gakkai, but has now opened its ranks to adherents who have no religious commitment; and, on the far Left, the various Maoist, Trotskyite and Anarchist groups who call themselves 'anti-Yoyogi' because they repudiate the leadership of the orthodox Communist Party which has its headquarters in the Yoyogi district of Tokyo. The divisions between these parties and groups have produced a situation in which, although it seems quite possible that at the next general election the Liberal Democrats may lose their absolute majority in the House of Representatives, it is difficult to see any government of the Left which could maintain itself on a parliamentary basis. There is here a striking contrast with West Germany, whose post-war politics have in general been similar to those of Japan. In Germany, as in Japan, the post-war economic recovery was achieved under the direction of a government which rejected the Nazi or militarist past, but was socially conservative; in Germany, however, there was one major opposition party, the Social Democrats, which with the support of a small centrist party, the Free Democrats, was able to form a government when the electorate denied a majority to the Christian Democratic Union. In Japan the Socialists, though still the largest opposition party, have no position comparable to that of the Social Democrats in Germany. They have been losing seats both to the Communists and to Komeito, and could be at best in a bid for power the nucleus of a Popular Front; but even this would be difficult to attain, because the Democratic Socialists have sworn never to enter into a coalition with the Communists and it is doubtful whether Komeito would agree to do so either. A combination of Socialists and Communists has had notable successes in electing governors (the equivalent of mayors because the largest cities count as prefectures) in Tokyo and Osaka, but has no prospect of carrying the country as a whole. A centre grouping of Komeito, the Democratic Socialists and breakaway factions from the Liberal Democratic and Socialist parties is a possibility for the future, but it is difficult to imagine that it would have much stability. If the Liberal Democrats, therefore, lose their present parliamentary majority, a period of weak and unstable government would be likely to ensue; if on the other hand they keep it, the firm government of the last two decades may be expected to continue, but with an increasing strain on a political system which apparently condemns the parties of the Left to permanent opposition and frustration.

The most remarkable development in recent Japanese politics has undoubtedly been the rise of Komeito. None of the parliamentary political parties of pre-war Japan had a religious basis, though the political order itself, centred on the divinely commissioned imperial dynasty, was bound up with the rituals of 'State Shinto'. This connection was abolished after Japan's surrender in 1945 and the Emperor himself formally repudiated any claim to divine origin. The collapse of the old order of things, with its complex of traditional beliefs, customs and loyalties, left a spiritual void, which was continually extended with the shrinking of the rural sector of society and the relocation of millions of uprooted peasants in the new urban areas. The general rise in material standards of living in a competitive money-making society did not compensate for the loss of faith and sense of collective dedication which the old *kokutai* nationalism had inspired. The vacuum was filled partly by the Marxist and Maoist creeds which flourished in the universities, but partly also by the emergence of new religious sects and revivals of old ones. The most successful of the latter was a revival of the Buddhist sect founded in Japan by Nichiren in the thirteenth century; an organization of its laity under the name of Soga Gakkai had an extraordinary expansion in the post-war period. As a faith rooted in traditional Japanese culture with emotional links with China and India, Soga Gakkai could commend itself as a factor of

Japanese and Asian resistance to the American cultural ascendancy of the post-war years, yet at the same time it could disclaim involvement in the discredited pre-war style of nationalism, for its founder, as an uncompromising Buddhist, had objected to compulsory State Shinto in the schools and the armed forces and had died in prison during the war as a result of his subversive activity. Soga Gakkai called for a moral regeneration of society, and on its entry into politics as the Komeito party concentrated on compaigning against the corruption all too prevalent under the rule of the Liberal Democrats; as a mass movement drawing its strength from a numerous petty bourgeoisie, it stood to the left of the Liberal Democrats, but rejected socialism and proclaimed its course to be 'middle of the road politics' (*chudo seiji*). Some observers, however, taking note of its fanatical disciplined enthusiasm and the highly organized propaganda of its meetings and rallies, saw in it a potentially fascist force capable of being directed in a crisis to a takeover of state power. Such a development might indeed take place in the future, but so far Komeito has no para-military forces nor does it repudiate the democratic system.

In Japan since the war there has been in the popular mind a close association between the ideas of democracy and pacifism. This was a natural consequence of the rejection of the pre-war system and of the army-sponsored policies which had led to war and defeat; the revulsion of feeling against militarism made the thorough disarmament and demobilization imposed by the victors generally acceptable at the time to the Japanese people, and the renunciation of armed forces was written into the constitution, thus making it an integral part of the new democracy. But when in the years after 1945 the cold war between Russia and the West replaced the alignments of the Second World War the Americans came to regret the creation of a power vacuum in Central Europe and another in Japan, and tried to promote a limited rearmament of both West Germany and Japan to assist in the task of containing the expansion of the new Soviet empire.

In West Germany there was no legal obstacle to this, but in Japan it involved either a breach or an evasion of a constitution, sponsored by the Americans themselves, which could not be altered except by what proved to be an unattainable two-thirds parliamentary majority. As a result of this situation there came about a paradoxical identification of nationalism and pacifism, so that the continuation of the war-time fight against America, the *revanchisme* of a defeated Japan, now took the form of pacifist demonstrations against the American military presence in Japan and resistance to the building of a Japanese 'self-defence force' denounced as a mere auxiliary of American imperialism. The campaign against the Japanese-American Security Pact and against Japan's own diminutive military establishment became a speciality of the Left. Where the Right, the residuary legatees of the tradition of Meiji nationalism, sought to make the best of the situation following the disaster of 1945 and accepted a relation of dependence on the United States for strategic protection, the Left kept on filling the streets with noisy demonstrations against American imperialism which again and again sank a metaphorical American fleet in a bloodless Pearl Harbour. This militant patriotic pacifism was particularly attractive to students; it could be combined with general Left-wing agitation against a government which might be charged with all kinds of sins but above all with being a puppet of the United States. On the other hand, the extreme Right, identified in the post-war years with anti-communism, could draw little benefit from the popular anti-American sentiments which sustained the Left, and its calls for stronger national armed forces seemed like a backing for American pressure on Japan to take a larger share in the cost of a joint strategy. A qualified pacifism also had its appeal for business interests, which in a period of booming expansion felt no need of arms programmes to sustain the economy and benefited from the relatively low state expenditure on defence. There was a general belief that Japan was better off without her pre-war military and naval power and could play a great part in world affairs in future through economic strength alone without a corresponding capacity in arms.

There are signs, however, of a change in Japanese public opinion on the question of national defence. The armed power of both Russia and China has greatly increased since 1965 while the isolationist trend in the United States has introduced an element of uncertainty into Japanese-American relations which have further been subjected to severe strain because of the development of economic conflict between the two nations. There is now, therefore, a stronger demand than at any time since 1952 for a more independent and self-reliant foreign policy, but this must raise the question of rearmament in an ever more acute form; is it to be an 'unarmed neutrality', as the Socialists urge, or a position in which a greater independence of policy is to be supported by much more powerful armed forces than Japan has now? The debate involves further the question of the existing constitution of the state; there would be nothing inherently undemocratic in an increase of Japanese armaments, which remain far below the level (relative to the GNP) of the major Western democracies, but the armed forces must remain, as they are, without formal status as regular services, unless there is a revision of the constitution to sanction it. The political situation involved, which was brought into an unpleasant prominence by Mishima Yukio's dramatic suicide, is discussed by G. R. Storry in a previous chapter of this book; it suffices here to point out that the extra-constitutional position of the Self-Defence Force does confront Japan with a serious political problem. So far no Japanese government since the war has needed to call in the Self-Defence Force to assist in the maintenance of internal order, and it has not itself shown any disposition to attempt a *Putsch*, but the ambiguity of its status cannot but be a grievance for those who belong to it and incline them against a political system which imposes it and political parties which prevent a revision.

Few observers anticipated that Japan's post-war democracy

would prove as stable and orderly as it has turned out to be. There has not so far been a serious threat to the regime from either the Right or the Left, and in spite of the spectacular quality of the student riots, so lavishly publicized by press and television, their violence has very seldom been lethal or more than a well-trained riot police have been able to cope with. The secret of the success has certainly been the fact that most Japanese have never had it so good. The land reform has, broadly speaking, satisfied the peasants who have remained on the land while the great industrial expansion brought general prosperity to the bourgeoisie and full employment for the working class. But it is doubtful whether the boom conditions can continue. The measures taken by President Nixon to protect the economic interests of the United States have dealt a severe blow to Japan's export trade in its most important market and, even if Japan can obtain an easing of the new restrictions through a revaluation of the yen, the competitive position cannot be as strong as it was before. Moreover, Japan has been hitherto among the nations least attentive to industrial pollution and it has now reached a point at which it is a menace to health as well as to amenity; it has suddenly become a political issue and the government is being compelled to take measures against it, but any effective action must add substantially to industrial costs. It may well be, therefore, that Japan is entering on a period of economic difficulty, which any downturn in world trade could turn into a serious crisis, and the setback to national prosperity would subject Japanese democracy to a strain more severe than any it has endured since national sovereignty was restored after seven years of foreign military occupation.

In Asia's other great democracy conditions are quite different, but certainly no less difficult. The strength of Indian democracy lies in its tradition, in the fusion of the ideas of democracy and national independence which was characteristic of the Indian nationalist movement long before independence; paradoxically it has a quasi-dynastic quality as represented by the three generations of the Nehru family from Motilal to Indira. Although the British retained supreme authority in India until 1947, the provincial elections of 1937 provided a real exercise in democratic practice before national independence; during the Pacific War India was not overrun or seriously invaded by the Japanese and after the War was over the transfer of power to a government of the Indian Congress Party was a peaceful one as far as Britain was concerned. By 1947 'indianization' had already gone far in the Indian civil service and army, so that the new government could start with effective instruments of central control; there was also a substantial capitalist class which had made considerable advances during the last years of British rule. India thus entered on the path of political democracy with advantages denied to French Indo-China or the Dutch East Indies, where there had been no preparation for democratic self-government before the Pacific War, where there was virtually no indigenous bourgeoisie, where the existing administrations had been wrecked by the Japanese invasions and where independence was only gained after fierce struggles against the returning forces of the metro-politan colonial power.

After independence, however, India was faced with two vast problems: the first, that of economic growth from a very low level of production, and the second, that of ethnic diversity and the aspirations of sub-nationalities. The Congress leadership was more aware of the former problem than of the second; as a new political elite which had rebelled not only against the British Raj but also against India's old social order, they were conscious of the need to initiate economic development and undertake social reforms, but as nationalists who had led a struggle against alien rule on behalf of all parts of India, they took the cohesion of the Indian nation too much for granted and underestimated the centrifugal forces of ethnic division, which were bound to be accentuated rather than diminished as the popular masses were more and more drawn into politics. As W. F. Crawley points out in his chapter of this book, the Congress Party was originally

283

opposed to the idea of recognizing any divisions of India on a linguistic basis and preferred to retain the old provinces of British India which often cut across linguistic boundaries; it was only in response to strong pressures from below that the principle of linguistic states was conceded as the basis for a federal 'Indian Union'. The rights granted to the states satisfied for the time being the aspirations of the sub-nationalities, but created new problems for the central government. The idea of making Hindi the national language of a united India was thwarted by the recalcitrance of the speakers of other important Indian languages, notably Tamil, and the autonomy of the states rendered central economic planning extremely difficult. Land reform remained under the control of the states and many large-scale economic projects required a degree of cooperation between the central government and one or more of the states which it was found impossible to achieve. Coordination of policies was difficult even when the Congress Party was in power both in the states and at the centre; when a Congress government in Delhi was confronted with non-Congress parties in office in the states, it became much harder. The ultimate sanction of armed force remained firmly in the hands of the central government and it was constitutionally able to impose direct rule on any state in an emergency, but every such intervention implied a failure in the working of the federal system.

The civil war in East Pakistan created an agonizing dilemma for India. Indian popular sympathies were strongly on the side of the insurgents and the burden of the millions of refugees on the finances of India and West Bengal provided a powerful incentive to intervention on behalf of Bangla Desh; on the other hand, it was inconceivable that an independent Bengali national state could be created in East Bengal without stimulating Bengali nationalism in West Bengal and thus threatening disruption of India as well as Pakistan. In the words of a perceptive Indian writer, 'Disintegration of Pakistan as a state, if it comes to happen, may lead to physical upheavals in the subcontinent far exceeding anything that has occurred so far.'[1]

As in Japan, one party has succeeded in spite of free elections in maintaining itself in power, but whereas the Liberal Democrats in Japan are the party of the Right with parliamentary opposition only on the Left, the Congress Party in India stands in the centre of the political spectrum with strong opposition from the Right as well as from the Left. The Jan Singh, a party with a Hindu religious basis, and the private-business-supported Swatantra have been reinforced by a substantial Right-wing secession from the Congress Party itself, but the possibility of government by a coalition of the Right was denied by the sweeping victory of Mrs Gandhi's Left-wing section of the Congress in the general election at the beginning of 1971. On the Left the main opposition to Congress leadership comes from the Communists, but their movement has split into three separate parties, two of which take part in legal politics, while the third, the Communist Party of India (Marxist-Leninist), is identified with the armed guerrilla revolt of the Naxalites (so called from the district of Naxalbari in Bengal, where its uprising began). Because Mrs Gandhi gained an absolute parliamentary majority in the elections she is not dependent on the Communists for support against the Right and can pursue at her discretion policies designed to implement the slogan of 'Banish Poverty' on which she won the election. The Pakistan civil war, however, and the vast exodus of refugees into India added new burdens to an already overstrained economy and even the military victory over Pakistan, though the war was very brief and brought about the repatriation of the refugees, has had to be paid for financially. On the other hand, the war has certainly strengthened not only Mrs. Gandhi's government, but also the democratic political system, in that it has shown that such a victory could be gained by an elected civilian authority, with no need for a military dictatorship.

In the adverse circumstances with which India has had to contend

[1] Bhabani Sen Gupta, *The Fulcrum of Asia*, p. 27.

the persistence of democratic government in India has been remarkable, and it is not surprising that it has been subjected to some restrictions. In Kashmir there has never been any real political freedom, since any party rejecting the union with India is outlawed, and no popular vote on the basic issue of Kashmir's position in relation to Delhi has been allowed. Kashmir, however, is marginal to the politics of India as a whole, and in general all parties, including the Communists, have been free to carry on their political activities and elections have been fairly conducted. A governmental power of detention without trial was introduced in 1962 at the time of the brief war with China, when the pro-Chinese wing of the Communists was suspected of treasonable actions; the power lapsed in 1969, but has been revived for use against the Naxalites. The struggle against the rural guerrilla revolt of the Naxalites is indeed one of formidable dimensions and there is no end to it in sight. K. C. Pant, the Minister of State for Home Affairs, declared on 22 July 1971 that Naxalite disturbances had been reported from West Bengal, Assam, Bihar, Andhra Pradesh, Punjab and Maghalaya. There is no indication so far that the Naxalites have been able to establish anywhere a secure base area of the kind required for the success of rural guerrilla communism on the Maoist model; in India they have to deal, not with a disintegrated state, such as China was in the twenties and thirties of this century, but with a strong central government commanding an effective unified army. Nevertheless, future developments such as war with Pakistan or national separation in Bengal could give the Naxalites their chance, and in the long run their potential threat can only be met by agrarian reforms more thorough than any that have yet been undertaken.

In Ceylon, where, as in India, a democratic political system has been operative since independence, the trend to the Left has been even more marked than in India and the constitutional order even more sharply challenged by the Ceylonese equivalent of Naxalism. Mrs Bandaranaike won the last general election with a

Left coalition of her own radical nationalist party with orthodox Communists and Trotskyites and formed a government on this basis; one of its first acts was to free from prison leaders of the revolutionary 'Guevarist' group who a few months later launched an armed insurrection and came close to success. The small Ceylon army was unprepared to meet such a rising, but was provided with needed arms and transport for crushing the revolt of the extreme Left by a strange international coalition which included, for diverse reasons, the United States, Britain, the Soviet Union, India and Pakistan. Reports from Ceylon indicated that there had been a revulsion of popular feeling against the Bandaranaike government in the months following the elections because it had made the most extravagant demagogic promises to the electorate and had been quite unable to fulfil them, even if it had had the will to do so. Events in Ceylon have indeed demonstrated in a dramatic way the perils of arousing hopes of rapid betterment in an underdeveloped country affected by widespread poverty, substantial unemployment of rural and urban workers and a large unemployed intelligentsia.

Communism in Asia

When in October 1949 the People's Republic of China was formally established, following the victory of the Chinese Communists in civil war, the most numerous people, not only of Asia but of the whole world, was officially enlisted in the 'socialist camp'. Since this result was achieved by a party committed to the principles of Marxism-Leninism, it should have meant an immense increase of prestige and strength for the cause of international communism, and so at the outset it appeared to be. In the event, however, things have not worked out as might have been expected. China has followed a path so divergent in theory and practice from other communist countries, and has been so self-assertive in its relations with the Russian elder brother, that not only has the solidarity of the international communist movement been seriously disrupted but the two leading communist

287

states have even—contrary to the vital doctrine that all wars are due to capitalism—engaged in limited military hostilities with each other.

The Chinese pursuit of such a separate 'road to socialism' has been partly the outcome of conditions prevailing in China at the time of the communist seizure of power and of the methods by which power was won. The prolonged experience of rural guerrilla warfare, and particularly the bitter duration of the Long March, when Mao Tse-tung gained the supreme leadership of the Chinese Communist Party, provided a background to the regime quite different from that of the Soviet Russian leaders, who came to power by a rapid *coup d'état* in the two principal cities—which were also the main centres of Russian industry—and continued to hold them during the subsequent civil war. For more than two decades the Chinese Communists had their own world in the territories they controlled deep in the interior of China—a world of villages and small towns without modern industry, of peasants, peasant soldiers who fought in the People's Liberation Army, and peasant craftsmen who provided the soldiers with small arms, clothing and other necessary supplies. It was a world of minimum professional specialization and maximum equality, of simple and frugal living and great solidarity in the face of manifold hardships and dangers. The men who from 1949 onwards undertook to govern, administer and industrialize the whole of China had been conditioned by their long years in the wilderness and their experience of a social organism which even in so preponderantly agrarian a society as that of China before 1949 had been one-sidedly rural and non-industrial. Their basic outlook, whatever their professed principles, had been nearer to Bakunin and the Russian Narodniks, who saw socialism emerging from a vast peasant *jacquerie* in a backward agrarian society, than to Marx and Lenin. They took with them to Peking what some American sinologists have called the 'Yenan syndrome', a nostalgia for the caves of Yenan and the virtues achieved there. Despite the theoretical conception of a revolu-

tionary progress from lower to higher things, Chinese communism, and particularly the form of it which came to be known
specifically as Maoism, revolved increasingly round the idea that
perfection, or something very near it, had already been achieved
in the good old days of the rural guerrilla war and that the
supreme task of the revolution was to avert a degeneration from
that standard. In consequence of this way of thinking the
intention of the Great Proletarian Cultural Revolution, which
was to convulse China in the late sixties, was not so much a move
forward into a new era as a redemption from Paradise Lost to
Paradise Regained.

The degeneration feared by the Maoists came from three main
sources: bureaucratism, a reliance on material incentives in the
economy, and professionalism in the army. Industrialization—
which had to be rapid if China was to emerge in good time from
her economic backwardness—involved tendencies towards
increasing specialization of functions, the formation of an élite
of managers and technicians and a sharp grading of salaries and
wages with special monetary rewards to stimulate productivity.
The Maoists desired the industrialization of China, but they
sought to attain it without appeal to even attenuated forms of the
profit motive; for them the spirit of economic development
should be that of an army on the march or a city under siege,
with all purposes of private betterment subjected to a dedication
to the common good. The inspiration for economic advance
must come from political faith and enthusiasm; hence the slogan
'Politics in Command', which became the watchword of the
Maoists against those whom they denounced as 'revisionists', the
more pragmatic Communist leaders who were ready to forget
about the heroic age of the Long March in the endeavour to make
the economy work by appealing to the less elevated desires of
countless individuals to get from it some material gain for
themselves.

A parallel choice presented itself with regard to military
affairs. It was obviously desirable for the new China to have

powerful armed forces in proportion to her size and population as a nation state, but this involved a risk in the eyes of the Maoists of losing the essential virtues of the army of the rural guerrilla—its close integration with the masses of the people, its egalitarian comradeship and its great strategic flexibility. The Maoists regarded with disfavour the formation after 1949 of a professional officers' corps on the Soviet model with titles and badges of rank independent of current functions of command, politically indoctrinated indeed, but increasingly absorbed in specialized military concerns at the expense of its political commitment. During the fifties the rival views on the proper shape and style of the armed forces under communism came to be personified in two leading military figures; Peng Teh-huai sought to build up highly trained regular armed forces with a corps of professional officers on the Soviet model, while Lin Piao, who had been Mao Tse-tung's closest military supporter in the days of the Long March, wished to preserve as much as possible of the character of the old guerrilla army in the new military system, counting on a dispersed 'people's war' to exhaust and defeat any invader of China. The People's Liberation Army, for the Maoists, should not be merely a military force; it should participate in political agitation and propaganda and engage in various kinds of economic construction, and if its technical military efficiency suffered to some extent through such diversions of effort, this would be less important that the gain for the revolution resulting from its political commitment and solidarity with the masses of the people. The inclination of the Maoists was to exalt political loyalty over technical training and morale over armaments. With regard to one kind of armament, however, the Maoists had more zeal than the professionals, and this was an issue which also involved fundamental questions of foreign policy.

In accordance with their aim of making China into a great power second to none they wanted her to have her own nuclear weapons; this was not incompatible with the idea of 'people's war' because it provided a means of hitting back at an enemy who might have a decisive superiority in conventional armaments. By her alliance with the Soviet Union, concluded in 1950, China would have the protection of the Soviet nuclear power in any war or confrontation with the United States—and did derive such an advantage from it during the war in Korea—but such dependence implied a degree of political subordination which the Maoists were unwilling to accept. The Soviet Union's failure to back up China in the confrontation with the United States over Quemoy in 1958, the refusal of support in the border clash with India in the following year, and Khrushchev's complete indifference to Chinese interests in his approach to America during the same year emphasized the price to be paid for looking to another country, even a communist one, for indispensable protection in international power conflicts. Peking's endeavours to get Soviet assistance in developing nuclear weapons proved abortive; the Soviet Union had no intention of building up China as a power of comparable, and perhaps in the end superior, strength to itself.

In 1959 the opposition to Maoism was embodied in Peng Teh-huai, who as Defence Minister was promoting what the Maoists later called 'the bourgeois military line' in the army, while in the Central Committee of the Party he became the foremost critic of Mao's twin brain-children, the Great Leap Forward and the Great People's Communes. The Great Leap Forward had been intended to speed up industrialization—and raise agricultural production at the same time—by mass mobilization of the people, putting everyone to work with the drive of an omnipresent exhortation and avoiding the problems of rapid enlargement of cities by bringing industry to the villages; it was a procedure which was meant to kill two birds with one stone, for the same decentralization of industry which was to make every peasant into a producer of industrial goods was designed at the same time to make China less vulnerable strategically to aerial attack, whether conventional or nuclear. The communes were to be the auxiliaries of this swift economic advance; they were to combine agriculture and industry in their localities and serve also as units of civil administration and military organization. After an enthusiastic start, however, the whole project went wrong; unforeseen hazards thwarted the over-ambitious plans, and in particular the scheme for doubling steel production in one year by using thousands of local 'backyard' furnaces came to grief after having 'at great cost produced steel resembling Swiss cheese, largely because no one had remembered that impurities in the firebrick contaminated the product'.[1]

In consequence of the failure of the Great Leap Forward Mao had to yield the office of Chairman of the Republic to Liu Shao-ch'i while himself remaining Chairman of the Party; he succeeded, however, by a tactical alliance with Liu and his followers in forcing the resignation of Peng Teh-huai as Minister of Defence and replacing him with his special *protégé* Lin Piao. For the next six years there was an uneasy compromise between the Maoists and their critics and during this period there was gradual, but substantial, economic progress. The compromise broke down, however, in 1965, and the crisis within the Party leadership was followed by the great upheaval of the so-called Cultural Revolution. The supporters of Liu Shao-ch'i had control of the Party apparatus, but Mao through Lin Piao had control of the armed forces, and fundamentally it was by the power of the army that the issue was decided. Mao was nevertheless unwilling to overturn the authority of the Party directly through a military *coup d'état* and preferred to carry out a political purge through the agency of bands of teenagers known as Red Guards, who were assisted and protected by the army, but gave the operation the character of a spontaneous mass movement of the younger generation in protest against the revisionist degeneration of the Party. In this way Mao hoped not only to remove his opponents from all positions of power but to raise up 'revolutionary successors' by giving young people who had never known the years of civil war the experience

[1] Robert S. Elegant, *Mao's Great Revolution* (1971), p. 59.

of 'making a revolution'. The idea did not, however, work out quite as intended; the Party was indeed purged and Mao's enemies swept away, but the fanatical pseudo-insurgency of the Red Guards soon declined into mere hooliganism and widespread violence between factions of the Red Guards themselves, so that the army had to step in to restore order. After youth had had its fling and the disorder had been quelled the People's Republic emerged as a different kind of society from that which had existed before the Cultural Revolution—one in which the Communist Party still retained a nominal supremacy but real power had passed into the hands of the army. The new state of affairs was reflected in the composition of the Party itself; of 170 full members of the Central Committee elected at the Party's Ninth Congress in 1969, 96 were from the army, and of 25 members and alternates of the Politburo 12 were soldiers. The army had taken over the direction of many economic enterprises and the supervision of schools and universities; its function as the indispensable guardian of revolutionary purity and internal order was at the same time reinforced by a sense of imminent danger in China's international situation.

However, a situation in which the army possessed such a preponderance of power was also one of danger for Mao Tse-tung, whose basis of authority was ideological and political and not simply military. Mao had exercised control of the army through Lin Piao as Defence Minister, and the latter had been formally designated as Mao's successor as Chairman of the Party, but this made him an over-mighty subject if any disagreement over policy should arise between the two men. Such a conflict apparently did arise in September 1971, as a result of which Mao carried out a drastic purge of Lin Piao himself and of the higher command of the armed forces. At the time of writing[1] a mantle of secrecy even more dense than that which surrounded Stalin's purges of the thirties still enshrouds these events, but an indication of their nature has been given by a radio

[1] November 1971.

broadcast assuring garrison troops that 'the leadership remains firmly in the hands of the central committee of the Communist Party headed by Mao Tse-tung'.

No publicity has so far been given to the issue on which Mao came into conflict with army leaders but it may well have been over the invitation to the President of the United States to visit Peking. Whatever the advantages to be obtained from the new course of foreign policy it must appear a highly dangerous one from a professional military point of view, for it risks an aggravation of the already tense relations with the Soviet Union and a war for which China is insufficiently prepared.

In the fifties the Chinese Communists' contention with the United States had been offset by their alliance with the Soviet Union which had provided them with both economic and strategic support. But from 1960 onwards the People's Republic was in conflict with both Russia and America simultaneously, and for good measure a bitter quarrel with India was added to the hostility of the two super-powers of the world.

The conflict with capitalist America was a natural one from a Marxist-Leninist point of view; although it had particular causes—Korea, Taiwan, Vietnam—the enmity could be regarded as inherent in the relations between American capitalism in its world-wide imperial expansion after the Second World War and the anti-imperialist revolution of the Chinese people. The conflict with the Soviet Union was of a different kind and hard to explain in Marxist-Leninist terms, since both the Soviet Union and the Chinese People's Republic were states governed by Communist parties which theoretically should be bound together by fraternal ties of international solidarity. If in fact their policies were not in harmony, this could only be because one or other of them had fallen into ideological error. Inevitably, therefore, clashes between the two Communist states took the form of charges and counter-charges of doctrinal heresy. In part the ideological controversies were unreal because they masked rivalries of interest and power between sovereign states which had nothing to do with communism and could have arisen between governments of feudal or bourgeois societies. But the ideological conflict was in part genuine because of the contradiction arising out of the very nature of the communist regime in China in contrast to that of the Soviet Union. Since communism had been victorious in China through a rural guerrilla revolution, this was a model which China could present to all backward agrarian societies, thus superseding Russian influence and inspiration throughout the 'underdeveloped' world of Asia, Africa and Latin America. The Russian Communists were undoubtedly closer to Marx in arguing that peasants could not make a real socialist revolution and that it was impossible to leap over whole epochs of economic development in order to arrive at the proletarian utopia. But the general reality of the international scene was that the advanced industrial countries outside the Soviet Union and its satellites afforded minimal prospects of conversion to communism, whereas the tensions of the 'Third World' gave promise of great revolutionary upheavals such as Marxist-Leninists were bound to hope for. The Russians suddenly found themselves confronted with a strongly self-assertive rival for leadership of the international communist movement in just those parts of the world where it seemed to have most prospect of success and they deeply resented the Chinese intrusion, while the Chinese on their side no less deeply resented the efforts of Khrushchev to reach a *modus vivendi* with the United States in which the special interests of Peking would be ignored. The Chinese ideological polemic against Russia from 1960 onwards therefore took the form of an accusation that Russia had succumbed to revisionism, had compromised with American imperialism and had abandoned the cause of world revolution which China would henceforth lead.

In practice the difference between Russian and Chinese policies has been by no means as great as the theoretical polemics would imply. Russia has matched Chinese support for the revolutionary war in Vietnam, while China has matched Russian willingness to sacrifice revolutionaries to *raison d'état* in foreign policy by its support for Pakistan; despite all the bluster Peking has not so far even tried to capture Quemoy since the abortive attempt in 1958, and with the invitation to President Nixon for a visit to Peking has made nonsense of its righteous indignation at Russian 'collusion' with America. But the 'Sino-Soviet Dispute' has not been assuaged because the Chinese world-revolutionary bite has fallen so far short of its bark; on the contrary, the tension has increased and this has been mainly the outcome of China's acquisition of nuclear weapons. As long as China was not a nuclear power, its aberrations could be regarded by Russia with annoyance rather than alarm; even its disruptive activities in the international communist movement were not a matter for fear. But if effective nuclear armaments were to be in the possession of a nation with a potential of military manpower three times that of the Soviet Union, a new super-power would be brought to birth in the not-distant future, and this would fundamentally alter existing relations of power, both in the continent of Asia and in the entire world. The situation has become still more alarming for Russia since the improvement of relations between Peking and Washington, which has meant that Moscow can no longer count on a permanent Sino-American antagonism and must reckon for the future with the possibility even of a Sino-American alliance. In these circumstances there is a strong temptation for Russia to embark on a preventive war against China with the aim of 'denuclearizing' China before the latter's nuclear capability becomes too dangerous to challenge. Already for some years now Russia has been faced with a two-front strategic situation instead of the one-front position assured in the fifties by the alliance with China and has had to transfer substantial forces from Europe into Asia; these forces, including their nuclear weapon components, are probably even now sufficient for a war with China, but it would be unwise for the Kremlin to force a showdown in Asia while there are still outstanding unsettled issues in Central Europe and the Middle East.

Settlements of these issues on the best terms that can be obtained appear, therefore, to be essential preliminaries to be completed before Russia is likely to embark on a trial of strength with the emerging super-power in Asia—though the course of events in the Indian subcontinent might bring about a crisis ahead of time. The alternative would be a reversal of policies both in Moscow and Peking which would bring about a real reconciliation and a revival of the never formally repudiated alliance; this is possible, but on present form hardly to be regarded as probable. In China the invitation to the President of the United States to visit Peking has been justified by reference to an old maxim of Mao's to the effect that it may be expedient in war to come to terms with a secondary enemy in order to prevail against the main enemy, the implication being that Russia is now China's principal foe with America only in second place. This is a state of affairs such as to make Marx and Lenin turn in their graves, but it corresponds to geopolitical realities; the United States, now in a political phase of increasing isolationism, can disengage from Asia— where its armed forces are not now at any point in immediate contact with Chinese Communist troops—while Russia is irrevocably in Asia with thousands of miles of land frontier with China and massive armies in direct confrontation.

All Asian Communist parties, both those in control of states and those which are in legal or illegal opposition to their countries' governments, have been deeply affected by the Sino-Soviet split. Of the three Communist-ruled states outside the Soviet Union and the Chinese People's Republic, Mongolia—in spite of competitive Chinese bidding through economic aid which for a time made the Mongols the most assisted nation in the world per head of population—has adhered firmly to the Soviet Union and has strong Russian forces stationed on its soil, while both North Korea and North Vietnam have tended to sit on the fence and avoid a definite commitment to either side. All three countries have mixed their communism with sentiments of fervent nationalism, and all have backgrounds of a recent feudal or colonial past with virtually no native capitalism prior to the period of communist rule; all have thus a national experience nearer to China's than to Russia's. For the Mongols, however, the former colonial power was none other than China itself, which still holds about half the total of the Mongol ethnic stock within its borders and continues to plant Chinese settlers on their lands, so that most Mongols regard the Russians as their protectors against a Chinese ascendancy; the North Korean and North Vietnamese communists, on the other hand, have been preoccupied since the foundation of their states with the reunification of their respective countries against the opposition of rival non-communist governments sponsored by America, and have sought support from both Russia and China for their political and military offensives. The leaders in both Pyongyang and Hanoi would probably prefer to see Russia and China reconciled in a militant anti-imperialist front; meanwhile they accept economic and military aid from both and take advantage of the rift between them to maintain a certain independence which they would not have if they were assigned to spheres of influence in a deal between Peking and Moscow.

With its re-emergence into the field of international diplomacy since the end of the xenophobic isolationism of the Cultural Revolution and its victorious entry into the United Nations, the Chinese People's Republic may yet come to exert a wide influence in Asia beyond the limits of the Communist world; nations which can no longer count on American protection seek to reinsure themselves by approaches to Peking—or alternatively look to Moscow for support. But an international situation which finds Russia and China dominant in Asia is not necessarily favourable to the spread of communism as long as these two powers are at variance, for non-communist governments of relatively weak countries are thus given considerable scope for independent policies and balancing manoeuvres. Apart from direct political pressures or material aid for Communist insurrections from Moscow or Peking there has been remarkably little in two decades of actual performance by ruling Asian Communists to inspire imitation by Asian peoples still outside the range of their political control. The achievement of China under Mao Tse-tung has been far from impressive in relation to the early expectations of his admirers and the claims of his propagandists. A totalitarian political system which has been even more suffocating than the Russian in its regimentation of intellectual and cultural life has not compensated its people for deprivation of political and personal liberties by a swift material progress—except, ironically enough, in the sphere of the most deadly of modern weapons of war. If Asians want political democracy as a condition of development, they can look to India for a model; if their concern is with advanced technology and high standards of living they can look to Japan; in China they can only find utopian ideology and a still backward economy which painfully drags itself upward with 'politics in command'. Yet there is still a potent appeal of Marxism-Leninism to the disinherited, and as long as there are in Asia so many unemployed intellectuals, landless peasants and destitute urban *Lumpenproletariat* a new Lenin or a new Mao may yet emerge in a country which is today outside the socialist camp.

Military governments in Asia
In Paris there used to be people who in times of political crisis would go on the streets and shout 'Vive l'Armée' even when there was nobody in high position in the army who had any intention of doing anything about the crisis. The idea that somehow or other in troubled situations salvation will come from a takeover of governmental power by the armed forces of the state is one which makes little appeal in societies which are—or imagine themselves to be—stable and secure, but is likely to be widely accepted in those beset by insecurity and instability. In any society the army, quite apart from the fact of having in its hands a monopoly or a preponderance of lethal weapons, is normally the most compact, orderly and disciplined section of

the body politic, and the more chaotic and disorderly are general social and political conditions, the more sharply do the qualities of military organization stand out in contrast. If the society is threatened from without, it is by the army that the task of repelling the foreign foe must primarily be undertaken; if the threat is one of disruption from within, whether through violent social strife or ethnic separation, it is the army which in the last resort must be called in to hold the society together. Moreover, the army often commands a degree of popular respect which is not accorded to the civilian leaders of either economic or political life; in contrast to landlords and capitalists pursuing their own private interests and party politicians fighting for the spoils of office and often feathering their nests with the proceeds of bribery and corruption, the professional soldier devoted to the service of the state and living on his pay can easily come to appear in the eyes of the masses as the embodiment of patriotic purpose and moral rectitude.

The vogue of military dictatorships in the countries of the Third World cannot be understood unless it is fully appreciated that such regimes draw their strength, at least initially, not only from the arms at their disposal but from a degree of popular support which sees the army as a saviour from weak and corrupt government, anarchy, and disintegration of the state, or from a tyrannical rule generally regarded as oppressive. Without some such support a military dictatorship has little chance of being successfully established or enduring for any length of time, because, basically, professional soldiers are not suited by training or normal habit for the exercise of political power and they can only take it and hold it in special circumstances which make the application of military force exceptionally important and urgent and cause the normal processes of politics to appear useless or irrelevant to large numbers of people outside the military profession. Military dictatorship is a real alternative form of government in critical situations in countries where traditional dynastic monarchies have disappeared or been greatly weakened and parliamentary democracy has not been established long enough or well enough to have taken deep root among the people at large. By this definition it can be distinguished from fascism. Fascism is essentially the dictatorship of a party which, even though it makes use of a para-military force, arises from civilian politics in a country with a relatively long history of parliamentary practice; it destroys democracy from within the democratic political system and, even though it may benefit from collusion from the regular armed forces of the state, creates a form of leadership which depends on party organization rather than direct military support. In Germany the Weimar Republic, which defeated the Kapp Putsch in 1920, succumbed to Hitler through a political process which at no point involved an armed *coup d'état*, and the regular army, though it had favoured the Nazis as the party which would carry through German rearmament, finally became the focus of resistance to Hitler after all civilian political opposition had been crushed by the Nazi terror. In Spain, on the other hand, the regime of the Popular Front was overthrown, not by the civilian Falange, but by the insurrection of the regular army; and the government of General Franco, which replaced democracy in Spain, although it was generally classified at the time as fascist, was something quite different from the dictatorships of Mussolini and Hitler. In Japan likewise the regime which turned back the tide of political liberalism running in the 1920s and led the nation into wars of conquest on the mainland of Asia was not, strictly speaking, one of fascism, but one of military rule which drew inspiration and popular acceptance from one side of a strong national tradition, for if the Meiji 'Restoration' sought to restore to the Emperor the power which had long been in the hands of the military *Bakufu*, the militarists of the 1930s in effect revived the tradition which made the monarchy sacred but powerless.

Since 1945 Japan after a total defeat in war has been, as already pointed out, the Asian country in which the armed forces have had the smallest share of the gross national product and the least political prestige or power. This state of affairs may change in the future, but it has been a fact, and politically a very important one, up to now. Elsewhere in Asia states have been as a general rule over the last two decades heavily armed in relation to their current resources and budgets, and their armed forces have held a position which, even where they have not intervened directly in politics, has made them indispensable to civilian governments for the maintenance of internal order.

Among the Asian countries in which military rule has been established the anti-communist sections of the three two-state countries of Asia—China, Korea and Vietnam—form a distinct group in which the basic condition of the army's power is a situation of permanent actual or suspended civil war requiring a rigorous suppression of hostile fifth-column activities. The communist sections of their countries are themselves highly militarized in that they depend on armed force, whether of regular army, militia or security police, to suppress all opposition to the dictatorship of the communist party; but it is basic communist doctrine that the party commands the gun, and the strength of the party organization and indoctrination of the armed forces normally ensures that this is so. In China, as already mentioned, the great weakening of the party during the Cultural Revolution and Mao's reliance on the army to restore order after the rampages of the Red Guards had brought the People's Republic near to anarchy has given the soldiers a degree of power which they do not possess in European communist regimes; even so, this power takes the form of membership of party committees rather than of direct exercise of state authority. On the other side of the lines, military governments have emerged because the only alternative to yielding to the revolutionary communist pressures has been to create state authorities stronger than can be provided, in the absence of any previous democratic tradition, by multi-party parliamentary systems.

In Korea, a country with no democratic tradition which for thirty-five years before 1945 had lived under an extreme form of colonial rule without politicians or administrators of its own nationality, the remarkable thing is not that parliamentary institutions should have worked badly under conditions of suspended civil war but that they should ever have worked at all. Under more favourable conditions, indeed, democracy might have taken root in Korea, for it was presented to the Koreans in the American zone of occupation after the end of Japanese rule as the ideological alternative to the communism promoted in the Soviet zone; moreover, Japan, the former overlord of Korea, was being transformed after defeat into a liberal democratic state. But the three years of war in Korea from 1950 to 1953 necessarily left South Korea with an overgrown military establishment; and this could not be disbanded, because the war had ended, not with any accepted peace settlement, but with only a truce, which did not prevent the North from infiltrating guerrilla cadres into the South even after the battle on the main fighting front had been stopped. In the end the army refused to be subject to parliamentary politics in Seoul and under the leadership of General Park took over control of the state. Park's rule as President was notable for a rapid economic growth, partly due to the fact that the assurance of strong and stable government attracted investment from abroad. He was not, however, inclined to claim a right of permanent military dictatorship for Korea and ran for re-election in 1970 against a civilian opponent in a Presidential contest, which even if not entirely free from official pressures, was hard fought verbally and piled up a large opposition vote. Park's power undoubtedly rests in the last resort on the support of the army, yet in a situation which keeps a hostile military power perpetually poised for action thirty miles north of the national capital, the rule of a military commander who has also shown marked ability as a political leader is widely acceptable to the civilian population in so far as it is moved by fear of fresh invasion or subversion from North Korea if there were to be a weakening of government in Seoul.

In Taiwan a military dictatorship was installed ready-made

when the residue of the armed forces of the former 'Nationalist' government of China was transferred to the island after the end of the civil war on the mainland. In China, after the manifest failure of the initial attempt to create a democratic republic on the ruins of the old dynastic autocracy, Sun Yat-sen prescribed a political process of transformation in three stages—first a military campaign by an army of the Kuomintang party to overcome the 'war lords' and re-unify the state; secondly, a period of party dictatorship or 'tutelage'; and thirdly, a transition to a full democracy with rights of political opposition and free elections. After the end of the Pacific War the period of tutelage was officially declared to be at an end, but with the country in a turmoil of civil war a real democratic process was out of the question; a general election was formally held in 1948 in the areas then controlled by the central government, but it was boycotted by the Communists. The Kuomintang deputies who were elected and subsequently went to Taiwan have continued to provide legitimacy to the rule of Chiang Kai-shek as President of a regime claiming to be the government of all China, but actually confined territorially to the single province of Taiwan. The army in exile, whose task it is to defend Taiwan against the Communist endeavour to 'liberate' it and notionally to 'return to the mainland' when the time is ripe, remains the main political factor in a situation complicated by frictions between the native Taiwanese and the immigrants from the mainland. On the other hand, there is no reason to believe that any substantial section of the people of Taiwan craves for the liberation promised by Peking; the agrarian conditions which gave the Communists their greatest advantage in the civil war on the mainland have been removed by a land reform which has been the most drastic in Asia after that of Japan, and two decades of economic growth with American aid have provided the Taiwanese with much higher standards of living than their compatriots on the other side of the Taiwan Straits.

In Vietnam the situation is very different in that, whereas

South Korea in recent years has been very little, and Taiwan not at all, disturbed by actual revolutionary violence, South Vietnam has been continually ravaged, and its economy disrupted, by the combined military operations of the Vietcong and invading North Vietnamese forces. In these circumstances no form of government other than a military dictatorship has been practically possible in South Vietnam in spite of the efforts of the American Embassy to promote civil liberties and free elections in order to counter the criticism in the United States which holds that American power has been used in Vietnam to prop up an unpopular and oppressive regime.

In Thailand an increased sense of external and internal danger following the American withdrawals from Vietnam, the cuts in American aid enacted by the United States Senate, and Communist China's spectacular triumph in the United Nations, appears to have prompted the latest military *coup*, which has reversed a previous trend towards parliamentary democracy. Thailand is unique in South-East Asia in having retained its traditional dynastic monarchy, but ever since the power of the monarchy was limited by a military *coup d'état* in 1932 there has been in Thailand a succession of army leaders who have governed in the name of the monarch while basing their authority on their military support. In 1969, partly under American pressure, steps were taken to transfer power to an elected parliament, but by the action of 1971 it was taken back into military hands and the parliamentary deputies were sent packing with payments in compensation for salaries and expenses. As the trend of American policy puts future American protection for Thailand increasingly in doubt, American influence in favour of democratization is correspondingly diminished and the tendency is to revert to a form of government which after nearly four decades of operation has become almost traditional.

In making a journey west from Bangkok to Islamabad the political observer moves from a region where confrontation with an expanding communism has provided the central issues of politics to one in which questions of nationality have been paramount. The state of Pakistan came into existence through the partition of a previously unified India against the will of the Indian Congress Party which rejected fundamentally the whole concept of national differentiation according to religion. Since India was the larger of the two succession states, Pakistan was from the beginning beset by a sense of insecurity and apprehension in dealings with New Delhi, and the tension was aggravated by the grievance over Kashmir; this situation was by itself sufficient to magnify the importance of the army as the guardian and champion of the new nation, and there was in addition the difficulty of holding together the two 'wings' of Pakistan, which were both geographically far apart and widely divergent in language and culture. For Pakistan to retain its national unity and stand up to India a strong central government was required, but it was hard to obtain this on the basis of a parliamentary democracy in which the people of East Bengal, forming a majority of the total electorate, were indifferent to the question of Kashmir, so traumatic for West Pakistan, and resentful of the political preponderance of the Punjabi Muslims who were the real *Staatsvolk* of the nation the Muslim League had brought into being. With such internal and external tensions the prospects for democracy in Pakistan were dim and the military dictatorships of Ayub and Yahya Khan a far from surprising outcome. Yet the pressure for a restoration of democracy was strong and Yahya Khan yielded to it. Having permitted free elections, he should logically have accepted their verdict; however, he seems not to have anticipated the overwhelming vote for the Awami League in East Pakistan and was not ready to concede a degree of autonomy which would have virtually ended the existence of Pakistan as a single sovereign state. Even so, some *modus vivendi* might have been reached but for the excesses committed against West Pakistan residents after the elections by the para-military auxiliaries of the Awami League; these led to the military repression which by its ruthlessness drove millions of refugees from East Pakistan into India and in turn provoked armed intervention by India with all its consequences for both nations.

If military dictatorship in Pakistan has had as its main purpose the maintenance of the unity of a state threatened with disruption, a similar motive can be discerned on a smaller scale in the Burmese dictatorship of General Ne Win. About half of the total territory of Burma is inhabited by national minorities, which, even though less numerous than the Burmese and lacking unity among themselves, have set a major problem for Burma's rulers ever since independence. Ne Win's predecessor in power, the civilian U Nu, sought to solve the problem by conceding to the minorities a far-reaching autonomy which was quite unacceptable to the more extreme nationalists; these found a leader in Ne Win whose policy after the *coup* was to enforce rigorously the control from Rangoon over the minority areas. Ne Win also continued with success the campaign against the insurgent communists which had already been undertaken under U Nu, but the anti-communist edge to his policy was much less than in Thailand; there can be no doubt that for him the communists were less of a danger to the state than the insubordination of the non-Burmese peoples. Ne Win's regime, moreover, was marked, in spite of its anti-communism, by a degree of socialism which to some foreigners seemed barely distinguishable from the product of People's China. Ne Win set up a Revolutionary Council which went in for nationalization in all directions. The ideology went back to the communist-influenced 'anti-fascism' which flourished in war-ravaged Burma at the time of the attainment of independence, but it emerged less from a native Burmese class struggle than from nationalism; in a country where virtually all big business was European and all small business Chinese it was possible to go a very long way in expropriating owners of capital without ever treading on the toes of a member of the Burmese race—indeed it was highly gratifying to a non-commercial agrarian people who had long been accustomed to associate wealth with alien minorities to see it being confiscated by a national leader. Since Burma produced more foodstuffs than were needed for its own population, there was no danger of starvation from Ne Win's experiments and if nationalization of (Chinese) retail trade led to tiresome shortages of many kinds of consumer goods, this was not too high a price to pay for soaking the Chinese merchant.

In Indonesia the army's rise to power took place in two stages. In the first it became powerful through the part it played under Sukarno's civilian political leadership, first in the war of independence against the Dutch, then in suppression of revolts in the Outer Islands against the ascendancy of Java, then in the campaign to get the Dutch out of Irian, and finally in the confrontation with Britain and Malaysia, which was still going on in the autumn of 1965. Gradually the army headed by Nasution acquired a degree of independent power unacceptable to Sukarno with his intense appetite for autocratic authority, and he resolved to cut it down to size by an operation in accordance with his own peculiar political style. Just as he sought to rule over a 'guided democracy' by leading a coalition of parties in which he played off the Communists against political groups of the Centre and Right, so he planned to organize and arm a workers' and peasants' militia, which would be virtually a military arm of the Communist Party, and which he could play off against Nasution and the regular army. The army, however, refused to provide equipment for the new militia, and there was no prospect of overcoming its resistance unless Nasution and other leading generals could be eliminated. It may never be known just how far Sukarno was himself involved in the plot to murder them, but the ambivalence of his attitude during the crisis fatally compromised him in the eyes of the army leadership, which, far from being crushed, was provoked into carrying out a complete takeover of governmental power, initiating ruthless repressive action against the communists, and driving Sukarno himself by degrees into political impotence. Nasution, though he survived the assassinations which were meant to include him, somewhat unexpectedly faded out of the picture and it was another general, Suharto, who became the supreme leader of the new military regime. Later on he made a gesture of restoring democracy and organized a new political party which won a majority of votes in a general election, but it was not doubted in Indonesia that he ruled by virtue of the support of the army and that his power was independent of any parliamentary mandate. The regime remains on guard against any revival of the former power of the communists, but also against any renewal of separatist tendencies in the Outer Islands; meanwhile it has done much to clear up the appalling economic mess left by Sukarno, though it will take far more than has yet been achieved to resolve the special problems arising from over-population in central and eastern Java.

A survey of recent examples of military rule in Asia shows wide variations of pattern in accordance with the social and political setting in each country, the nature of the particular crisis leading to a military *coup*, and the personalities involved. What they have in common, however, in spite of their frequency, is what may be called their abnormality, the sense shared by the military rulers themselves and those whom they govern that their regimes are merely provisional and transient creations. Military government is not really an ideological and institutional alternative to democracy and communism. It is even for those who welcome it an emergency solution, something like a fire-engine which is expected to go away again when the fire has been put out. There is a feeling that an army is not doing its proper job when it assumes responsibility for civil government, and indeed professional soldiers cannot perform leading political functions in society over a long period of time without losing their identity as soldiers. In the past, when dynastic monarchy was the normal form of government, the leader of a successful military revolt would found a new dynasty, and Riza Khan did just that in Iran in the 1920s, but in the Asia of the seventies this is hardly a political possibility. The military dictator in the contemporary world lacks legitimacy and when faced with dangerous unrest or the problem of assuring a succession to his own personal power seeks to legitimize his position either by restoration of an old monarchy, as Franco has done in Spain, or where—as is usual—there is no such monarchy to restore, by a controlled return to parliamentary democracy. The quest of legitimation through popular election has been pursued with considerable success by Park in South Korea and Suharto in Indonesia, but had disastrous consequences in Pakistan. There is no golden rule for military dictators in their endeavour to make good, but the political devices to which they have resorted in order to consolidate their governments or wind them up without a collapse of state authority must be seen as recognition of the fact that merely moving tanks into the streets of a capital city does not assure any stable permanence of power thus acquired unless it can somehow be given root either in an accepted traditional right or in a democratic consent. There will no doubt be more military *coups d'état* in Asia, more Suhartos and Yahya Khans, yet there is no reason to expect army rule anywhere to be an enduring form of government. In the modern world, when the kings depart, the captains cannot make the kingdoms their own; the basic choice is only between a popular sovereignty with free elections and the rule of a *parti unique* dedicated to the creed of Marx, Lenin and Mao.

NOTES ON CONTRIBUTORS

G. F. HUDSON is a Fellow Emeritus of St Antony's College, Oxford; he was a Fellow of the college and Director of its Centre of Far Eastern Studies from 1954 to 1970. He served in the Research Department of the Foreign Office from 1939 to 1946. Publications include *Europe and China* (Edward Arnold, 1930), *The Far East in World Politics* (Oxford University Press, 1936) and *The Hard and Bitter Peace* (Pall Mall Press, 1966).

DR W. KLATT, O.B.E., is an agricultural economist who served with H.M. Government from 1940 to 1966, the last fifteen years of this period as economic adviser at the Foreign Office. He edited and contributed to *The Chinese Model* (Hong Kong and Oxford University Press, 1965). He also contributed to *Asia Handbook* (Penguin, 1969) and *The Far East and Australasia* (Europa Publications, 1972). He is at present engaged in a study on agricultural development in Asia.

W. A. C. ADIE was a Research Fellow in Chinese Studies at St Antony's College, Oxford from 1960 to 1970, and since 1970 has held a post in the Research School of Pacific Studies in the National University of Australia at Canberra. He has made a special study of the Chinese press and of the policy of the Chinese People's Republic towards African countries.

RALF BONWIT studied Chinese in Frankfurt, Paris and London. He later took a degree in Japanese, but the war interrupted his postgraduate studies at the School of Oriental Studies in London and also prevented him from taking up a scholarship at Sendai Tohoku University in Japan. After wartime service with the BBC he transferred to another department where his work kept him in constant touch with current developments in the Far East. He has been for several years closely associated with the Far Eastern Seminar of St Antony's College.

RICHARD STORRY taught at the Otaru College of Commerce in Japan from 1937 to 1940. He served in the army in India and Burma during the Pacific war, and after a period of work sponsored by the National University of Australia became a Fellow of St Antony's College, Oxford, in 1955. He has been Director of the Centre of Far Eastern Studies in the college since 1970. Publications include *The Double Patriots* (Chatto & Windus, 1957), *A History of Modern Japan* (Penguin, 1960), with F. W. Deakin *The Case of Richard Sorge* (Chatto & Windus, 1966) and *Japan* (Benn, 1969).

W. F. CRAWLEY was a research student at St Antony's College, Oxford, from 1967 to 1970, and wrote a doctoral thesis on the politics of the former United Provinces in India during the period 1880 to 1921. He graduated from Trinity College, Cambridge, in 1964 and taught at St Stephen's College, Delhi University, for two years. He now writes and broadcasts on current South Asian affairs.

MISS H. KHUHRO graduated from Girton College, Cambridge, and afterwards obtained a Ph.D. at the University of London. She taught for several years at the University of Karachi and contributed to *A History of Sind*. From 1969 to 1972 she was a Fellow in Pakistani Studies at St Antony's College, Oxford.

DR. L. H. PALMIER, an anthropologist and historian with a special interest in Indonesia, has been a Research Fellow of St Antony's College, Oxford, since 1965 and has also been teaching at the University of Bath. Publications include *Indonesia and the Dutch* (Oxford University Press, 1962) and *Indonesia* (Thames & Hudson, 1965).

INDEX